Governance in Russian Regions

"This book greatly enriches our understanding of policy-making processes in authoritarian Russia. The authors show convincingly that the state depends on resources of non-state actors to manage policy challenges. Their fine, deeply-researched study analyzes how the resulting governance networks vary across Russia's regions and policy areas. The book makes a unique and valuable contribution to scholarship on Russia, governance, and the complex politics of contemporary authoritarian regimes."
—Linda J. Cook, *Professor of Political Science, Brown University, USA*

"*Governance in Russian Regions—A Policy Comparison* is a significant theoretical and empirical contribution to interdisciplinary research on multidimensional aspects of subnational governance in today's Russia. Its innovative approach reveals the combination of 'vertical' hierarchy with 'horizontal', collaborative networks and interactions between the state agencies, society and private interests. Presented case studies (HIV prevention, policies towards NGOs, climate change, child welfare, ethnic conflicts) corroborate an important theoretical conclusion that there are common features of governance that transcend regime types."
—Andrei Melville, *Dean of the Faculty of social sciences, Higher School of Economics, Moscow*

"An original, refreshing entry into the analyses of Russian state-society relationship. Instead of usual statist top-down design, the authors apply network governance theory into the Russian case. The book provides a diversified picture of the dynamics how Russian state and civil society interact. Additionally, it makes a significant contribution to our understanding of how federalism, tripartite government, policy making and implementation really work in contemporary Russia. The developed, systemized framework is useful to studies of other hybrid regimes as well."

—Meri Kulmala, *Academy of Finland Research Fellow, Aleksanteri Institute, University of Helsinki*

Sabine Kropp · Aadne Aasland
Mikkel Berg-Nordlie · Jørn Holm-Hansen
Johannes Schuhmann
Editors

Governance in Russian Regions

A Policy Comparison

Editors
Sabine Kropp
Otto Suhr Institute of Political Science
Freie Universität Berlin
Berlin, Germany

Aadne Aasland
Norwegian Institute for Urban
  and Regional Research (NIBR)
Oslo, Norway

Mikkel Berg-Nordlie
Department for International Studies
  and Migration
Norwegian Institute for Urban
  and Regional Research (NIBR)
Oslo, Norway

Jørn Holm-Hansen
Department for International Studies
  and Migration
Norwegian Institute for Urban
  and Region
Oslo, Norway

Johannes Schuhmann
Institute of German and International
  Party Law and Party Research
Heinrich Heine University Düsseldorf
Düsseldorf, Germany

ISBN 978-3-319-61701-5   ISBN 978-3-319-61702-2   (eBook)
DOI 10.1007/978-3-319-61702-2

Library of Congress Control Number: 2017945788

Cover credit: Crispyicon/iStock/Getty Images Plus
Cover design by Akihiro Nakayama

Printed on acid-free paper

This Palgrave Macmillan imprint is published by Springer Nature
The registered company is Springer International Publishing AG
The registered company address is: Gewerbestrasse 11, 6330 Cham, Switzerland

CONTENTS

1 **Preface**   1
Sabine Kropp

2 **The Russian State as Network Manager: A Theoretical Framework**   7
Mikkel Berg-Nordlie, Jørn Holm-Hansen and Sabine Kropp

3 **Adjusting the Scope of Interaction Between State and Civil Society: HIV Prevention Among Drug Users**   43
Aadne Aasland and Anastasia Y. Meylakhs

4 **Environmental Impact Assessment: Between Facilitating Public Contribution and Arbitrary Involvement of NGOs**   73
Johannes Schuhmann and Sabine Kropp

5 **Climate Change Adaptation: Governance in a Fragmented and Unsettled Policy Area**   105
Jørn Holm-Hansen and Mikkel Berg-Nordlie

6 **Child Welfare Policies in Russia—Civil Society Contributions Without Return?**   131
Jørn Holm-Hansen

7   Imitation and Enforced Cooperation: State and Civil
    Society in Ethnic Conflict Management   155
    Sabine Kropp and Johannes Schuhmann

8   Substitution in Sápmi. Meta-Governance and Conflicts
    Over Representation in Regional Indigenous Governance   189
    Mikkel Berg-Nordlie

9   Patterns of Governance in Russia: Feedback of Empirical
    Findings into Governance Theory   219
    Sabine Kropp and Aadne Aasland

Index   247

EDITORS AND CONTRIBUTOR

About the Editors

Sabine Kropp holds the Chair of German Politics at the Otto Suhr Institute of Political Science, Freie Universität Berlin. Her main research interests are comparative federalism, legislative studies, governance and public management and East European, especially Russian politics. Recently, she has been the leader of a 5-years project on governance in Russia. She was also partner in the project on network governance in Russia led by Aadne Aasland.

Aadne Aasland is a senior researcher at the Norwegian Institute for Urban and Regional Research (NIBR), Oslo and Akershus University College of Applied Sciences. His main research interests are welfare and migration, with a special focus on Russia and the Baltic countries. Recently, he has been the leader of international multi-partner projects on network governance in Russia and HIV prevention in Northwest Russia.

Mikkel Berg-Nordlie is a researcher at NIBR. His research is mainly on Russian politics, indigenous politics, ethnic minority policy, minority organization, state-civil society interaction and media analysis. He is currently doing research on Russian Sámi politics, indigenous urbanization, Russian immigrant integration, Russian education reform and Nordic indigenous political representation. Recent books: *Bridiging Divides:*

Ethno-political leadership among the Russian Sámi (with Indra Overland, 2012); *Indigenous politics: Institutions, representation, mobilization* (ed. with Jo Saglie and Ann Sullivan, 2015).

Dr. Jørn Holm-Hansen is a political scientist at the Norwegian Institute for Urban and Regional Research (NIBR-HiOA). His main research focus is on Russian and Polish politics and society. Among the policy areas he has studied in Russia is housing and utility services, local climate change adaptation, environmental protection, child rights and history politics.

Johannes Schuhmann is a postdoc researcher at the University of Dusseldorf. Prior to this, he worked as a representative of the Free University of Berlin at the Institute for International Relations of the Russian Foreign Ministry (MGIMO) in Moscow, as a lecturer for Political Science at the University of Munich and as a research assistant at the Center for Applied Policy Research (CAP) in Munich.

Contributor

Anastasia Meylakhs MA is a researcher at the National Research University Higher School of Economics and Centre for Independent Social Research. She specializes in qualitative research on Russian government programs in substances abuse and HIV-infection prevention and treatment, high-risk social networks, social policy" and medical services quality monitoring.

LIST OF FIGURES

Fig. 7.1   Meta-governance in the Russian multilevel context   170
Fig. 9.1   Subtypes of Russian state-dominated governance networks   227

LIST OF TABLES

Table 4.1   Patterns of collaboration and meta-governance in EIAs   95

Table 5.1   Meta-governance tools and the climate adaptation networks   127

Table 7.1   Platforms for state-civil society collaboration in ethnic policy   158

Table 7.2   Meta-governance: tools for governing platforms in Krasnodar and Stavropol   181

Table 9.1   Governance networks typology   230

CHAPTER 1

Preface

Sabine Kropp

In the past decades, governance theory has been among the most inspiring and rapidly growing research areas in social science. As it emphasises the limited statehood of modern states, the theory lies at the heart of international relations but was also frequently used and further developed by policy studies disclosing that state authorities have to engage with autonomous private actors in order to cope with complex social, economic and political problems. More specifically, '…governance implies that private actors are involved in decision-making in order to provide common goods and that non-hierarchical means of guidance are employed'.[1] In such cooperative, network-based arrangements, command and control are considered inappropriate. State authorities are expected to direct networks by mainly using 'soft' techniques of governing. As regards the quality of the state, governance theory uncovered that the 'state' hardly ever appears as a homogeneous, unitary actor, but should rather be conceived as a network in and of itself. The modern state comprises various organisations and actors which are only partially linked to each other by simple hierarchies. Empirical research inspired by governance theory has substantiated this convergence towards

S. Kropp (✉)
Otto Suhr Institute of Political Science, Chair of German Politics,
Freie Universität Berlin, Ihnestraße 22, 14195 Berlin, Germany
e-mail: sabine.kropp@fu-berlin.de

© The Author(s) 2018
S. Kropp et al. (eds.), *Governance in Russian Regions*,
DOI 10.1007/978-3-319-61702-2_1

1

collaborative relations involving public and non-public actors and the linking of different government levels. Considering these ascribed characteristics, it is not surprising that networks have been acknowledged as a mode of governance typical for *western* societies.

As a departure from this mainstream thought, this book takes the theory out of its genuine context and investigates the emergence and working of governance networks in contemporary Russia where there is a system which has frequently been designated as 'hybrid' or increasingly authoritarian.[2] Our point of divergence was the assumption that governance networks are a ubiquitous phenomenon and do not occur just in democracies. At first glance this basic notion may appear to be somewhat counterintuitive because non-democratic regimes are usually associated with subordination, control, coercion, and, generally, 'vertical' styles of governance. Nonetheless, when starting our research, we considered our argument as conclusive for at least three reasons. Firstly, even non-democratic regimes featuring strong hierarchies cannot effectively respond to complex policy problems without activating the resources of private actors. Secondly, there is widespread consensus that networks are just one ideal-type mode of governance besides hierarchy and the market; the strict dichotomy between 'horizontal' and 'vertical' governance modes is therefore an over-simplification and should be replaced by approaches delving into 'patterns of the mix'.[3] Following this, the theory opens up for an analysis of non-democratic regimes since it becomes plausible that in all systems vertical modes mingle with horizontal ones, albeit featuring strong differences in how these modes are mixed and linked to each other. Thirdly, the normative undertone usually accompanying governance network theory, stressing equality and trust among actors, tends to obscure the fact that networks in democracies are rarely shaped by horizontal, trust-based relations, but often feature asymmetries and hierarchies working in favour of the state authorities. We postulate that all these arguments make network governance theory an obvious approach for investigating empirical cases across various regime types. Last but not least, the motivation for this book also arose from the empirical observation that governance networks do emerge in Russia. In fact, over the past decade the Russian federal government has spent considerable effort to nurture and incorporate a 'constructive' civil society into policy-making. Collaboration with non-state actors has become an officially sanctioned policy. It was a central question underlying this book as to how this formalised working-together is vitalised in everyday politics and implemented across various policy issues.

We believe that shifting the research perspective on Russian politics in this direction enables us to gain a deeper understanding of hybrid and 'new' authoritarian regimes. In studies on Russian politics and society, however, the term 'network' often has a negative connotation because it is strongly associated with informal, dark power networks, such as patronal politics, clientelism, or corruption. These structures may well indeed be crucial for understanding the nature of Russian politics. Yet we argue that this is just half the battle when debating the meaning of networks. Like other regimes, Russia must solve concrete policy problems in order to stabilise or increase its legitimacy. At the same time, its capacity to tackle these problems is limited, especially at the regional level and in the communities where policy problems become visible and concrete.[4] Significantly, social welfare tasks and health issues have been transferred to the subnational levels, but tax money is predominantly allocated from the federal level. Effectively then the regional governments lack fiscal and organisational resources. In such situations, it is an obvious strategy for incumbents to resort to the resources provided by non-state actors and establish formal collaborations. The individual chapters will show, however, that the real functioning of institutionalised networks is rather divergent, and the articles will give explanations for similarities and differences.

The research provided in this volume is located at the interface of governance theory and regime hybridity (respectively 'new' authoritarianism) which represent independent, but combinable strands of research. On the one hand the book attempts to widen the angle of governance theory. On the other hand, as the volume links the theory to the ongoing debate on regime hybridity and authoritarian rule, it helps to refine our knowledge about what is characteristic of these regimes. Despite the continuously growing stock of contributions, scholars have pointed out that research still lacks profound insights into how authoritarianism and regime hybridity work in practice. This book argues that network governance theory may help to fill this gap. It claims to bring some new insights to light by addressing the following questions: How are we to understand the real functioning of governance networks? More specifically, how are various policies made and implemented within networks, which types of actors interact and of what kind are their relations? Which patterns of—more or less mixed—governance modes have emerged in Russia? Which invariant features of governance networks can be carved out, and which functions do governance networks fulfil in an increasingly authoritarian regime?

For grasping the specific 'mixes' of governance modes in Russia, the abundant theoretical debate had to be confined, but at the same time it was indispensable to widen the perspectives on network governance. Considering the hierarchical character of Russian politics, theories explaining how governance networks are guided 'from above' were consulted. Correspondingly, the individual chapters examine in detail which tools the state authorities utilise in order to govern networks. This theoretical angle, which was labelled 'meta-governance' in the second wave of governance research, precisely matches the Russian context: even though the regime aims at cooperating with loyal private actors, it at the same time tightens control, often mistrusts non-state actors, and bends the rules if it regards it to be necessary. Hence, the authors expected to discover a broad range of 'soft' and 'hard' tools used to direct governance networks.

This volume endeavours to meet the questions outlined above by comparing governance networks across various policies and Russian regions. The data was gathered by two project teams, one based in Oslo, and the other one in Dusseldorf and Berlin. In total, both teams conducted more than 20 case studies in seven Russian regions. In regular meetings the theoretical framework was debated and empirical findings were discussed, evaluated and compared. This procedure not only enabled us to integrate the case studies into a coherent theoretical framework which was finally applied to all policy chapters in this volume, but it also facilitated tying the empirical findings together and allowed for feeding the results of the case studies into governance theory.

The chapters can be grouped into two sets, namely those providing the empirical observations in various policy areas, and those preparing the research field on theoretical grounds and further systematising the empirical results. As governance theory is a slippery ground, a conceptual clarification was indispensable. The existing stock of literature resembles a maze of intermingled, sometimes conflicting conceptions, and is often underlain by normative-laden assumptions. Chapter 2 therefore strides across this minefield by undertaking definitions and demarcating the research field. It discusses which strands of governance theory are feasible for being transferred to our object of investigation, and reconsiders how the theory is to be contextualised when analysing governance networks in Russia. Case selection and methodology are also debated in this introductory chapter. Chapter 9, again, systematises the empirical findings by comparing them across regions and policy areas. This final chapter maps different types and functions of governance networks and elaborates new perspectives on governance theory by applying it to an increasingly authoritarian regime. In doing so, we believe that the ideas and findings elaborated in both these chapters are conducive to developing fresh views on governance theory. The second group of chapters, again, comprises six policy areas, ranging from social issues such as HIV prevention and child care, to the investigation of environmental impact assessments and climate change adaptation, to problems of ethnic policy and indigenous representation. All policy chapters use the theoretical framework worked out in Chap. 2 and compare governance networks within one and the same policy area either across regions or over a period of time. They were designed to tell 'thick descriptions', but at the same time all the authors attempted to make sure that all chapters were wrought by the same theoretical framework and that they generate comparable findings. The book can thus be read by scholars of Russian politics as an integrated monograph; but since the theoretical concept is also briefly clarified within each policy chapter, it also provides an added value for experts engaged in a respective policy area.

The work on this book has stretched over years. It would have been impossible to conduct the research without the generous funding given by the German Metro Foundation and the Norwegian Research Council's NORRUSS programme. Empirical fieldwork is always an uncertain endeavour and can be successful only if many partners are willing to cooperate and support the research. We are thus very grateful to all actors coming from state and non-state sectors in Russia for sharing their expert knowledge with us and providing useful information. We would also like to thank our colleagues, Elena Bogdanova, Jonathan Davies, Vadim Kononenko, Karina Mikirova, Asbjørn Røiseland and Olga Tkach for their various contributions to the research that forms the basis of this book.

Notes

1. Héritier, Adrienne. 2002. Introduction. In *Common Goods. Reinventing European and International Governance,* ed. Adrienne Héritier, 1–12, Lanham: Rowman & Littlefield, at p. 3.
2. Since the empirical research of the authors has streched over years, it reflects the recent development of the Russian system becoming increasingly authoritarian. Therefore, the book also touches the contested issue whether Russia is better categorised as a hybrid regime which combines formally democratic institutions wautocratic practices, or whether it is more convincing to assign it clearly to the regime type of authoritarianism. Both approaches put forth plausible arguments.

Regarding the functioning of governance networks in Russia, it can either be argued that their existence mirrors regime hybridity as they provide a new variant of—albeit 'managed'—public participation, or that governance networks highlight an important aspect of what is 'new' about authoritarian rule.

3. Davies, Jonathan S. 2011. *Challenging Governance Theory: From Networks to Hegemony.* Bristol: The Policy Press, at p. 57.
4. Melville, Andrei, Denis Stukal and Mikhail Mironiuk. 2014. 'King of the Mountain', or Why Postcommunist Autocracies Have Bad Institutions. *Russian Politics and Law* 52 (2), 7–29.

CHAPTER 2

The Russian State as Network Manager: A Theoretical Framework

Mikkel Berg-Nordlie, Jørn Holm-Hansen and Sabine Kropp

Governance networks are usually associated with democratic forms of government. In this book, network governance theory is used as a tool to analyse the relations between state and non-state actors in a hybrid regime. The chapters in this volume investigate various governance networks in Russia and seek to answer the following questions: Who is allowed the right to participate in the networks; why do these actors participate; and what precisely sets the limits to the influence actors obtain through the networks? What characterises

M. Berg-Nordlie (✉)
Department for International Studies and Migration, NIBR Institute of Oslo and Akershus University College, Holbergs Gate 1, 0166 Oslo, Norway
e-mail: Mikkel.berg-nordlie@nibr.hioa.no

J. Holm-Hansen
Department for International Studies and Migration, Norwegian Institute for Urban and Regional Research NIBR-HiOA, Holbergs Gate 1, 0166 Oslo, Norway
e-mail: jorn.holm-hansen@nibr.hioa.no

S. Kropp
Otto Suhr Institute of Political Science, Chair of German Politics, Freie Universität Berlin, Ihnestraße 22, 14195 Berlin, Germany
e-mail: sabine.kropp@fu-berlin.de

© The Author(s) 2018
S. Kropp et al. (eds.), *Governance in Russian Regions*,
DOI 10.1007/978-3-319-61702-2_2

governance networks and how are these networks governed by the Russian authorities? The overarching argument underlying this book is that examining Russian politics through the prism of network governance theory helps to obtain a more nuanced understanding of how regime hybridity and 'new' authoritarianism work in practice (Way 2010: 335; Levitsky and Way 2010; Hale 2011). By clarifying and discussing different theoretical concepts of high relevance to all studies collected in this book, this chapter develops a framework for studying the relations between state and non-state actors in contemporary Russia.

To this point, the prevailing approach of most studies on Russian politics has been to focus either on formal institutions establishing strict hierarchies or on informal, 'dark' power networks, such as patron-client relations and corruption (Hale 2015; Holmes 2012). In accordance with the 'power vertical' and the extensive recentralisation which was set up after President Vladimir V. Putin had come to power in 2000, many analyses have adopted a distinct top-down view spotlighting the dominant role of state actors in policy-making processes. This perspective seems to correspond to the authoritarian turn Russia has gradually undergone since the early 2000s. In the course of this the Russian authorities have applied a versatile toolkit comprising formal and informal instruments so as to keep society and the elites at the different territorial levels and from various sectors under control. Nevertheless, there is plenty of evidence that authorities in hybrid (Robertson 2009, 2010) or non-democratic regimes not only resort to command, threat and control, but also rather often prefer incentives and collaborative practices over direct intervention (Wintrobe 1998). Even in distinctly centralised regimes like Russia, policies are perceived as being so complex that the authorities acknowledge the need to combine top-down approaches with horizontal modes of governance. By drawing on resources and actors from the non-state sector, the state thus creates and sustains governance networks in which various types of actors are able to exchange resources.

The book takes this observation as its point of departure, arguing that it is worth letting the governance concept travel to contexts outside the western world. Its basic conjecture is that Russia is not exceptional. Significantly, research on other regimes featuring extreme hierarchies such as China (e.g. Teets 2013), has recently revealed that their governments also experiment with governance networks. While official rhetoric focuses on Russia's need to follow its own political path, the Russian government in the past has repeatedly modelled reforms on international examples (Benevolenskiy and

Shumlevich 2013; Davies et al. 2016). Why, then, should Russian authorities refrain from following the international trend of collaboration with non-state actors, particularly since these actors have access to resources seen as essential for solving complicated policy problems?

By exploring interactions between state and non-state actors, the theoretical approach of this book focuses on the strategies and role perceptions of actors involved in networks. Without denying the dominating role of the state in contemporary Russia, our analysis lets various actors 'speak' by tracing their interactions, and thus partially departs from the prevailing top-down perspective. The power inherent in the state's role as network manager is explored by applying the concept of 'meta-governance'. The book examines governance networks where they emerged, i.e. in concrete policies and in concrete locations. Accordingly, the case studies in the following chapters cover various policy areas and different regions of Russia, providing a wide selection of actor constellation types and 'mixes' of governance modes. It should also be noted that all case studies focus on governance networks which are legal and institutionalised. Certainly, any formalised state-private collaboration is more or less closely linked to informal structures. Informality inevitably comes into play because formal rules always remain incomplete and thus need to be supplemented. Under this consideration, the analysis also contributes to the ongoing debate on the role of informality in Russian politics.

In the remainder of this chapter, we will first discuss concepts of network governance relevant to the Russian practice. With this, the normative 'baggage' associated with network governance theory is critically debated before we move on in the second part to reasoning about the meaning of meta-governance for the analysis of governance networks in Russia. In the third section, the theoretical framework is adapted to the specific context of Russian governance by relating it to some noteworthy aspects of Russian 'managed' democracy, the role of informality, and the links between network and multi-level governance. In the final section, the case selection and some issues of methodology are discussed.

2.1   NETWORK GOVERNANCE: CONCEPTS AND NORMATIVITY

2.1.1   Discourses on Network Governance

Academic literature on governance has emerged in Europe since the late 1970s and began to flourish from the early 1990s (Mayntz 2004; Torfing and

Sørensen 2014: 2–4). The literature constructs a fundamental division between hierarchical government through the state's traditional chain of command and 'new practices of coordinating activities through networks, partnerships, and deliberative forums' which involve a wide range of actors including 'labour unions, trade associations, firms, NGOs, local authority representatives, social entrepreneurs and community groups' (Hirst 2000: 18–19). As the governance concept captures quite different phenomena, the literature is so multifarious to the extent of being slippery. It ranges from the lexical 'running things and organisation to run things' to denoting the minimal state, but also involves 'good governance', 'new public management', or self-organising networks. Within this academic discourse, again, there are different operational definitions of these concepts—some broader, some narrower (Hirst 2000: 14–19; Jung 2010: 352; Osborne 2010; Torfing and Sørensen 2014: 5–6). Among the broader ones we find Kooiman (2010: 73), wherein 'interactive governance' is defined as 'the whole of interactions taken to solve societal problems and to create societal opportunities, including the formulation and application of principles guiding those interactions and care for institutions that enable and control them'.

In the contemporary governance discourse, it is common to posit that there is a difference between an old model for research on politics which takes the state structures as the point of departure, and a new model, which 'looks more generically at the coordination and various forms of formal or informal types of public-private interaction, most predominantly the role of policy networks' (Peters 2000: 39). In short, the analytical focus has shifted from being state-centric to being network-centric.

The entire concept of 'network governance' was originally developed to account for an assumedly non-hierarchical and qualitatively new type of close interaction between state authorities, non-state actors, and business. In such settings, policy instruments are tailored to collaborative or at least deliberative ways of operating. The hierarchical aspect of state power appears softened, because the measures applied by the authorities within the network cannot rely on direct command alone. Through the net-working of key individuals coming from different groups and institutions, the distinctions between politics and administration, private and public, civil society and state, civic groups and business, state administration and local self-government become less clear-cut and more blurred. When actors interact within a model of network governance, they become mutually interdependent in the sense that they rely on each other to achieve their objectives.

The rationales for network-type arrangements can roughly be divided into 'problem-centred' and 'actor-centred' types (Jessop 2004; Davies et al. 2016: 136; Myhre and Berg-Nordlie 2016: 193, 210). The former claims network governance to be necessary because of contemporary societal complexity, while the second asserts that network governance could be seen as a pragmatic response to deregulation, fragmentation and specialisation that followed neo-liberal reforms (Rhodes 1997). In the problem-centred line of argumentation, the challenges to be handled by network governance are problems so complex and even 'wicked' (Rittel and Webber 1973) that joint efforts of multiple actors from different sectors are required. Top-down approaches are considered obsolete, and the inclusion of non-state actors are thought of as useful. Yet, some contributions to governance theory countered that problem-solving is not always the primary objective of networks which may be designed just to preserve or extend power (Mayntz 2004). Narrowing the focus down exclusively to the problem-centred approach may thus run the risk of ending up in a functionalistic fallacy (Jessop 2004). The actor-centred approach, for its part, understands network governance as a response to political and administrative fragmentation and specialisation or to the state's reduced direct involvement and the cutback of state and administrative capacities which were highlighted by concepts of the 'lean' or 'hollow' state (Rhodes 1994). In this line of argumentation, network governance is necessary damage control in a situation where the state fails to steer society properly, abandons responsibility, or when institutions are fragmented. In addition, it has been argued that governance networks may be vehicles for collaborative innovation in the public sector (Sørensen and Torfing 2016). Such innovation is helpful in finding ways to cut costs in more acceptable ways for the affected groups. Under this line of thought, network governance helps to improve democratic performance by providing a supplementary channel for participation of intensely affected actors (Berg-Nordlie 2015; Sørensen and Torfing 2016). This position has been criticised because networks may have the opposite effect of capturing potentially oppositional voices within networks where they are unable to make a genuine difference (Davies 2011).

The concept of network governance applied in this book aims to be concise, concrete and easy to operationalise. We draw a basic distinction between the frequently cited three ideal types (modes) of governance (e.g. Bähr et al. 2007): hierarchy (vertical); market; and network (horizontal). In the first type, a policy issue is considered the exclusive domain of the state and relations are usually based on institutionalised subordination which significantly curtails the autonomy of subordinate actors (Scharpf 1997). The links between the actors are tight, if not rigid in this model, which is, among others, typical for the traditional Weberian bureaucratic organisation. In the second type, the state defines the phenomenon as best managed without its direct participation, allowing private actors to regulate the field through competition. Coordination of autonomous actors is achieved mainly by mutual adaption. In the last type, the state permits and enables actors from civil society and private business to participate in policy-making and policy-implementation, ideally on relatively equal footing. Coordination among actors is achieved by mutual influence and resource dependency. In practice, of course, a policy issue will often be treated through a mix of governance modes (Winsvold et al. 2009: 408–421). For the purpose of this book, we further limit the definition of network governance to the *legal* utilisation of networks transcending the state/non-state divide to govern, and thereby consider the utilisation of illegal or hidden networks as a separate, though often in practice connected, form of governance. The networks we investigate are formalised, or at the very least their existence has been publicly declared (see above). This does not mean that informal practices and channels were blended out while the formalised bodies were studied, but the point of departure was to examine openly declared networks.

Our understanding of governance networks is narrower than, for example, that of Torfing and Sørensen (2014: 6), who do not considerate it necessary for both state-based and non-state actors to take part. Simultaneously, it is narrower and broader than their general definition of governance: they do not strictly define informal networking as being on the outside of the 'governance' concept, but they do delimit the term to situations where there is a fundamental position of common interest on part of the involved actors ('in accordance with common goals'; see also Héritier 2002: 3). We, on the other hand, do not assume any notion of a common goal among governance network participants since actors may have different reasons for participating in the same network. As mentioned above, it is not unusual for definitions of governance to take a degree of mutual dependency between state and non-state actors for granted and to operate from an expectation that interactions will not be characterised by much hierarchical power wielded by the state, while more generally acknowledging that network processes usually occur 'in the shadow of hierarchy' cast by the state (Scharpf 1994: 40; Héritier and Lehmkuhl 2008; Bekkers et al. 2007; Rhodes 2007: 125; Vabo and Røiseland 2008: 91). The assumption of equality between actors in networks has also been discussed critically since there is an inherent power imbalance between state- and non-state sectors, and also because traditional and well-established elites may exert power over others within networks (Davies et al. 2016). In line with these general reservations, the authors of this book do not consider civil society-based actors in governance networks as operating on equal terms with state-based actors.

2.1.2   *Normativity in Network Governance Theory*

Early contributions to the network governance literature tended to be normatively inclined in favour of their object of investigation. The phenomenon was portrayed as something qualitatively new, or at least a practice that had assumed proportions that made it a qualitatively new type of policy-making. It was emphasised that this governance mode provides considerable structural innovation, where 'production, financing and decision-making are all moved around in a new configuration to reshape the system that determines what is produced, how it is financed, and whose values are given emphasis in guiding the process of social production' (Moore and Hartley 2008, 2010: 62). Relationships within networks are said to feature a high level of trust (Provan and Kenis 2007: 238; Sørensen and Torfing 2009a: 236). It is also argued that collaboration between self-governing actors creates benefits for all sides so that win-win situations arise (Sørensen 2006: 101). Moreover, it is commonly assumed that 'horizontal' forms of governance increase the effectiveness of policy-making (Provan and Milward 2001) and thus enhance output legitimacy. From a discursive, associational or elite-democratic angle, it has been argued that networks contribute decisively to improving the input legitimacy (Sørensen and Torfing 2009a: 244) by incorporating affected or competent groups into policy-making.

Contrariwise, it has been pointed out that the academic interest in interactions between state- and non-state actors is not something invented by the network governance literature, and that today's discourse and practice are but the contemporary incarnation of something very old (Davies et al. 2016). It is more novel that decision-makers and academics now talk explicitly about governance networks as one of the most 'efficient and legitimate mechanisms of public governance' (Torfing and Sørensen 2014: 7). The development of this normative position is reflected in the further spread of governance networks at various levels of politics, which in turn makes governance networks an increasingly interesting object of research.

Research on governance has been divided into two generations, the first of which focused on demonstrating that this new type of governance exists and on defining the phenomenon. The second already took its existence as a point of departure for further investigations (Torfing and Sørensen 2014: 11–14). Soon the concept was revised, predominantly by pointing to the permanent role of the state as the 'meta-governor' of governance networks. Meta-governance studies are sometimes considered as a second wave in governance research and which shares the view of the first wave that a shift has occurred from hierarchy to markets and networks. But they are less ambitious and normatively laden in that the role of the state is more strongly emphasised. In this perspective, the state appears particularly in its capacity as meta-governor which coordinates a myriad of self-regulating governance mechanisms and remains an accountable body of last resort in case of governance failure (Bevir and Rhodes 2010; Davies 2012: 2689). This concept can be understood as an approach pointing to the need of coordination by designing and managing sound combinations of the three basic governance modes. Ideally, meta-governance would help to overcome some of the shortcomings inherent in each single governance mode (Jessop 2004). This issue, and its relationship to the potential democratisation aspect of network governance, will be discussed below.

In addition to the concept being revised and made less normative, the practice of network governance has also been criticised by researchers on more fundamental grounds. While network governance emerges for various reasons—such as problem complexity, social fragmentation and resource interdependence—it creates new problems, notably limited pluralism and deficient representation, loss of influence of elected officials as well as being informal and lacking visibility. It has also been observed that networks, although facilitating representation, inhibit accountability because networks activities are often deliberatively informal in style, and opaque, in order to achieve compromise (Papadopolous 2012: 116). Papadopoulos (2013: 130) as well takes issue with networks' conception as 'irenic' entities, meaning that they produce harmony and provide reconciliation-seeking bodies. It was also demurred that this view obscures power relations among their members as well as between members of, and outsiders to, the network. Networks are often a result of power struggles on whose claims are reckoned to be legitimate, and who are therefore considered credible stakeholders. Furthermore, it has been argued that governance networks are easily subject to network closure and creeping managerialism. It was also emphasised that they often fail to cultivate the dispositions actually envisaged by the neo-liberal hegemonic project, namely citizen-activists capable of energetically solving policy and management problems through a trust-based, de-politicised discourse (Davies 2011: 132). Different techniques and principles of state meta-governance have been promoted as ways of solving some of these issues: for example, how to prevent power slipping too much from elected representatives, and how to ensure that non-state participants represent the interests of their groups and organisations. Simultaneously, state meta-governance is also accused of having potential for helping traditional elites entrench their dominance despite the inclusion of barely audible groups (Berg-Nordlie 2015: 215–216; Davies 2011: 62–64; Røiseland and Vabo 2012: 62–63; Sørensen and Torfing 2009a: 246–247, 251).

While the theoretical literature on network governance is often imbued with normativity regarding the phenomenon it describes, it nevertheless provides a solid theoretical core which focuses on the systematic involvement of actors outside the state sector in policy-deliberation, policy-making, and implementation. Our point of departure in this book is that governance networks in Russia do exist and can be described by using the terminology of network governance theory, although one should not expect actually-existing governance networks to be characterised by egalitarian interrelations, trust, or good faith. The existence of governance networks in Russia has already been documented by case studies utilising network governance theory (Aasland et al. 2016; Berg-Nordlie 2015; Berg-Nordlie and Tkach 2016; Bogdanova et al. 2016; Davies et al. 2016; Kropp and Schuhmann 2014, 2016; Myhre and Berg-Nordlie 2016). Yet, there is still a need for more literature which systematically compares such networks, both in Russia and in other countries, from a critical angle that focuses on meta-governance and power asymmetries. The chapters collected in this book provide structured comparisons for investigating such networks.

2.2   META-GOVERNANCE AND THE SO-CALLED NATO MODEL

Research has given plenty of evidence that the state plays a prominent role in governing and coordinating network activities. Considering that, it seems more than plausible that state authorities in hybrid regimes are even more inclined to keep network activities under control than their counterparts in democracies. Consequentially, applying network governance perspectives to Russia requires a careful account of how the state exerts influence in the networks. The so-called *NATO* model suggested by Hood (1983)[1] highlights four capabilities that enable an actor to exert control. The NATO model was originally used to describe the state's resources for governing, but may also be utilised to specify the resources non-state actors may draw on. 'NATO' is an acronym for nodality, authority, treasure, and organisation. *Nodality* refers to an actor's centrality in information networks and social networks. Through its nodal position, the state may not only gather relevant information to gain an edge over non-state actors, but also to send out messages which facilitate its control, or withhold and suppress information to its benefit. *Authority* denotes the usage of legal authority to make decisions. An actor may also resort to its *treasure*, or its *organisation*—referring to the access to economic resources and human or material resources. The reader may note that these resource types fortify one another—the possession of one may be utilised to strengthen one's control of the other. For example, organisation is relevant for most of the state's meta-governance since it tends to be performed by state employees, who are again paid through treasure.

Vabo and Røiseland (2012) developed the NATO model further in their studies of network governance and meta-governance, pointing to the possibility of drawing on these resources in 'hard' or 'soft' ways. Hard utilisation involves maintaining a monopoly on nodality and treasure: other informational nodes can be prevented from appearing and opportunities for financing can be restricted. Authority can be exerted in ways that unwanted forms of action are completely prevented; one's organisational resources can be used in order to directly make decisions while the network is bypassed or instructed from the inside. Softer utilisation of these resources involves giving information and setting incentives in a context in which no actor disposes of a monopoly. It implies relying on guidelines and non-binding regulations rather than instructions and using organisational resources to participate inside networks in a non-authoritarian fashion.

Five concrete meta-governance techniques which one may relate to these capabilities are: formal framing; economic framing; rhetorical framing; participant selection; and direct participation (for this typology see Sørensen and Torfing 2009: 246–247, 251; 2016; cf. also Davies 2011: 62–64; Røiseland and Vabo 2012: 62–63, 80). In addition, we distinguish between the concepts 'meta-governor' and 'network governor', the latter referring to the actor that formally has the responsibility for managing the network, if such an actor exists. The former is simply a participant who tries to steer the network—a role that all participants in a network may attempt to take.

Formal framing refers to how a network's activities are organised. All formalised governance networks possess a certain degree of this feature since they are established to address some pre-defined issue and the level of authority is mostly pre-determined. Formal framing can be done so 'hard' that it effectively prevents network members from raising problems or proposing solutions the network manager does not want to see discussed. Under these circumstances, certain types of criticism are essentially blocked. Formal framing is a function of the authority to decide the tasks and responsibilities of governance networks. *Economic framing* points to the practice of regulating the network's access to resources. It is quite common for networks not to have their own budget. Instead, they have to go through the network governor, a practice that obviously empowers the latter. Applying this observation to the NATO framework, it is a function of not only the treasury, but also of authority, since the available sources of funding a network may be regulated through formal framing. Meta-governors may also utilise *rhetorical framing* to determine what is to be considered 'constructive', 'proper', 'realistic' etc. for network participants to do and say. Actors who choose to enter governance networks run the risk of being ensnared by a pre-set discourse's definitions of the problems and the options (Davies 2011: 62–64). In a similar vein, rhetorical framing was discussed when describing how authorities can control governance networks by articulating ideas about the network's common identity and mission (Røiseland and Vabo 2012: 62, 80), attempting to 'determine [its] political goals … and discursive story-line' (Sørensen and Torfing 2009: 246; 2016). Rhetorical framing can be regarded as an effect of an actor's nodality, both in the concrete governance networks and for the society in which the governance networks operate.

Participant selection refers to the network governor reserving for himself the power to decide who participates in the network. In some cases, the entire network consists of individuals chosen by the network governor, while in others NGOs or other 'constituencies' are invited to elect or select their own representatives. This difference is rather important since the latter practice increases the likelihood of network participants who consider themselves beholden to an outside constituency rather than to just the network governor. This will be an advantage, if it is a goal in itself to ensure the genuine representation of certain groups in the network. Moreover, it reduces the chances of participants refraining from constructive criticism from the fear that they will be removed from the network by the governor (Berg-Nordlie 2015: 216–218; Røiseland and Vabo 2012: 63–64; Sørensen and Torfing 2009a: 244–245). On the other hand, the absence of participant selection by the network governor may make it more difficult to reach agreements or lead constructive debates if participants consider themselves locked into the positions of their constituencies and value representing these positions over actually coming to agreement. The ability to design a network with respect to participant selection, again, is a function of authority. Finally, *direct participation* of the network governor or its representatives inside the network is also a quite common technique to guide—or censor—the activity of other network participants. This is both a product of network design and hence authority, as well as being a function of organisation, since direct participation generally necessitates human resources, again paid in many cases through treasure.

All these techniques can be practiced in 'hard' or 'soft' ways. If the first option is realised, asymmetrical relations within the network become self-evident. If the second option materialises, then this probably results in networks which are to varying extents horizontal in structure, and whose actors are also to varying extents able to give creative and critical input. In addition, if all meta-governance techniques fail, then the state is, in most cases, free to ignore input from network governance arenas or the actors included—bypassing networks in this fashion are a hard utilisation of NATO-resources. The state can ignore such input unless it has committed itself to give non-state actors a veto right, has delegated decision-making authority to them, or has a weak position vis-à-vis the non-state actors. Generally, though, the power imbalance between state- and non-state actors can be expected to lean in the state's favour.

Furthermore, it should be noted that certain meta-governance techniques relevant to investigating non-democratic contexts are often not mentioned in common models: The informal or implicit threats of negative consequences must not be underestimated as *de facto* methods of keeping network participants under control (Sect. 2.3). Another shortcoming of the above practice is that actors are often treated as 'totalities' in the words of Hood (1983), who underscores that this is a substantial simplification. As the chapters of this book will make clear the Russian state is, indeed, a conglomeration of multiple actors, several of which may adopt a role in the establishment of governance networks and their meta-governance, while others may not. Within the state organisation, different agencies with different interests exist, and different levels of the state may pursue various goals. The chapters will show that multi-level governance can be particularly relevant in Russian network governance, due to relationships between the federal, provincial, and municipal levels. This will be further addressed under Sect. 2.3.

As noted above, meta-governance can be seen as an opportunity for the state to secure control in a situation where non-state actors have been given the chance to influence policy-making or policy implementation. It is also applied in order to ensure the legitimacy of governance networks' activities. Yet, it can in addition be used as a method for state-based actors and other traditional elites to maintain their dominance despite the emergence of mechanisms that involve subaltern groups in policy-making. Especially when the governance networks are supposed to facilitate the empowerment of minorities and other marginal groups, the critical view on meta-governance can be very relevant. Furthermore, in states like Russia, where one must question that institutions of representative democracy are effective or not, the argument that meta-governance secures representative-democratic power becomes less applicable. In such regimes, the inclusion of civil society actors in governance may even be one of the few possibilities for authorities to receive genuine input from below. Nevertheless, even in hybrid or authoritarian regimes, the state can be popularly perceived as the legitimate wielder of political power, and governance networks are consequently not acknowledged as legitimate unless the state exerts control over them. In the Russian context, some non-state actors consider the absence of state involvement in their network as a signal for the network's irrelevance, while others want the state to be hardly involved, in order to discuss matters more freely (Aasland et al. 2016; Berg-Nordlie and Tkach 2016). Differing positions therefore may reflect differing strategies and indicate a difference between actors interested in pragmatic politics on the one hand and actors primarily oriented towards compromise-free expression of their movement's interests on the other.

The effect of meta-governance depends on how, and for what reasons, it is practiced. It can prevent a network from becoming chaotic and dysfunctional or stifle creativity and criticism. It can be used to facilitate a sense of equality between actors, but also to cultivate favoured actors at the cost of the marginalisation of others. It can keep discussions from veering off course and becoming unproductive, or it can delimit the frames for discussion to such an extent that only details are left to the network with all matters of importance being decided elsewhere. An often cited typology to rate the power of non-state actors in cooperation with state-based actors is the ladder of citizen participation, which divides types of participation into non-participation, tokenism, and citizen power (Arnstein 1969). Arnstein's typology is quite strict classifying as mere 'tokenism' all arrangements where the non-state actors lack the power to make actual political decisions, or at the very least have the power to block decision-making until they give their consent. In practice, it is very rare and often illegal for state bodies to give non-state actors the kind of power that Arnstein holds up as the ideal (cf. Schmidt et al. 2011). Another typology of non-state influence, simplified from Arnstein's typology, uses the participation types *manipulative or symbolic inclusion*, with non-state actors having no detectable impact on decisions; *effective consultancy*, when it can be shown that non-state actors have influenced decisions; *negotiating power*, which is exercised when decisions cannot, formally or informally, be made without non-state actors' acceptance, and true *decision-making authority* (Berg-Nordlie 2015).

The chapters of this book will primarily utilise an approach which forgoes the 'ladder' format and instead suggests a typology showcasing different, non-exclusive activities that governance networks may perform (see Chap. 9): *monitoring*, which means systematically observing politics and giving critical comments to state-based actors and/or to the public; *advice*, which points to a formalised recommendation system; *coordination*, which aims at distributing tasks and avoiding duplication of activities; *implementation*, and *decision-making* (cf. Howlett and Newman 2010; Aasland et al. 2016). In addition, we also utilise the type *conflict management*, as this is an intended function of many Russian governance networks (Berg-Nordlie and Tkach 2016; Kropp and Schuhmann 2014). Individual chapters may also refer to the other typologies listed above.

2.3   Network Governance in Russia

This book does not proceed from the assumption that Russian public administration is permeated with networks of benign, trust-based relations among actors with equal voice and resources which contribute to social inclusion and participatory democracy. As argued by Davies (2011, 2012), this is not an adequate description of network governance in the West either: existing power structures can and do use governance networks in order to reinforce themselves. This revision of the governance literature, which emphasises the role of the state as meta-governor and highlights that governance networks are often established as tools to assist the state in governing, allows us to take network governance theory out of its original context and apply it for discussing how and why the Russian regime sets up consultative platforms and financing mechanisms for interaction with non-state actors. At the same time, the empirical investigation of governance networks in Russian regions requires a careful contextualisation of the approach, taking into account the given institutional setting and the specific constellation of actors.

In fact, governance networks have become a widely accepted tool of policy-making in Russia. A study of Russian media debates on inclusion of non-state actors in several different policy fields found it to be treated as natural and expected that non-state actors participate in, or perhaps one should rather say 'contribute to', governance (Myhre and Berg-Nordlie 2016). The findings also included also Russian debate on non-state actors' involvement in politics as leaning heavily towards presenting actors as being obliged to help the state reach its goals, rather than as actors who represent their own interests and opinions. Interviews have also found there to be a prevalent attitude among participants in network governance, state- and non-state alike, that the state has the role of 'lead partner' and that the non-state actors are considered as 'invited expertise' rather than as representatives of their groups' interests (Aasland et al. 2016; Berg-Nordlie and Tkach 2016). At the same time, it was often openly claimed that the Russian state is incapable of solving certain problems without non-state actors. The debate hence leans towards the 'problem-centred' discourse that presents sector-transcending networking as a necessity produced by social and political complexity, and a hegemonic discourse of mutual dependency. Thus the reader may note that the governance networks described in this book have been established in a context where it is almost expected that such networks be problem-centred rather than actor-centred, as well as being actively steered by the state.

2.3.1   Managed Civil Society and Managed Democracy

Russia is one of several states that combine formally democratic institutions, including a (managed) multi-party system, with authoritarian techniques of governance, among others: electoral manipulation, large degree of control over mass media, and discrete harassment. These so-called 'hybrid' (Petrov et al. 2014; Robertson 2010) or 'competitive authoritarian regimes' (Levitsky and Way 2010) do however seek to avoid direct and open use of repressive measures as a standard tool. Opposition parties compete, albeit under conditions that are not on a level playing field. Even when opposition parties gain a considerable share of seats in the national assembly, the hybrid regime does not take the risk of letting the freely elected representative organ play an independent role. Instead, they substitute (Petrov et al. 2014: 11) the representative organs with various types of consultative bodies composed of non-elected, individual members who are tasked to represent public opinion, provide sector-specific insights and, to a certain degree, bring forward special interests. The substitution phenomenon is also known outside of hybrid and new authoritarian regimes: networks as substitutes go together with the 'lean state' often associated with the Anglo-Saxon mainstream.

In the Russian version of 'managed democracy', the government controls elections so that voters can exercise their rights but generally have no substantial impact on policy outcomes. In addition to such electoral politics, governments in hybrid regimes also aim to manage the landscape of civil-society organisations, cultivating and promoting NGOs that are supportive and loyal to the regime. As coercion and threat do occur in Russian politics (Gel'man 2015), the Western public debate has come to discuss the Russian regime's attitudes towards NGOs as being predominantly hostile and suppressive. This image has been underpinned by amendments to the NGO legislation in 2012—the so-called 'foreign agent law'—which made NGOs financed from abroad objects of tight scrutiny, and which is often cited as a prime example of the government's authoritarian turn. This law was mainly a reaction to the 'colour revolutions' in certain neighbouring post-Soviet countries, after which the Russian government aimed at taming 'antagonistic' NGOs with international connections, suspecting that these could undermine the government's authority and threaten domestic stability (Chikov 2014; Crotty et al. 2014). The 'foreign agent law' is an important aspect of state-NGO interrelations in Russia, but should not be consulted as the benchmark for evaluating the regime's general attitude to civil society—rather, it is mainly evidence of the regime's distinct 'fear of foreign influence' (Davies et al. 2016: 134).

Restrictive policies against NGOs with foreign connections have been combined with diverse grant schemes that create new opportunities for perceived 'loyal' NGOs. Many Russian NGOs suffer from weak financial and organisational resources. In responding to these deficiencies, several programs have since 2005 aimed at extending domestic funding for civil society organisations. The authorities have provided support for 'socially oriented' NGOs, mainly in social and environmental policy (Law 7-FZ, 2010), and have granted tax relief for enterprises financing charitable NGOs (Law 40-FZ 2010), thereby setting incentives for businesses to establish collaborations with civil society and demonstrate their loyalty to the state (Ulybina 2014). Authorities want NGOs to play a constructive role, mainly in supplying social services, improving housing conditions, mediating social conflicts, or contributing to environmental protection. During the same period, various arenas for managing societal initiatives and NGOs have been institutionalised. With the law designated as 'On the Public Chamber' (FZ-32, 2005), a new institution was introduced at both the federal and regional levels. Its tasks are to provide expertise to state authorities, exert control on incumbents, administrations, and legislation, and recommend how to distribute grants to civil society organisations. Its control functions were thwarted with the 2014 'Law on Public Control' (Law 212-FZ, 2014; Flikke 2016). The public chamber also presents an annual assessment on civil society activities (Petrone 2011; Tarasenko 2010).

In addition, the Russian government has promoted the establishment of platforms for sector-transcending deliberation in various policy issues. Since regional and local executives 'can shape these institutions to their own purposes' (Richter 2009: 15), these platforms differ significantly with respect to their objectives, composition, and organisation. Such platforms —often referred to as councils (*sovety*) or chambers (*palaty*)—may have the function of allowing non-state actors to monitor regional administrations, to co-opt civil society, to keep criticism internal rather than public, and not least of all to make regional policy-making more effective by involving non-state actors into policy-making. They are also, and not seldomly, created by regional-level administrators simply in order to fulfil a demand for civil society-input which comes from above (Aasland et al 2016; Berg-Nordlie and Tkach 2016; Evans 2008; Mikirova 2016). Another tendency of note during the current regime is a certain blurring of the distinctions between state and non-state through the growth of state-owned institutions (*uchrezhdenija*) which resemble New Public Management-inspired semi-public institutions in the West. In Russia, these are often owned by provincial authorities (*oblasntnye uchrezhdenija*). They are tasked with implementing policy, and—to differing extents—operate semi-autonomously, although under a clear set of demands from the state, and whose tasks can often include managing relationships with relevant civil society actors (Aasland et al. 2016; Berg-Nordlie 2015).

These examples illustrate that Russia's managed democracy has experienced a remarkable increase of formalised arenas enabling state and non-state actors to establish collaborations for policy-making and implementation. Studies suggest that civil society activism is relevant, and cooperation between state and non-state actors is pursued by state actors as long as the issues or solutions raised by non-state actors are not fundamentally controversial, and the non-state actors do not have foreign ties considered suspicious (Kleman et al. 2010; Hemment 2012). Yet, the government sets the limits and defines the scope of collaboration (Aasland et al. 2016; Ljubownikow et al. 2013; Mamonova and Visser 2014; Chebankova 2013). This leads to asymmetrical relations and strengthens the nodal position of state actors within governance networks from where the state can spread information and distribute other resources. Correspondingly, it has been pointed out that the new arenas involving civil society organisations were institutionalised to establish a so-called 'constructive' civil society. The type of civil society Russian authorities are trying to create is one that either practices compliance with the regime's policies or enforces what Cheskin and March (2015: 266) refer to as 'consentful contention'—when political activism protests policy but does not aim to replace the people in authority, particularly when coming in the form of well-intentioned advice. The regime is interested in feedback on its policy, but wants to crack down on 'dissentful contention', particularly if it is practiced by groups connected to international networks.

Notwithstanding these constraints, a broad variety of civil society organisations exists in Russia. In the steadily growing bulk of literature on state-society relations, the following ideal types of organisations are often mentioned: *Grassroots NGOs* emerge spontaneously in response to local policy problems, often related to housing and utilities, and generally feature a low professional level (Kleman et al. 2010: 135). *Professionalised NGOs* dispose of staff and are characterised by being relatively permanent. They typically voice their criticism publicly and do not refrain from taking legal steps against administrations and businesses. Quite a few of them can be characterised as dissenting, and many of them have at some point received funding from abroad. This makes them prime targets of the state. *GONGOs* (Government Organised Non-Governmental Organisations) are non-governmental organisations that were founded by state institutions. These are often made to attract international funding or simply just to mimic public participation (Mikirova et al. 2013). For some readers the term 'GONGO' has connotations of dishonesty and corruption. For the purposes of this book we ask the reader to shed these connotations, as the term is here used as a neutral description of the organisation's historical background. *State affiliates,* for their part, are organisations which are closely entangled with state structures in less formal ways (Schuhmann 2012: 101). They often consist of former employees of state administrations, for example people who were dismissed due to privatisation or staff reductions, and offer policy expertise and knowledge to the state. They can be adequately described as consenting but not necessarily as subordinate or obedient. Investigating the conflicts and interaction patterns within governance networks, variation is likely to reflect differences in types of NGO involved. The above list of ideal types does, of course, not give justice to the variation found within the world of Russian NGOs. Case chapters will, nevertheless, utilise these terms when they appear to describe the empirical data. The concluding chapter debates the extent to which this map fits the landscape.

Overall in the literature one can find a broad consensus that Russian NGOs have had to move closer to the state in order to pursue their goals. This finding has some relevant implications for the investigation of governance networks. On the one hand, during the last decade Russia has created a favourable legal and institutional environment for nurturing and sustaining governance networks. On the other hand, all previous findings suggest that Russian networks are shaped by asymmetrical relations between the actors and a corresponding lack of equality, promoting the emergence of state-dominated networks. State-based actors take full awareness of their nodality, authority, treasury and organisational capabilities, and use the complete range of meta-governance techniques listed in this chapter. They also apply coercive tools onto NGOs within networks (Kropp and Schuhmann 2016), but often it is the mere potential and not the immediate application of coercion and threat that is sufficient to make non-state actors behave according to the authorities' will. Some of these features, however, partially apply for governance networks in Western democracies as well, and these have been assessed more critically in the recent past (Davies 2012). Our analysis therefore argues that one should not think in a clear-cut dichotomy between Russian and 'Western' network governance, but place governance networks found in Russia on a continuum ranging from a pronounced state dominance to a more equal cooperation.

2.3.2   Informality and the Rule of Law

Taking the analytical perspective of network governance 'out of area' in order to apply it to Russia requires a discussion of how Russian practices of informality affect the ways formal governance networks operate. In Russia, a culture of informality is widely noted to be pervasive and likely to pattern both how governance networks are perceived externally and how they operate internally. Ledeneva (2011), who uses the term *sistema* ('the system' for the Russian culture of informality, characterises it as an open secret: every citizen knows about how the system really works and takes part in its practice. Some studies go even further, describing the Russian state as a 'network state' (Kononenko 2011: 6) where informal networks 'permeate virtually all areas of policy-making' and '[informal] network-based governance defines what the Russian state is, in effect, all about.' This, however, ignores the concurrent presence of strict formality in Russian policy-making and public administration. The marked co-existence of lively informality and strict formality is captured by analyses portraying Russian politics as being characterised by the parallel existence of a 'constitutional' or 'normative' state and an 'administrative regime' of day-to-day behaviour where state-based actors deviate from the formal rules (Sakwa 2010a, b, 2014).

Most cases collected in this book are strictly formal in the sense that they take place in clearly defined arenas with explicitly stated network memberships and transparent meetings. In fact, the relations between state and non-state actors in Russia are marked by a strong penchant for meticulous formalisation of the respective roles (Benevolenskiy and Shumlevich 2013; Makovetskaia 2016). As such they are part of the 'normative state', but the elements of informality inherent in the concept of network governance may materialise in specific, perhaps even reinforced, ways, not least of all because the rule of law is weakly institutionalised. Informality, therefore, can be expected to be a permanent factor influencing network member selection and exclusion. The processes behind the acknowledgement of which stakeholders' claims are considered legitimate (Papadopoulos 2013: 130)—a process which may cause 'network closure' (Davies 2012: 132)—are often informal and non-transparent. Moreover, policy-making in networks remains often amorphous and informal, with the details obscured for outsiders (Papadopoulos 2013: 137).

Informality has often been described as 'parasitic' on the structures of the constitutional state, while acknowledging that the picture of informal institutions living at the expense of formal institutions is all too black-and-white (Lauth 2000). Unlike formal institutions, informal ones can neither be easily identified nor their relative impact measured. In fact, the term 'informal institution' encompasses a wide variety of behaviours. Even if formal and informal institutions diverge, the informal ones do not always challenge formal rules but may *accommodate* deviant behaviour. Relations between formal and informal institutions may also be *complementary* in that they reinforce and support each other mutually; informal institutions may also substitute the formal ones and become functionally equivalent to each other (*substitutive*); but the two systems sometimes also become incompatible and *compete* with each other (Helmke and Levitsky 2004).

Network governance institutions in Russia are highly formal and codified but network governance practices are likely to be influenced by the different types of informal institutions. The authorities setting up the networks may wish to draw on complementary and substituting informal mechanisms to strengthen policy formulation and implementation. Likewise, even formalised governance networks may be used by actors who wish to accommodate the existing formal institutional arrangement to their own needs rather than to obtain certain goods. Moreover, clientelist or clan-based practices may occur within governance networks in Russia. While the culture of informality allows state-based actors to exert influence beyond their formal capacities, it simultaneously enables non-state actors to take inordinate advantage of the legitimate institutions of the state. Informality hence constitutes a two-edged sword for the state: it helps the state achieve concrete political goals, but simultaneously de facto undermines its position of supreme authority in the longer run by making the formal system less relevant than the informal system.

The relationship between formal and informal networks can turn different ways. On the one hand, being included in a formal governance network could serve as a stepping stone on the way to becoming included in an informal network (Evans 2008: 358). On the other hand, an individual may be invited into a formal governance network as a consequence of his or her prior involvement in an informal network. Formal governance networks can hence be used both to recruit people to informal networks and to formalise pre-existing unofficial networks by providing a legitimate meeting arena for government officials and non-state actors who were already involved with one another. Certain participants in Russian formal governance networks have articulated that they themselves do not know what ultimately led to their invitation into a network—their formal association with an organisation or institution, their informal connections to certain insiders, or their individual expertise (Berg-Nordlie and Tkach 2016; Aasland et al. 2016). Moreover, it is possible to find individual participants who have been included in governance networks as a result of informal networking, but are still recognised as representing their group's interest by many members of the represented organisation.

Participation in governance networks can obviously have benefits for non-state actors, just as the refusal to participate might have negative consequences. The state does not necessarily willingly share its treasury with actors who have refused to cooperate, and the possible benefits associated with close collaboration are not only symbolic. This does not mean that one's organisation is given favour only when grants and other financial support is to be handed out. It can be much subtler such as having a personal connection to someone inside the authority structures when a problem needs to be solved. These problems are not necessarily just matters of one's personal interest, but as well may be problems experienced by members of an informal network that the formal network participant is part of the group which the participant ostensibly represents (Berg-Nordlie and Tkach 2016). The patron-client mode of social interaction cultivates this kind of behaviour, as people in sector-transcending informal networks utilise formal organisations or other organs to work for their interest. The widespread practice of informal networking, the mixing of political and economic interests, and of individual and collective interests, adds a whole new layer to political analysis. Because of this muddled state of affairs, it can sometimes be a challenge to understand which interests are, ultimately, being pursued by the various state- and non-state actors in a network, and where decisions are really being made.

2.3.3   Multilevel Governance, Federalism, and Regional Specifics

Governance networks are embedded into the institutional framework of the Russian multilevel system. Between both arenas—the federal setting and governance networks which are usually located at the subnational levels—multifarious linkages, more or less tightly coupled, may occur. The Russian regions provide an excellent laboratory for studying this broad variety of governance modes. Due to the vast territory and the economic, ethnic and cultural diversity of Russia, most civil society organisations focus their activities on the municipal and regional levels rather than on the federal level (Richter 2009: 12). Policy-making takes place within the same institutional framework because most policy issues are shaped by federal laws (Art. 71 Const. RF) or by powers constituting spheres of joint juris-diction (Art. 72 Const. RF; Kahn, Trochev and Balayan 2009). At the same time, the federal subjects are granted residual authority over some reserved policy areas not provided for in art. 71 and 72 (Ross 2010: 168). Moreover, federalised policies are subject to regional interpretation, and governance structures differ considerably across the regions due to various socio-economic conditions. While, for example, some federal subjects are dominated by oil, gas and other resource extractive branches, others possess a diversified regional economy. Such differences affect the governance patterns: the more diverse the regional actor constellations, the better the chances for non-state actors to form coalitions with other private actors as well as with regional and local elites. It seems plausible that network relations feature higher complexity in regions providing some economic diversification (Schuhmann 2012: 27).

A distinction relevant to policy networks is also the extent to which the region in question is 'securitised', for example due to the existence of key resources in the area, or in the area's military-strategic value. In certain regions, issues which are not controversial elsewhere in Russia may be subject to security-related thinking from the side of state-based actors, and therefore attract more attention from Russian security structures. Finally, what kind of governance networks emerges and how networks are used are not least of all affected by the degree of democratic quality found in a specific federal subject and by the autochthonous strength or weakness of civil society. Regional comparisons demonstrate that the federal subjects differ remarkably in these dimensions (Petrov and Titkov 2013).

The Russian version of multilevel governance with its de facto inter-twined responsibilities offers plenty of opportunities for federal authorities to intervene in regional issues. Federal-regional relations have, in fact, witnessed a rigorous recentralisation after president Putin came to power in 2000 (Obydenkova and Swenden 2013). In order to contain centrifugal developments and to prevent further destabilisation in the federation, Putin promoted the concept of a 'power vertical' in order to form the backbone of multilevel governance. The 'power vertical' comprises tools of coercion and control but also includes selected incentives used to make subnational elites adapt their behaviour to the federal government's goals.

One of the most prominent measures was the foundation of 'United Russia' (*Yedinnaya Rossiya*), which was designed as a dominant party in order to co-opt the leaders at the different territorial units (Reuter 2010; Reuter and Remington 2009) and to strengthen the vertical ties within the federation. In general, the vertical integration of the party system is a key variable for understanding the true working of federal states (Riker 1964; Hepburn and Detterbeck 2013). Yet, to date Russian elite party members do not necessarily share the same policy positions when it comes to con-crete issues. United Russia by no means constitutes a homogeneous actor pursuing coherent policies. The party is rather characterised by diverging policy positions and territorial interests while also being patterned by internal conflicts. This, albeit limited, intra-party heterogeneity gives NGOs at least some opportunities to form coalitions with selected state actors (Kropp and Schuhmann 2016: 186). In addition to United Russia, several Kremlin-attached, 'in-house opposition' parties have been allowed a place in parliament—parties that practice not just compliance to the regime, but also consentful contention. Representatives of the Communist Party and 'A Just Russia' (*Spravedlivaya Rossiya*), for instance, also par-ticipate in networks with non-state actors desiring to affect policy-making.

Putin's federal reforms have altered the formal rules to govern centre-regional relations without completely changing their substance. Although the federal government is even able to encroach on policies which are under the jurisdictions of the federal subjects, heads of regions still have some leeway within their territory for shaping policy-making and applying different governance styles. Accordingly, the degree to which NGOs are actually involved in policy-making varies significantly across the regions, as the chapters in this book reveal. One should generally be careful not to overestimate the capacity of hierarchical, centralised regimes to exhaustively control lower territorial entities. Multilevel governance rarely appears as a uniform setting; this was not the case even in the extremely centralised Soviet federation (Kropp 1995). Compared to unitary systems, multilevel settings possess a more fragmented institutional structure which, again, provides a certain number of 'access points' (Bouwen 2004) for NGOs trying to influence decisions. However, differing from democratic federations and multilevel governance structures such as the EU (Jessop 2004), state actors in Russia still operate as immediate holders of sovereign authority, notwithstanding the hierarchical command structure which is opened for governance networks. In this regard, the case studies in this book illustrate that NGOs have tried to exploit different positions within the 'power vertical' to their own advantage, but they also substantiate the argument that federal authorities attempt to overrule the lower ones and encroach on regional responsibilities, if they regard it as being useful or necessary. Considering the complex interactions among actors at the various territorial levels and their individual linkages with governance networks, it can, however, be summarised that Russian multilevel governance is not strictly shaped by a military-like chain of subordination and command running from the centre to the regions, although the official discourse on the 'vertical of power' may suggest this. Even though regional power has been undoubtedly curtailed under Putin (Sharafutdinova 2013), multilevel relations have also been characterised by negotiations between actors and non-interventions.

In fact, it would result in considerable transaction costs to supervise the federal subjects continuously and extensively. At the outset of this study, we therefore expected to find selective, rather than systematic federal encroachments upon subnational governance networks. Basically, such encroachments can go in two directions: the federal government can apply vertical tools in order to either enforce collaboration between state authorities and non-state actors at subnational levels or to constrain the creation of networks. In the Russian multilevel setting, regional authorities act as agents of two principals (Sharafutdinova 2009): On the one hand, the federal government wants regional leaders to prevent protest, to ensure mass loyalty by developing the regional economies and providing social welfare, and to deliver favourable election results (Gel'man and Ryzhenkov 2011: 456). While the direct election of the governors was reintroduced in 2012 (Golosov 2012), the president still has power to secure an 'uncompetitive field' in advance of gubernatorial elections in order 'to guarantee the desired outcome' (Goode 2013: 10). On the other hand, regional elites need to gather legitimacy and ensure output efficiency by accounting for the needs and demands of the region's citizens. In such constellations, governance networks may provide an institutionalised arena for regional elites where they try to balance the outlined agency problems.

2.4   Case Selection and Methodology

As this book tries to capture the complexity of interactions within governance networks and asks how these networks are governed by the authorities, a qualitative research design was chosen (Yin 2014). The individual chapters build on comparisons of formal governance networks which were selected for their differences. Some of these networks form part of *policy fields*, i.e. the issues they deal with are constructed as targeted specific action by the authorities and include specialised institutions, experts and interest groups which aim to influence the issue. This concerns the governance networks in ethnic conflict management (Kropp and Schuhmann, this book), child protection (Holm-Hansen, this book), and the indigenous policy field (Berg-Nordlie, this book). Other chapters analyse governance networks operating in a relation to a *policy issue* that does not enjoy the same level of institutionalisation, where the actors involved are often specialised to deal with other issues, and the political attention to the issue can be weak. This includes the chapter on HIV prevention and HIV treatment (Aasland and Meylakhs, this book) and the chapter on climate change adaption (Holm-Hansen and Berg-Nordlie, this book). Finally, one of the chapters deal with governance networks formed as part of a *policy tool*—a method to implement policy. This concerns the networks formed as part of the procedures for performing environmental impact assessments (Schuhmann and Kropp, this book). Examples of Russian governance networks are also drawn from a wide variety of Russian regions: from Arkhangelsk and Murmansk by the White Sea, St. Petersburg by the Gulf of Finland, Samara on the banks of the Volga, Krasnodar and Saratov near the Caucasus Mountains, and Irkutsk at Lake Baikal in Siberia.

Systematic variation between the cases has made it possible to create and test a broad range of hypotheses on governance in Russia. All studies provide a comparative perspective, comparing approaches to network governance in different regions, different levels, and at different points in post-Soviet Russian history. This case-study approach (Gerring 2008) allows for controlling for inter-case variances that cannot be traced back to the characteristics of the specific policy. Even if the cases are strikingly dissimilar, Russian network governance exhibits interesting commonalities and permits some theoretical generalisations. These differences and similarities alike will be showcased in the final chapter of this book (Kropp and Aasland, this book).

As governance networks are usually created in response to complex problems, only those policies characterised by a high complexity were chosen for this book. Apart from that, the modes of politics that the governance networks work with are rather different, but in all case studies we find that the issues have generated more or less high levels of conflict. EIAs are a policy tool normally applied to large-scale infrastructure projects with high economic impact. The clash between environmental interests and economic interests which may be in mutual opposition, something such as tourism versus heavy industry, can create conflicts that may put EIAs high on the political agenda. The same is true for ethnic conflict management, more so for those cases related to the larger ethnic groups ('nationality policy') than for the native and small-numbered groups ('indigenous policy'). But observing the latter policy field it becomes evident that it is also far from harmonious as it involves elements of both inter-ethnic conflict, economic interest conflicts, and internationalised dissenting contention.

The term 'securitisation' is again relevant: in several of the cases dealt with in this book, political issues are discursively transformed into matters of security against threats to the realm, a framing enabling authorities to resort to extraordinary measures. This is relevant particularly for indigenous policy. On a more general level, the securitisation of international contacts as such is relevant for all the political issues dealt with in this book, since many non-state actors (and for that matter, also parts of the state apparatus) have, or have had, projects and programs subsidised by international partners. However, after the 'foreign agent law' of 2012, non-state actors who were dependent on international networks and/or international funding experienced setbacks. This applies particularly to EIAs, indigenous policy, and HIV prevention among drug users (Chaps. 3, 4, 8). Incidentally, the reader must be aware that the securitisation of internationalised arenas also affected the research for this book, since we experienced during our field work that it became increasingly difficult to obtain interviews with state-based actors or even consenting actors, presumably since these actors deemed it unwise to discuss Russian politics with foreign researchers. Not wanting to have our findings skewed by an unrepresentative number of dissenting interviewees, some of the cases saw the need for interviews with consenting or state-based actors to be performed by Russian partners.

Differences of governance networks relating to political specifics can also be traced back to the formal institutional setting. Like in all multilevel systems, the distribution of responsibilities between the federal level and the regions in Russia varies from policy to policy. Some issues, such as the environmental impact assessments (EIAs) are strictly regulated on the federal level. By contrast, the regional platforms tackling ethnic problems are under the jurisdiction of the federal subjects, providing scope for establishing and governing regional and local networks in a different manner. Others, such as drug prevention, are shaped by shared responsibilities. Legal regulations, of course, explain the real working of networks just partially. Moreover, irrespective of the given policy-specific distribution of responsibilities, all governance networks are subject to regional and local interpretation. Case-related variations within a federal entity or a single policy may also occur if the federal government selectively applies the tools of the 'power vertical' in order to enforce its targets to its own discretion (Kropp and Schuhmann 2016).

The case studies used method triangulation, drawing upon more than 200 semi-structured interviews conducted between 2007 and 2015 with deputies in local and regional parliaments, officials in regional administrations and federal agencies, academics, journalists, NGOs, and representatives of businesses. When interviewees had reservations about being recorded, the content of the interview was written down and evaluated afterwards. The interviews were coded along a categorised scheme, an approach which allowed adding categories which were subsequently extracted from the empirical data. For ethical reasons, all interviews were anonymised. We hence refer only to the region and place, the policy area, and, if possible, the organisation of the respondent. The project teams also attended meetings and public hearings between 2007 and 2016. Regional and federal legal documents as well as local and national media and newsletters of state and non-state actors completed the database.

The scale of this study, based on a medium number of cases, provides some systematic variation. Therefore, some generalisations on the systemic role and the functioning of governance networks as well as the way these networks are governed (meta-governance) in hybrid regimes can be drawn. In addition, the scope of this book offers detailed descriptions of the actors and their preferences and enables the reader to delve into each single case study; the last chapter summarises the basic findings and offers a systematic overview on the types of governance networks presented in the policy chapters. It also gives explanations for why similarities and differences occur. The findings are finally fed back into governance theory.

NOTES

1. The name of this model is somewhat unfortunate, when our purpose is to study Russian politics. Yet, we find the model useful enough that we utilise it despite the name's potential for controversy in a Russian context. For clarity, neither the model nor its origin has any connection to the North Atlantic Treaty Organisation, the acronym stands for 'nodality, authority, treasure, and organisation'.

REFERENCES

Aasland, Aadne, Mikkel Berg-Nordlie, and Elena Bogdanova. 2016. Encouraged but controlled: Governance networks in Russian regions. *East European Politics* 32 (2): 148–169.

Arnstein, Sherry R. 1969. A ladder of citizen participation. *Journal of the American Planning* 35 (4): 216–224.

Bähr, Holger, Gerda Falkner, and Oliver Treib. 2007. Modes of governance. Towards a conceptual clarification. *Journal of European Public Policy* 14: 1–20.

Bekkers, Viktor, Geske Dijkstra, Arthur Edwards, and Menno Fenger. 2007. *Governance and the democratic deficit.* Hampshire: Ashgate.

Benevolenskiy, B. Vladimir, and Ekaterina O. Shumlevich. 2013. Gosudarstvennaia podderzhka sotsial'no orientirovannykh NKO v svete zarubezhnoi opyta. *Voprosy gosudarstvennaia i munitsipal'nogo upravleniia* 3: 150–175.

Berg-Nordlie, Mikkel. 2015. Who shall represent the Sámi? Indigenous governance in Murmansk Region and the Nordic Sámi Parliament model. In *Indigenous politics. Institutions, representation, mobilisation*, ed. Mikkel Berg-Nordlie, Jo Saglie, and Ann Sullvian, 213–253. Colchester: ECPR.

Berg-Nordlie, Mikkel, and Olga Tkach. 2016. You are responsible for your people: The role of Diaspora leaders in the governance of immigrant integration in Russia. *Demokratizatsiya* 24 (2): 173–198.

Bevir, Mark, and R.A.W. Rhodes. 2010. *The state as cultural practice*. Oxford: Oxford University Press.

Bogdanova, Elena, Olga Tkach, and Aadne Aasland. 2016. Network governance in Russia: Costs and benefits. *Demokratizatsiya* 24 (2): 139–142.

Bouwen, Peter. 2004. Exchange access good for access. A comparative study of business lobbying in the EU institutions. *European Journal of Political Research* 43 (3): 337–369.

Chebankova, Elena. 2013. *Civil society in putin's Russia*. London: Routledge.

Cheskin, Ammon, and Luke March. 2015. State–society relations in contemporary Russia: New forms of political and social contention. *East European Politics* 31 (3): 261–273.

Chikov, P. 2014. *Čerez god ni odna nynešnjaja NKO v Rossii ne budet rabotat' v prežnem formate*. https://openrussia.org/post/view/1158/. Accessed September 7, 2016.

Crotty, Jo, Sarah Marie Hall, and Sergej Ljubonwnikow. 2014. Post-soviet civil society development in the Russian Federation: The impact of the NGO law. *Europe-Asia Studies* 66 (8): 1253–1269.

Davies, Jonathan S. 2011. *Challenging governance theory. From network to hegemony*. Bristol: Policy Press.

Davies, Jonathan S. 2012. Network Governance Theory: A Gramscian Critique. *Environment and Planning* 44 (11): 2687–2704.

Davies, Jonathan S., Jørn Holm-Hansen, Vadim Kononenko, and Asbjørn Røiseland. 2016. Network governance in Russia: An analytical framework. *East European Politics* 32 (2): 131–147.

Evans, Alfred B. 2008. The first steps of Russia's public chamber: Representation or coordination? *Demokratizatsiya* 16: 345–362.

Flikke, Geir. 2016. Resurgent authoritarianism: The case of Russia's new NGO legislation. *Post-Soviet Affairs* 32 (2): 103–131.

Gel'man, Vladimir. 2015. The politics of fear. *Russian Politics & Law* 53 (5–6): 6–26.

Gel'man, Vladimir, and Sergei Ryzhenkov. 2011. Local regimes, sub-national governance and the 'power vertical' in contemporary Russia. *Europe-Asia Studies* 63: 449–465.

Gerring, John. 2008. Case selection for case study analysis: Qualitative and quantitative techniques. In *Oxford handbook of political methodology*, ed. J. Box-Steffensmeier, H. Brady, and D. Collier, 645–684. New York: Oxford University Press.

Golosov, Grigorii V. 2012. The 2012 political reform in Russia. *Problems of Post-Communism* 59: 3–14.

Goode, Paul J. 2013. The revival of Russia's gubernatorial elections: Liberalization or Potemkin reform? *Russian Analytical Digest* 139.

Hale, Henry E. 2011. Hybrid regimes – When autocracy and democracy mix. In *Dynamics of democratization: Dictatorship, development, and diffusion*, ed. Nathan J. Brown, 23–45. Baltimore: John Hopkins University.

Hale, Henry E. 2015. *Patronal politics. Eurasian regime dynamics in comparative perspective*. CUP: Cambridge.

Helmke, Gretchen, and Steven Levitsky. 2004. Informal institutions and comparative politics: A research agenda. *Perspectives in Politics* 4: 725–740.

Hemment, Julie. 2012. Redefining need, reconfiguring expectations: The rise of state-run youth voluntarism programs in Russia. *Anthropological Quarterly* 85 (2): 519–554.

Hepburn, Eve, and Klaus Detterbeck. 2013. Federalism, regionalism and the dynamics of party politics. In *Routledge handbook of regionalism and federalism*, ed. John Loughlin, John Kincaid, and Wilfried Swenden, 76–92. Abingdon: Routledge.

Heritiér, Adrienne. 2002. Modes of governance in Europe. Policy-making without legislating? In *Common goods: Reinventing European and international governance*, ed. Adrienne Heritiér, 185–206. Lanham: Rowman and Littlefield.

Heritiér, Adrienne, and Dirk Lehmkuhl. 2008. The shadow of hierarchy and new modes of governance. *Journal of Public Policy* 28: 1–17.

Hirst, Paul. 2000. Democracy and governance. In *Debating governance. Authority, steering, and democracy*, ed. Jon Pierre, 13–36. New York: Oxford University Press.

Holmes, L. 2012. Corruption in Post-Soviet Russia. *Global Change, Peace & Security* 24 (2): 235–250.

Hood, Christopher. 1983. *The tools of government*. London: Macmillan.

Howlett, Michael, and Joshua Newman. 2010. Policy analysis and policy work in federal systems: Policy advice and its contribution to evidence-based policy-making in multi-level governance systems. *Policy and Society* 29 (2): 123–136.

Jessop, Bob. 2004. Multi-level governance and multi-level meta-governance. In *Multi-level governance*, ed. I. Bache, and M. Flinders, 49–75. Oxford: Oxford University Press.

Jung, Tobias. 2010. Policy networks: Theory and practice. In *The new public governance?: Emerging perspectives on the theory and practice of public governance*, ed. Stephen P. Osborne, 351–364. London: Routledge.

Kahn, Jeffrey, Alexej Trochev, and Nikolay Balayan. 2009. The unification of law in the Russian federation. *Post-Soviet Affairs* 25: 310–346.

Kleman, Karin, Ol'ga Miriasova, and Andrei Demidov. 2010. *Ot obyvatelelei k aktivistam – zarozhdaiushchiesia dvizhenia v sovremennoi Rossii*. Moskva: Tri kvadrata.

Kononenko, Vadim. 2011. Introduction. In *Russia as a network state: What works in Russia when state institutions do not?*, ed. Vadim Kononenko, and Arkady Moshes, 1–18. Houndmills: Palgrave Macmillan.

Kooiman, Jan. 2010. Governance and governability. In *The new public governance?: Emerging perspectives on the theory and practice of public governance*, ed. Stephen P. Osborne, 72–86. London: Routledge.

Kropp, Sabine. 1995. *Systemreform und lokale Politik in Rußland*. Opladen: Leske + Budrich.

Kropp, Sabine, and Johannes Schumann. 2014. Hierarchie und Netzwerk-Governance in russischen Regionen. Beziehungen zwischen Staat und privaten Akteuren im Policy-Vergleich der Umweltpolitik und ethnischen Konfliktregulierung. *Zeitschrift für Vergleichende Politikwissenschaft, Comparative Governance and Politics*, Special Issue (Von Government zu Governance. Informales Regieren im Vergleich, eds Stephan Bröchler and Hans-Joachim Lauth): 61–90.

Kropp, Sabine, and Johannes Schumann. 2016. Governance networks and vertical power in Russia—Environmental impact assessments and collaboration between state and non-state actors. *East European Politics* 32 (2): 192–214.

Lauth, Hans-Joachim. 2000. Informal institutions and democracy. *Democratization* 7: 21–50.

Ledeneva, Alena V. 2011. Can Medvedev change sistema? Informal networks and public administration in Russia. In *Russia as a network state. What works in Russia when state institutions do not?* ed. Vadim Kononenko and Arkady Moshes, 39–61. Houndsmills: Palgrave Macmillan.

Levitsky, Steven, and Lucian A. Way. 2010. *Competitive authoritarianism: Hybrid regimes after the cold war*. New York: Cambridge University Press.

Ljubownikow, Sergej, Jo Crotty, and Peter W. Rodgers. 2013. The State and civil society in Post-Soviet Russia: The development of a Russian-style civil society. *Progress in Development Studies* 13 (2): 153–166.

Makovetskaia, Svetlana G. 2016. Uchastie ob"edinenii grazhdan i biznesa v so-upravlenii sotsial'noi sferoi—institutsional'nye vozmozhnosti, izderzhki i bar'iery dostupa. Paper presented at the XVII April international academic conference on economic and social development, higher school of economics Moscow.

Mamonova, Natalia, and Oane Visser. 2014. State marionettes, phantom organisations or genuine movements? The paradoxical emergence of rural social movements in post-socialist Russia. *The Journal of Peasant Studies* 41: 491–516.

Mayntz, Renate. 2004. Governance im modernen Staat. In *Governance—Regieren in komplexen Regelsystemen. Eine Einführung*, ed. Arthur Benz, 65–76. Wiesbaden: VS-Verlag.

Mikirova, Karina. 2016. *Governance structures for regional ethnic policy in the Russian federation. Interactions between state and non-state actor within negotiation platforms*. WVB: Berlin.

Mikirova, Karina, Kathrin Mueller, and Johannes Schuhmann. 2013. The influence of civil society activism on regional governance structures in the Russian federation: Cross-regional and policy comparison. In *Civil society activism under authoritarian rule. A comparative perspective*, ed. Fracesco Cavartorta, 111–134. New York: Routledge.

Moore, Mark, and Jean Hartley. 2008. Innovations in governance. *Public management review* 10 (1): 3–20.

Moore, Mark, and Jean Hartley. 2010. Innovations in governance. In *The new public governance? Emerging perspectives on the theory and practice of public governance*, ed. Stephen P. Osborne, 52–71. London: Routledge.

Myhre, Marthe, and Mikkel Berg-Nordlie. 2016. "The state cannot help them all". Russian media discourse on the inclusion of non-state actors in governance. *East European Politics* 32 (2): 192–214.

Obydenkova, Anastassia, and Wilfried Swenden. 2013. Autocracy-sustaining versus democratic federalism: Explaining the divergent trajectories of territorial politics in Russia and Western Europe. *Territory, Politics, Governance* 1 (1): 86–112.

Osborne, Stephen P. 2010. The (new) public governance: A suitable case for treatment? In *The new public governance? Emerging perspectives on the theory and practice of public governance*, ed. Stephen P. Osborne, 1–16. London: Routledge.

Papadopoulos, Yannis. 2012. Accountability and multi-level governance—More accountability, less democracy? In *Accountability and European Governance*, ed. Deirdre Curtin, Peter Mair and Yannis Papadopoulos, Oxon: Routledge.

Papadopoulos, Yannis. 2013. *Democracy in crisis? Politics, governance and policy*. Houndmills, Basingstoke: Palgrave.

Peters, B. Guy. 2000. Governance and comparative politics. In *Debating governance. authority, steering, and democracy*, ed Jon Pierre, 36–54. New York: Oxford University Press.

Peters, B. Guy. 2010. Meta-governance and public management. In *The new public governance?: Emerging perspectives on the theory and practice of public governance*, ed. Stephen P. Osborne, 36–51. London: Routledge.

Petrone, Laura. 2011. Institutionalizing pluralism in Russia: A new authoritarianism? *Journal of Communist Studies and Transition Politics* 27 (2): 166–194.

Petrov, Nikolay, and A. Titkov. 2013. *Rejting demokratičnosti regionov Moskovkogo centra karnegi: 10 let v stroju*. Moskva.

Petrov, Nikolay, Maria Lipman, and Henry E. Hale. 2014. Three dilemmas of hybrid regime governance: Russia from Putin to Putin. *Post-Soviet Affairs* 30 (1): 1–26.

Provan, Keith G., and Brinton H. Milward. 2001. Do networks really work? A framework for evaluating public-sector organizational networks. *Public Administration Review* 61: 414–423.

Provan, Keith G., and Patrick Kenis. 2007. Modes of network governance: Structure, management, and effectiveness. *Journal of Public Administration Research* 18: 229–252.

Reuter, Ora John. 2010. The politics of dominant party formation: United Russia and Russia's Governors. *Europe-Asia Studies* 62: 293–327.

Reuter, Ora John, and Thomas F. Remington. 2009. Dominant party regimes and the commitment problem: The case of United Russia. *Comparative Political Studies* 42: 501–526.

Rhodes, Rod A.W. 1994. The hollowing out of the state: The changing nature of the public service in Britain. *The Political Quarterly* 65 (2): 138–151.

Rhodes, Rod A.W. 1997. *Understanding governance: Policy networks, governance, reflexivity and accountability*. Maidenhead: Open University Press.

Rhodes, Rod A.W. 2007. Understanding governance: Ten years on. *Organization Studies* 28: 1243–1264.

Richter, James. 2009. The ministry of civil society? The public chambers in the regions. *Problems of Post-Communism* 56: 7–20.

Riker, William. 1964. *Federalism: Origin, operation, significance*. Boston: Little Brown.

Rittel, H.W.J., and M. Webber. 1973. Dilemmas in a general theory of planning. *Policy Sciences* 4: 155–169.

Robertson, Graeme. 2009. Managing society: Protest, civil society, and regime in putin's Russia. *Slavic Review* 68 (3): 528–547.

Robertson, Graeme. 2010. *The politics of protest in hybrid regimes: Managing dissent in Post-Communist Russia*. Cambridge: Cambridge University Press.

Røiseland, Asbjørn, and Signy Irene Vabo. 2012. *Styring og samstyring—governance på norsk*. Bergen: Fagbokforlaget.

Ross, Cameron. 2010. Federalism and inter-governmental relations in Russia. *Journal of Communist Studies and Transition Politics* 26 (2): 165–187.

Sakwa, Richard. 2010a. *The Crisis of Russian Democracy—The dual state, factionalism and the Medvedev succession*. Cambridge: Cambridge University Press.

Sakwa, Richard. 2010b. The Dual state in Russia. *Post-Soviet Affairs* 26 (3): 185–206.

Sakwa, Richard. 2014. *Putin redux. Power and contradiction in contemporary Russia*. Houndmills: Routledge.

Scharpf, Fritz W. 1994. Games real actors could play: Positive and negative coordination in embedded negotiations. *Journal of Theoretical Politics* 6 (1): 27–53.

Scharpf, Fritz W. 1997. *Games real actors play. Actor-centered institutionalism in policy research*. Boulder: Westview Press.

Schmidt, Lene, Jon Guttu, and Lillin Knudtzon. 2011. Medvirkning i planprosessen i Oslo kommune. *NIBR-rapport* 2011: 11.

Schuhmann, Johannes. 2012. *Governance-Strukturen in der regionalen Umweltpolitik Russlands. Verhandlungen zwischen Staat, Wirtschaft und Zivilgesellschaft*. Wiesbaden: VS-Verlag.

Sharafutdinova, Gulnaz. 2009. Subnational governance in Russia: How putin changed the contract with his agents and the problems it created for Medvedev. *Publius: The Journal of Federalism* 40: 672–696.

Sharafutdinova, Gulnaz. 2013. Gestalt switch in Russian Federalism: The decline in regional power under putin. *Comparative Politics* 45 (3): 357–376.

Sørensen, Eva. 2006. Metagovernance: The changing role of politicians in processes of democratic governance. *American Review of Public Administration* 36: 98–114.

Sørensen, Eva, and Jacob Torfing. 2009. Making governance networks effective and democratic through metagovernance. *Public Administration* 87: 234–258.

Sørensen, Eva, and Jacob Torfing. 2016. Metagoverning collaborative innovation in governance networks. *American Review of Public Administration*: 1–19.

Tarasenko, A. V. 2010. Deyatelnost' obshchestvennykh palat v regionakh Rossii: Effektivnost' vs. fiktivnost'. *Politiya* 56 (1): 80–88.

Teets, J.C. 2013. Let many civil societies bloom. The rise of consultative authoritarianism in China. *The China Quarterly* 213: 19–38.

Torfing, Jacob, and Eva Sørensen. 2014. The European debate on governance networks. Towards a new and viable paradigm? *Policy and Society* 33 (4): 329–344.

Ulybina, Olga. 2014. Interaction, cooperation and governance in the Russian forest sector. *Journal of Rural Studies* 34: 246–253.

Vabo, Signy Irene, and Asbjørn Røiseland. 2008. Governance på norsk. Samstyring som empirisk og analytisk fenomen. *Norsk statsvitenskapelig tidsskrift* 24 (1/2): 86–101.

Vabo, Signy Irene, and Asbjørn Røiseland. 2012. Conceptualizing the tools of government in urban network governance. *International Journal of Public Administration* 35 (14): 934–946.

Way, Lucian. 2010. The new authoritarianism in the former Soviet Union. *Communist and Post-Communist Studies* 43: 335–337.

Winsvold, Marte, Knut Bjørn Stokke, Jan Erling Klausen, and Inger-Lise Saglie. 2009. Organisational learning and governance in adaption in urban development. In *Adapting to Climate Change: Thresholds. Values. Governance*, eds W. Neil Agder, Irene Lorenzoni and Karen L. O'Brien. Cambridge: Cambridge University Press.

Wintrobe, Richard. 1998. *The political economy of dictatorship*. Cambridge: CUP.

Yin, Robert K. 2014. *Case study research. Design and methods*, 5th ed. London: Sage.

CHAPTER 3

Adjusting the Scope of Interaction Between State and Civil Society: HIV Prevention Among Drug Users

Aadne Aasland and Anastasia Y. Meylakhs

3.1 INTRODUCTION

The HIV rates in the Russian Federation have increased quite dramatically during the past decade and is among the world's top-ten countries with the fastest growing incidence of HIV/AIDS. The official number of registered HIV infections in Russia reached one million in 2015, while the actual number of HIV positive is likely to be considerably higher.[1] Furthermore, Russia is the only country in the G20 and BRICS where infection rates

A. Aasland (✉)
The Norwegian Institute for Urban and Regional Research (NIBR), Oslo and Akershus University College of Applied Sciences, St. Olavs plass, 0130 Oslo, Norway
e-mail: aadne.aasland@nibr.hioa.no

A.Y. Meylakhs
International Centre for Health Economics, Management, and Policy, National Research, University Higher School of Economics, Saint Petersburg, Russian Federation; Centre for Independent Social Research, Saint Petersburg, Russian Federation, Kantemirovskaya St., 3 A, office 406, Saint Petersburg, Russian Federation194100
e-mail: nastia.meylakhs@gmail.com

© The Author(s) 2018
S. Kropp et al. (eds.), *Governance in Russian Regions*,
DOI 10.1007/978-3-319-61702-2_3

continue to grow (Sidibé 2014). Though sexual transmission is becoming more pervasive, the majority of HIV positive people have been infected through the use of contaminated needles (Burki 2015). Of Russia's around two million injecting drug users (IDUs) 37% are estimated to be HIV positive, but regional variation is considerable, and in some regions HIV prevalence among IDUs reaches up to 75%.[2]

The quality of governance, understood broadly to encompass the interface between the state and non-state actors, is widely recognised to be crucial in tackling HIV (UNDP 2007; Moran 2004). With due recognition of the importance of the federal level and national leadership (Putzel 2004b), health policy in Russia, including HIV prevention, is rather decentralised with considerable regional variation (Moran and Jordaan 2007; Aasland et al. 2013). This chapter investigates governance challenges in preventing HIV among drug users in two federal subjects of Russia highly affected by the epidemic, St. Petersburg and Samara.

The chapter addresses the interaction between the authorities and non-state actors in HIV prevention among drug users, most importantly in civil society organisations. It looks into the mix of vertical structures of governance (dominated by health authorities, including the regional AIDS centers, and drug control authorities) and aspects of network governance where both state and non-state actors collaborate on policy-making and implementation. Findings are based on a thorough examination of concrete formal governance networks in St. Petersburg and Samara where issues relating to HIV and drug prevention are on the agenda.

After a presentation of the policy field and the main federal and regional actors, the chapter assesses the role of governance networks in the policy system surrounding HIV prevention. Meta-governance techniques applied by the state to retain control while at the same time encouraging input from non-state actors are then analysed. A recurrent theme is the reduced role of collaboration with international actors and the non-application of internationally recognised HIV prevention methods, a theme which has had a huge impact on the interaction between the state and civil society in the field.

3.2   Data and Methodology

Data for the chapter have mainly been collected through the project *Network Governance: A Tool for Understanding Russian Policy-Making*. Apart from a general literature review, we build on fieldwork in St. Petersburg and Samara between 2013 and 2015. The two regions were selected as being areas with high HIV incidence and widespread drug abuse. According to official statistics at the time of data collection, they were respectively number 2 and 8 among Russia's 85 regions (federal subjects) with the highest share of HIV infected in relation to the total population.[3] With more than 1% of the population being HIV-infected, both these regions qualify as territories with a generalised epidemic (Pisani et al. 2003). As will be shown, the two regions are rather different, however, when it comes to civil society landscape for HIV prevention and collaboration between authorities and civil society.

Exploratory fieldwork in the two regions was conducted in the spring and summer of 2013. We first conducted eight interviews with experts (academics, journalists, activists) to identify the main institutions, civil society organisations and collaborative structures operating in the field in each of the two regions. Then we conducted 19 semi-structured interviews with government officials and policy-makers, representatives of professional groups, civil society organisations (mostly NGOs), as well as with independent stakeholders who work in the field of HIV and drug prevention. Common interview guides were elaborated for the informant interviews, but with ample room for adaptation to specifics of each type of informant and local conditions.

Project researchers also conducted observations of five network meetings to which they had gained access. The aim of the observations was to identify participants, and to examine agenda-setting, presence or absence of debate and critical voices, negotiations and decision-making.

In addition to data collection from the above project we also made use of transcripts of nine semi-structured interviews with policy-makers and other key stakeholders at federal level that one of the authors conducted during the implementation of a project on HIV prevention in North-West Russia in 2008–2010 (for details on the project, see Aasland et al. 2011).

The interviews were recorded[4], transcribed (in Russian) and coded in Nvivo 11 Pro. Due to ethical concerns and especially taking into account the controversial nature of the issue, informants were promised anonymity. Thus, for citations in this chapter we only refer to region and category of respondent.

3.3   The Policy Field

After many years of neglect and denial, from the mid-2000s Russia started to devote significantly more attention and funding to curb the HIV epidemic (Aasland et al. 2013). Despite this political commitment, the response has until now been too limited in scale and coverage to be adequate (Pape 2013: xiv). While most of the Russian state HIV funds have been concentrated on detection and treatment of HIV infected, a lower priority has been given to other forms of prevention, and especially to targeted measures towards risk groups such as drug users. Substitution therapies, such as the use of methadone, are forbidden in Russia.

A comprehensive prevention strategy has never been adopted, though it is now finally in the making.[5] The strategy looks into different types of prevention, and besides prevention towards the general population it also stresses prevention measures towards 'key' (target) groups such as drug users. According to the strategy, such prevention should involve enhancing their motivation for being tested and for rehabilitation from drug use. However, no mention is made of evidence-based harm reduction strategies, such as needle exchange or distribution of condoms which have proven efficient internationally, and are recommended by supranational organisations such as UNAIDS and WHO in curbing HIV from spreading.[6]

From the mid-2000 onward, Russia became strongly integrated into supranational governance structures on HIV and AIDS. The country received funding from the Global Fund to Fight AIDS, Tuberculosis and Malaria, which insisted on targeted measures directed towards risk groups such as drug users, and provided funding to NGO-coordinated programmes to support such prevention efforts. Though harm reduction remained controversial, there were at least some programmes of needle exchange and distribution of condoms in many Russian regions, but these were almost exclusively supported by international donors.

With the conservative turn in Russian politics, and scepticism towards foreign funding of NGOs, international programmes in the HIV and AIDS sphere have been cut drastically. Since 2012, the Russian health minister has consistently discouraged needle exchange programmes and other targeted HIV prevention measures towards drug users and has supported more general prevention measures such as promotion of a 'healthy lifestyle' (Pates and Riley 2012) which has significantly reduced the provision of harm reduction in the Russian regions. A few small-scale programmes may still operate in Russian regions, however, typically forming a small part of more complex prevention programmes. Still, the negative attitudes of the authorities have made many organisations rethink their activities.

Until recently, socially-oriented organisations have been exempt from registering as foreign agents even if they have received foreign funding.

However, in the spring of 2016 one could see the first cases of the foreign agent label being attached to organisations working on HIV prevention. So far (September 2016) five organisations across Russia working on HIV prevention have been compelled to register under this label, as their promotion of harm reduction methods is considered a political activity. Russian legislators have recently discussed a broadening of the definition of political activity, which currently is rather vague, thereby making it even harder for organisations with a harm reduction approach to HIV prevention to find Russian donors for their activities. The following actions could count as 'political' activities: having previous international funding, distributing funding to other NGOs with a foreign agent status, conducting sociological studies within IDU- and HIV-positive communities, reporting study results to local governments, (re)publishing 'political' documents on the internet, publishing of NGO members' personal opinion, and the distributing of condoms and clean needles.

Anti-retroviral medication (ART) is used both for treatment of patients with HIV but also for the prevention of new infections. Until 2013, the Ministry of Health ran a centralised system for distribution of ART to HIV positive people. However, from mid-2013 the authorities decided to hand over the responsibility for ART distribution to the regional authorities. As a result of shortages of ART, patients in a number of Russian regions have been deprived of life-sustaining medicines, and federal and regional authorities have blamed each other for the shortages. Drug users, who are widely suspected of not being able to adhere to the strict medication regimes required for ART medication to be effective, are often low on the list of priority of users when supply is scarce.

The widespread stigma and discrimination associated with both drug use and HIV make many drug users reluctant to be tested for HIV and to consult medical institutions for treatment (Kuznetsova et al. 2016). Severe criminalisation of drug use also distances these groups from the authorities and health services. Thus, the most effective prevention programmes targeting them are often delivered through non-governmental organisations (NGOs) in the form of peer or professional outreach, drug user self-organisation and drug user network interventions. Such targeted prevention measures towards drug users are, however, not a priority of Russian authorities, neither at federal nor regional levels. Even during the height of Global Fund[7]-sponsored activities in Russia, few Russian drug users were covered by prevention activities.

Despite the negative attitudes towards harm reduction, some recent initiatives indicate that HIV prevention again is to be devoted more attention by Russian authorities, probably induced by the disturbing increase in new HIV infections. In late 2015 Prime Minister Medvedev ordered the Health Ministry to speed up the preparation of a strategy for combating the spread of HIV which, when adopted in October 2016, was the first national strategy on HIV prevention.[8] The budget for the fight against HIV doubled from 2015 to 2016—mainly in the form of more funding to treatment—despite many other cuts in the Russian budget.[9] At the time of this writing there are nevertheless reports of further budget cuts.[10] While the government advises that Russia could learn from best practices of other countries, such as Germany, they have made no mention that their policies on evidence-based harm reduction methods will be reconsidered.

3.4   THE LEGAL FRAMEWORK, FORMAL INSTITUTIONS AND STATE POLICY

The main legislation surrounding HIV and AIDS prevention among drug users in Russia is the 1995 Federal AIDS Law.[11] The law states that the federal government is responsible for the HIV response, including prevention. It also guarantees the human rights of people living with HIV (PLWH). The law is in general considered to be in line with international recommendations and best practice; the challenges are more a matter of its implementation than about the text of the law itself (Pape 2013: 76).

More problematic for HIV prevention among drug users is Russian drug legislation. Russia has adopted many punitive measures towards drug users (Lunze et al. 2015). According to Russian legislation, those who obtain or possess drugs are to be incarcerated or forced into treatment. Russian authorities persistently argue that methadone and other drug substitution therapies encourage drug use. Instead of methadone, the country relies on detoxification, psychotherapy and prescription medication to reduce the reliance on drugs (Burki 2015).

At the federal level the main institution in the field of HIV is the Federal AIDS Centre, which is in charge of surveillance, prevention, diagnosis and treatment. Under its umbrella there are eight interregional AIDS centers in the federal districts (macro-regions) and AIDS centers in each of the regions and in some larger municipalities. The structure is integrated into the Federal Service for Surveillance on Consumer Rights Protection and

Human Well-being (*Rospotrebnadzor*). This agency is subordinate to the Ministry of Health and Social Development, although the ministry also has its own AIDS department.

During the fieldwork the most important institution for dealing with drug policy in Russia was the Federal Drug Control Service (FSKN), with a hierarchical set-up of institutions in all federal subjects and regional and local territorial units. In April 2016 FSKN was dissolved and its functions and authority transferred to the Main Drugs Control Directorate of the Ministry of Internal Affairs. The Directorate is responsible for drafting state policy, legal regulation, control and monitoring of virtually all aspects of drug policy. While historically FSKN was mainly concerned with stopping the supply of illicit drugs, the agency, and now the Directorate, has also been given the responsibility for drug use prevention, rehabilitation and re-socialisation, i.e. all aspects of drug issues except the medical treatment of drug users.

Legislation in the HIV and drug sphere is centralised, and the opportunity for the regions to propose major policy initiatives is quite limited. However, both in terms of drug and HIV prevention there is some scope for regional variations in the implementation of the federal policy and when it comes to social aspects of the policy issue, such as drug rehabilitation, re-socialisation, work with drug users' families, and the prevention of substance abuse at all levels.

There has been a dramatic decrease in the number and size of grant schemes specifically targeted at HIV prevention among drug users, especially since much of the international funding in this area has been withdrawn from the country. Our informants in Samara and St. Petersburg, however, apprised us that there are still funding schemes available for NGOs operating in the area, something which is not the case in many other Russian federal subjects. The profile of the grant schemes and the projects selected for funding is quite different from the profile of previously available international grant schemes, hinting at differences between the discourses that are seen as relevant by authorities in Russia and international funding agencies. There is much more attention devoted to primary prevention directed at youth and the general public, instead of prevention measures targeted at risk groups. The Russian government strategy for the fight against HIV and AIDS for example highlights the need to involve civil society, including socially oriented non-commercial organisations. Their focus is then, however, on the general population and on a 'healthy lifestyle':

It is necessary to involve civil society organisations, prominent figures of science, culture, art, and media to prevent HIV infection among the population in order to create in the public opinion positive attitudes to socially responsible and safe behavior.[12]

Many of the NGO representatives themselves support the government's policy priorities and are opposed to controversial harm reduction measures. Others secretly support distribution of condoms and needle exchange programmes but are pragmatic and realise that it is futile to promote such measures in today's situation. In their opinion, it is better to devote their efforts to issues where they can make a true difference. Only a few openly continue to work with and promote controversial harm reduction, even with the risk of being counteracted and intimidated by the authorities.

3.5   REGIONAL STAKEHOLDERS AND GOVERNANCE NETWORKS

At a regional level, while Samara oblast has its own Ministry of Health and Social Development responsible for HIV prevention, in St. Petersburg HIV is the responsibility of the Committee of Public Health which acts as a regional ministry. As in other parts of Russia, most HIV-related activities, i.e. testing, prevention and treatment, are undertaken at specialised AIDS centres, and these therefore play a key role in the HIV response. In Samara the AIDS centre is at regional level, while in St. Petersburg it is at the city level.[13] While medical workers in the AIDS centers are professional in dealing with various aspects of the HIV epidemic, HIV has not been mainstreamed into other parts of the health system where knowledge is limited and discriminatory attitudes towards HIV positive and drug users prevail. In the drug sphere, the FSKN has had a hierarchical set-up from the federal to the regional and local levels, a structure that is likely to be transferred to the new drug directorate under the Ministry of Internal Affairs.

The number of NGOs dealing with HIV in St. Petersburg and Samara is quite limited, and particularly small in the latter. In 2013 about 30 organisations dealt with aspects of HIV in St. Petersburg (Pape 2013), but this is likely to have sunk since then. Based on our own observations we noted that the related number of organisations in Samara amounts to only handful. Very few NGOs in both the two regions are specifically centered on prevention of

HIV among drug users. Furthermore, without stable foreign funding these few organisations now are having a hard time to survive. In a situation of resource constraints, most NGOs have to work much closer with the authorities and compete for funding from state-sponsored grant programmes. The only way they can get state support is through implementation of a very limited number of activities that are planned in federal programmes or through even scarcer regional funding.

The decline in funding from international donors in combination with a priority of Russian policy-makers in the sphere towards general rather than targeted prevention has led not only to the collapse of many non-state organisations but also to a change in the activity profile of many NGOs. One result is the shift of focus from drug use prevention to more general HIV infection prevention measures or to other ways of aligning their activities with the state's priorities. Very few NGOs in the two cities are staying pro-activist, centered on drug users' rights, while a few express direct opposition to government policies. In recent years the Russian Orthodox Church has also entered the scene to become a much more involved actor in HIV prevention and drug rehabilitation (Myhre and Berg-Nordlie 2016). The majority of the organisations are legally registered as 'public associations', including 'public charity foundations'. The majority are regionally based, though in St. Petersburg some also work towards the federal level. The sizes and resources of the organisations vary considerably. Many of them are established to provide services to PLWH. Grass roots organisations such as self-help groups and interest groups among PLWH are not uncommon and exist in both cities, though during our fieldwork in Samara this organisation was not open in the public for fears of stigma and discrimination.[14] Over the past few years, there has been a trend of increasing specialisation of civil society organisations. If earlier they had a wide scope of activities, they now typically specialise on one issue, such as monitoring of HIV medication, provision of social and health services to women and children, rights protection, rehabilitation of drug users, etc. Pure GONGOs are not common in the sphere, though there is a widespread overlap between civil society groups and the state in terms of personnel transfer and distribution of tasks.

To a considerable degree, HIV and AIDS in Russia are still, viewed primarily as a medical challenge, and inter-sectoral cooperation has remained poorly developed (Aasland et al. 2013). HIV prevention, however, is a complex issue and the international experience has shown that it requires a multi-sectoral approach with involvement of a number of ministries and agencies as well as civil society actors (Putzel 2004a). Today there are inter-sectoral AIDS committees at both the federal level and, in some regions, involving both state and non-state actors. These committees were originally established as the result of Russia's then deepening involvement in international HIV and AIDS work. In St. Petersburg such a coordination council was established in 2008 and is still in operation. Samara never set up a similar council devoted to HIV, however. Likewise, while St. Petersburg still operates with a targeted cross-sectoral programme for HIV prevention[15], in Samara a corresponding programme operating in the region between 2012 and 2014 has been mainstreamed into the general health programme for 2014–2018.[16]

Besides these coordination bodies specifically targeted at HIV, there are also a number of other bodies which deal with HIV-related issues albeit on a more occasional basis. The most important arenas for coordination of drug policy initiatives, sometimes raising HIV among drug users as a topic, are the regional and municipal anti-drug commissions, which are under the FSKN (now directorate) umbrella. The anti-drug commissions have rather fixed memberships, with all sectors involved in drug prevention represented. At regional levels it is headed by the governor and has high-level representatives from a variety of regional ministries. In both Samara and St. Petersburg the commission includes one member from the regional Public Chamber. Moreover, the commission invites a variety of state and non-state experts for participation in commission meetings. At municipal levels the membership is less fixed, with some commissions including permanent non-state members, while others only invite them in as experts for reports on specific issues.

Other governance network arenas that deal with HIV issues include the regional Public Chambers, where HIV policy issues have been on the agenda in both federal subjects, at the plenary level as well as in specific thematic sections, though none is devoted to HIV issues exclusively. The Regional Dumas in Samara and St. Petersburg have public consultative councils attached to them where issues relevant for HIV prevention have also been occasionally raised. In addition, both NGOs and state institutions have organised round-table discussions where state and non-state actors meet to discuss HIV-related issues for exchange of information, or for the initiation of joint actions. Youth parliaments and on-site seminars are other initiatives where state and non-state actors collaborate about HIV and anti-drug activities. Conferences and round-tables organised by civil society have, however, become rarer as a result of reduced funding of NGOs (i.e. international funding), necessitating many of them to make stricter priorities of their use of funding. We should also mention that there are various state-run grant schemes through which non-state actors may implement projects, e.g. within service delivery, for the state authorities.

Thus, in the two regions there is a variety of arenas where state and non-state actors may come together to approach the topic of HIV prevention among drug users. In reality, however, with the possible exception of the HIV coordination council in St. Petersburg, the issue is not high up on the agenda in these various consultative bodies. In line with the government priorities the issue is usually only touched on indirectly in connection with broader HIV or drug prevention efforts. Still, since it is mainly NGOs that push for targeted HIV prevention among drug users, it is largely arenas where such organisations are involved that the issue has a chance to be brought up and discussed.

3.6   Governance Networks and the Policy Process

As has been shown, there are no governance networks in St. Petersburg or Samara that deal exclusively with HIV prevention among drug users, but several networks cover the issue when dealing with HIV or drug use in general, or with broader topics in the social sphere. The following discussion refers to findings from the governance networks in the two federal subjects that regularly deal with HIV and drug prevention: the HIV Coordination Council in St. Petersburg, the Anti-Drug Commissions in both regions, and the consultative councils under the regional legislatures, which frequently have HIV and drug issues on their agenda. We will, however, refer to individual networks only when there are substantial differences between them.

In this section we examine these governance networks' role in the policy process with emphasis on decision-making; policy advice; coordination; policy implementation; and evaluation and control (Chap. 1; Aasland et al. 2016). It should first be noted that none of the above-mentioned governance networks has a *decision-making* function. Key decisions in the field are made elsewhere, whether at federal (most drug issues) or regional level (most HIV issues) within the designated state structures. Since HIV is a complex issue cutting across a large number of policy fields, there is, however, great need for *coordination* between the government structures.

This is one of the core tasks of the governance networks, i.e. to organise and systematise the relevant stakeholders' interactions and divide their tasks in order to smooth decision-making processes and policy implementation. Since non-state actors are much closer than the authorities to the target populations (HIV-positive, drug users), civil society can supplement the authorities with actions for which direct contact with such groups are needed. High-level stakeholder participation in the networks furthermore ensures that decision-making actors get access to the relevant information they need from a variety of institutions, which in turn helps to provide for better-informed decisions.

Another important aspect of the governance networks is to give *advice* to the authorities on various aspects of policy-making and implementation. Such advice is given within the broad consensus on government policy in the field, so bringing up controversial issues about e.g. harm reduction, is futile and only risks reducing the scope of a member's or organisations' influence. But within this explicit and, sometimes, implicit consensus that all actors are aware of and few challenge, there is still room for expert opinions, professional input, methodological recommendations and insights gained from access to the target groups. It is important to note that policy advice is collected not only during the network meetings, but also in between meetings when decision-makers can contact a network representative directly with a concrete policy problem and ask for his or her input.

In addition to policy advice, the networks also have important functions regarding *policy implementation*. A regional authority when given a task by a federal authority, or simply when planning for the implementation of a policy measure, often uses the network arena to divide responsibilities for its implementation. This can take the shape of formal or informal command (the latter involves pressure on the institution without a direct order), or true voluntary contributions from the network actors. Typically, at a later meeting the involved participants will report back to the network about the execution of their tasks, but this can also take place in working groups that are set up to solve a specific issue during a specific time period and can work and meet outside the confines of the network meetings.

A second dimension of policy implementation is the state's use of grants to civil society organisations, typically the so-called 'socially oriented non-profit organisations'; the law on such organisations was enacted in

2010 (Krasnopolskaya et al. 2015). For-profit service providers can usually also participate in these grant competitions. The non-state actors are brought in as welcome additional expertise and knowledge that can help the state to provide affordable services of a high quality. Though the direct connection with the governance networks is not always evident, there can be no doubt that these two instruments reinforce one another. Firstly, loyal civil society organisations that are present in networks have, according to our informants, a better chance of winning the grants than organisations outside the networks. This is a result of their formal and informal links with the authorities. The organisations are considered to be loyal and trustworthy by those administering the grants (reducing the risk of awarding them the grant), and they pick up useful information and have the familiarity with the field that help them make better applications and come up with better project ideas than they would without these links. Secondly, the grant schemes themselves are normally administered by institutions of the network, usually its core institution, and the networks quite often have a role in the formulation of the call, providing expertise in the processing of applications, following up on the activities of the winners of the call, etc. Several of the informants in the HIV field questioned the transparency of the grant allocation procedure.

A final element in the policy process is systems of feedback to decision-makers on implemented policy and ways of exerting public control over a policy field. This *monitoring* and *control* function is ambiguous in the case of HIV prevention among drug users in the two regions, as is also the case in other policy fields in Russia. In theory, public scrutiny over government policy is one of the main features of governance networks justifying their formation (Owen 2015). In practice, however, our governance network informants found it hard to give concrete examples of how they exert such a function. The advisory nature of the networks, with policy recommendations rather than decision-making taking place in the network arenas, does not require government institutions to take these recommendations into account or not even to report back to the networks as to whether or not they were implemented in some way (Olisova 2015). Some of the consultative councils did perform a level of monitoring to see if their recommendations had been taken into account. In reality, however, there is little public access to the fora where the actual decisions are made. We observed different practices as to whether higher level authorities needed to react to recommendations from governance networks at all, or give feedback regarding their implementation. At the time of our fieldwork the Public Control Law

(Federal Law No. 212-FZ) which stipulates procedures for how the public can exert control over authorities had not yet been implemented, and it remains to be seen if this law will change established practices.

3.7   Meta-Governance and Other Governance Tools—The NATO Taxonomy

In this section and the next, we examine the governance tools applied by Russian authorities when they use governance networks in policy-making in the field of HIV prevention among drug users. As mentioned earlier, there are different ideologies and practices among the responsible stakeholders as to how to approach this complex issue. In order to assess how the authorities apply meta-governance in the field, it is important to stress that one can observe different interests among federal and regional levels, and among stakeholders in drug control, health authorities and other government actors, but also within each sector. While all of them, at least vocally, recognise the importance of preventing HIV, there is no uniform agreement on ways to deal with the issue, how much of the resources to spend and the main priorities for spending them, whether and how to reach out to specific target groups (as opposed to a general approach) and whether and how much to involve non-state actors. The head of the Federal AIDS centre, Vadim Pokrovsky is, for example, a long-time critic of Kremlin's HIV policy and a proponent of targeted measures towards drug users. This means that there will be no uniform meta-governance strategy applied by Russian authorities on the issue. Furthermore, it leaves opportunities for both state and non-state actors to form alliances with the likeminded to pursue their goals.

Applying the NATO taxonomy described in Chap. 1 (Hood 1983; Hood and Margetts 2007) to meta-governance on HIV prevention among drug users, we start with *Nodality*. Nodality denotes the use of government information resources to influence and direct policy actions through the provision or withholding of 'information' or 'knowledge' from societal actors. With two nodes—one based in drug control (FSKN) and another in health authorities (including the federal and regional AIDS centres) there are two competing information sources both of which control their own sphere but which do not individually have a monopoly on information. Each of the nodes are quite hierarchically structured and have some vertical control, but while in the drug control sphere there is mostly one line of government policy from the federal to the local level, the health sector is more open to regional variations, something which also affects practices of gathering and distributing information. For example, both Samara and St. Petersburg have been more open to collaborating and involving non-state actors in providing service to vulnerable groups and to sharing information with them than is the case in many other federal subjects.

At the time when Russia was more involved with international collaboration on HIV prevention, actors both at federal and regional levels involved in such projects would receive information and knowledge from international sources such as UNAIDS, WHO and, especially in the case of Samara, USAID. The change of focus from international to domestic funding not only reduced the presence of such actors in Russia but also watered down the relevance of this information and knowledge (e.g. on harm reduction) for the Russian actors. The nodality function of the Russian state institutions was thereby strengthened. Alternative information (i.e. Western influence) was not made illegal, but acting upon it is was strongly discouraged by the authorities and its allies, emphasising the particularities of Russia that '[take] into account the cultural, historical, and psychological characteristics of the Russian population, and is based on a conservative ideology and traditional values'. The threat of being labelled a 'foreign agent' puts additional pressure on actors in the field to conform to the knowledge and information provided by the state.

Another constraining factor for the manoeuvring room of governance networks is the high degree of normative acts surrounding drug and HIV policy. Participants need to have a good grasp of legislation. Informants from local anti-drug commissions have said they often struggle with their initiatives not complying with regulations and have called for more legal experts as commission members. The actors that have the best grasp of the legislative framework also have the most influence on decisions made—and these are typically the government institutions, which have more legal resources. Resistance to initiatives from the non-state sectors is sometimes based on Russian officials not being accustomed or willing to working outside the framework of prohibitions and restrictive controls (Malakhov 2014: 1067).

This brings us to the *Authority* aspects of Hood's model. The Russian power vertical provides the framework within which state and non-state actors operate. The authorities apply a combination of hard and soft tools, while legislation sets clear limits as to what the different actors can do. That drug substitution therapies are forbidden in Russia, for example, makes this harm reduction method, successfully applied in most Western countries, impossible to apply in a Russian setting. In other cases, it is up to regional authorities to decide (such as in the case with needle exchange programmes) though the recommendations from the federal level are clearly negative. To operate against the federal recommendations is something the majority of actors seeks to avoid for fear of losing access to networks, money and other resources. In St. Petersburg during fieldwork there were still some NGOs that ran such harm reduction programmes According to our informants in the city, these programmes still operate, and in some respects have been easier to implement after the dissolution of FSKN. While in other parts of Russia a few HIV-related NGOs promoting harm reduction have been compelled to register as 'foreign agents', in St. Petersburg the organisations most at risk have re-registered as 'foundations' or 'networks' thus avoiding this label. Also in Samara some organisations continue to collaborate with the authorities.

In some cases, and for some issues, there can be diverging interests and opinions among drug control and health authorities, and the question is then who decides on issues where there are such conflicts. For example, many HIV and AIDS experts within the health sector focus on access to services for drug users, whereas the authorities in the drugs control sector tend to view HIV among drug users as a criminal issue that should be met with punishment and isolation. Since the health authorities occupy a lower place within the governance hierarchy than those responsible for public security, informants told that the latter tend to win through with their approaches in case of opposing views:

> Let's take harm reduction, for example. Such programs have to be approved by the Ministry of Health and Social Development as well as the drug control authorities. In many cases, at both the federal and regional levels, the Ministry [...] remains neutral until the drug control people have expressed their views—and their attitude to such programs are negative and repressive. In that way, a criminality approach comes to take precedence rather than an approach focused on Public Health [Federal NGO representative].

This also has implications for how the governance networks operate, and especially since the more securitised aspects of HIV and drug issues are not open to much influence from more liberally inclined actors inside the networks.

Sakwa's (2010) differentiation between the normative and the administrative state (see Chap. 1) also has relevance for governance networks on HIV. In a country where these two operate in tandem, informal relations and personal influence of support from individuals can be decisive in getting acceptance for a given policy. For example, regionally the quality of the cooperation between the local governor (or whoever has been charged with coordinating HIV at the regional level) and the head of the regional AIDS centre is often important. This means that governance network representatives usually need to weigh their intentions and goals against their relations to the local authorities.

In terms of *Treasure*, Russian HIV prevention is clearly underfunded. Most of available HIV funding goes to treatment and testing (which are, of course, also important elements of HIV prevention since detected HIV positive on treatment are much less likely to pass on the virus). Of the limited funds for more traditional prevention measures, the bulk goes to prevention towards the general public with a special focus on youth. Funding for targeted prevention towards most-at-risk groups, such as drug users, is minimal. The tendency towards relatively higher rates of sexual transmission, surpassing transmission by intravenous drug use in both St. Petersburg and Samara, as well as the slow 'dying out' of many of the heavy drug users, are additional factors explaining this focus.[17] Still, despite the transmission of HIV through needle exchange declining in relative terms, the absolute numbers are still high and need to be given continued attention.

The state does have a few grant programmes that non-state actors can apply to in order to carry out HIV prevention programmes among drug users, both at federal and regional levels. It is then important for non-state actors participating in such competitions to propose measures that the state, whether explicitly or not, finds to be worthy of support, i.e. that are in line with government priorities. Our fieldwork found that formal and informal networking with state authorities, such as through the aforementioned governance network arenas, makes non-state actors better positioned for winning grants. This is due to the information that they pick up in the network setting, the connections that they establish with key officials, and the status and legitimacy they obtain among important actors simply by being network members associated with the authorities:

> We have people [in the government], somehow interested in us, that know that we are professional, that we can implement it. Apart from conducting

research I, for example, take part in various commissions, give presentations, tell how the situation is here. I have in mind various government commissions, including the anti-drug commission. [...] That is, there are people who are loyal towards us, that know us and would like to see us as a stable winning organisation [of government grants], however competition is competition [Local NGO representative, Samara].

International funding, which was a welcome alternative source of funding in the HIV area, though never plentiful, was available between 2005 and 2011, has now more or less also disappeared from the scene in the two regions. In Samara there is no more international funding and limited collaboration with international partners, while in St. Petersburg there are still some initiatives that are being funded through international organisations, some in collaboration with international partners. Since the Russian organisations now need to direct their attention towards domestic funding, they also must adjust their activities in line with the priorities of federal and regional policy-makers. HIV prevention measures towards drug users, which is not high on the priority list of the authorities, then need to be buried within more complex programmes such as support to children of mothers with HIV or other initiatives that sound more acceptable to the authorities.

But if we talk about our role in drug policy, we try through those channels that may work. For example, women and children. But [...] drug users, they are not interesting to anyone, because they are often [considered] to have the blame themselves. From which side do we approach this? There are women and children. There are effects, because these services are indispensable, because where there are children, they cannot be blamed, so one has to provide assistance through their mothers, including those using drugs, during pregnancy and birth, and during social rehabilitation. We look for ways of arguing that could work. Women and children, that's a good argument in my opinion [Federal NGO representative, St. Petersburg].

Not all organisations working on HIV prevention see the withdrawal of international funding as something negative, however, as indicated by the following statements:

As long as we had international funding, everyone strived to receive a grant [...]. A huge minus with these grants was that they were completely unsystematic. That is, for some time you worked in one direction, the next day you were moving in a different direction. The only thing that was positive was that you were paid for this work. Nothing remained here, nothing new was invented. [...W]e have lost the money, but in return the opportunity to work in a targeted manner has emerged [Professional worker, Samara].

Finally, when it comes to *Organisation* there is a considerable interaction of state and non-state institutions in HIV and drug prevention. As is the case with other welfare policies, Russian authorities encourage involvement of non-state actors and especially civil society organisations, in various aspects of the policy process. The fact that several governance network arenas that involve such actors have been set up is in itself a sign that their involvement is encouraged by the authorities. From the point of view of the authorities, motivations for this collaboration are mixed. For some it seems that governance network arenas at regional level is a requirement by the authorities at a higher level, and so the local actors are simply fulfilling their duty. More often, however, the resources and input provided by non-state network participants are really valuable to authorities for solving pressing issues. Some challenges have to be addressed by professionals, and some events have to be organised. Of not the least of importance, the authorities may lack resources to implement all the policy measures for which they are responsible. We have already seen that major policy decisions are usually not made in the network but elsewhere. The tasks of the networks and their non-state participants is to bring in expertise, advise on policy, implement policy on behalf of the authorities (e.g. in service delivery) and, not least, to act as contact points for the authorities to approach the hard-to-reach target groups. Building legitimacy for the state policy is another motivation, though this is expressed implicitly rather than explicitly by government officials.

Thus, the state has a leading role in nearly all the governance networks with HIV and drug on the agenda, and the organisation of the networks reinforces this power imbalance. The main trend is that the state controls agenda-setting and membership (more on this below). Observations of network meetings have shown that power asymmetries are reflected even in the set-up of the meetings. In such meetings the sitting arrangements tend to be formal, with highly-ranked officials taking up the seats near the chairman at one end of the hall or round table, while lower-ranked officials and NGO representatives are seated at the other end. Representatives from the state dominate the proceedings (except in platform specially designated for NGO involvement such as the consultative councils under the regional

Duma). Network meetings are typically very formal, with previously-prepared statements by participants followed by comments by other attendees. Participants rarely comment on issues which are not directly linked to their area of responsibility or recognised 'expertise'. On rare occasions the participants vote, but more often decisions are made unanimously without voting. The nature of the issue determines to what extent diverging views are tolerated.

3.8   Issue Framing and Control Over Participation

The governance networks that we have looked into have all been set up by the state, and thus it is the state that sets the agenda of the meetings. Usually there is a troika consisting of the head of the network, his or her deputy, and a dedicated secretary, all representatives of the state, that are responsible for the agenda and for the day-to-day running of the network between meetings. Even if nothing formally restricts them from doing so, according to network members, there are few instances where the non-state actors make their own initiatives or raise issues themselves. Rather, they see as their function the providing of expert input on issues raised by the chairman or the leadership troika. In some cases the regional or municipal level has been given an assignment from federal authorities that should be fulfilled at lower levels. It is possible for network members to propose topics for discussion in the networks, but they will usually be filtered by the network governor or the network troika prior to the meeting. Raising issues spontaneously at a meeting is, according to our informants, almost never done.

The sequence of a network meeting, as observed by project researchers and confirmed by informants, sheds some light on the formal framing of the networks. Normally the head or designated head of the network first presents the issue or issues on the agenda and also conveys what is expected from the network on the issues that are raised at the meeting (information sharing, cross-sectoral coordination, input into policy processes, etc.) and the required output. More information about the issues is often presented by experts giving more thorough accounts or briefings. The expert could either be someone from within the ranks of the network itself, or a speaker invited externally. This person is not considered as representing a specific organisational or political interest: rather it is the 'neutral and objective' expert input that is called for.

Usually the expert presentation will be followed by an exchange of statements, often prepared in advance, by some of the network members present. There is considerable variation as to whether discussion and critical comments are expected and welcomed, but we have observed few cases of open and fierce debate. More disagreement is prevalent, however, in networks set up by health authorities than in anti-drug commissions. Indeed, many network participants appreciate that networks strive for consensus rather than conflict. When asked whether disagreements are common in the commission, a member of the anti-drug commission in Samara, for example, answered:

> Thank God, we have not had any[...]. They didn't occur, because the key feature of the anti-drug commission is that everyone understands, that if a specialist, an expert in a given field, speaks out, that means that the person doesn't just talk without a purpose. Therefore, to interfere, and say that he is not right, that's not good behaviour [Public administration, drug policy, Samara].

A representative of the HIV coordination council in St. Petersburg said:

> Everything is quite unanimous. This is because the members are mostly professionals. [...] Now there is a tendency towards more cohesion with the representatives of the civil society organisations, they have all got used to one another. So, they collaborate quite well. At least, I have never heard from civil society organisations that there were complaints [...] [Public administration, HIV coordination council, St. Petersburg].

The seeming lack of diverging views is also a sign that serious discursive issue framing takes place in governance networks in the field. There are many controversial topics where methods of harm reduction (substitution therapy, needle exchange, condom distribution) appear to be the ones that the governance networks are most eager to avoid, or rather, which are simply not touched on in what seems to be a tacit agreement between the actors. By looking at the agendas of governance networks in the field over an extended period, these issues have never appeared on the list of items to be discussed, though they are high up of the agenda among nearly all international actors engaged in HIV prevention in Russia. The avoidance of Russian federal authorities to address harm reduction thoroughly is probably one reason why it is not covered at regional levels either. Second, there is a considerable self-censorship in that organisations that would be in favour of such measures avoid bringing the issue up for fear of losing their position. Furthermore, some argue that the issue is lost anyway and impossible to do anything about. In their view it is then better to direct one's efforts towards activities where the chances of success are more achievable. The fact that some of the few organisations promoting needle exchange have been forced to register as foreign agents can be interpreted as a warning for others not to do the same. Finally, persons or organisations openly advocating liberal harm reduction methods would be very unlikely be invited into the networks anyway.

This is because network *participation* also tends to be controlled by the state authorities in charge of the networks. For some of the governance networks, such as the anti-drug commissions and the HIV Coordination Council in St. Petersburg, the membership is quite fixed. According to the principle of cross-sectoral collaboration, certain listed institutions should be represented. In some networks it is up to the invited bodies to choose their own candidates from among their staff, though in practice the level of representation tends to be high-level; normally the head of the institution or his or her deputy are council members. Practice also differs as to whether participants are invited to represent their institutions, or as designated individual experts in the field. In addition to the prescribed institutions, there is also room for membership in the networks 'by agreement' *(po soglasovaniyu)*. These are typically representatives of specialised agencies. State institutions dominate, but representatives of civil society organisations are usually included in cross-sectoral governance networks on HIV and drug issues from the 'by agreement' list. According to informants in both regions, there is also an informal practice of recruitment to the networks: 'the one who works and is visible in the field, that is the one who is selected'. Furthermore, only those organisations that are considered to be loyal and supportive of the priorities of the state are invited to join the networks.

Another observation in both Samara and St. Petersburg is that it is mostly professional organisations that are invited into the networks. A few grassroots organisations do participate, however. For example 'Anonymous drug users' are considered by the Anti-Drug Commissions to be a major actor in the programme for rehabilitation and resocialisation and are in this connection regularly invited to their meetings. The same goes for so-called patient groups in HIV-related networks.

3.9   REGIONAL DIFFERENCES

Despite strict federal control over the most securitised aspects of HIV and drug policy, such as issues relating to drug traffic and drug use, there is considerable leeway for regional authorities to formulate and implement regional policies on various aspects of HIV prevention. This also opens up a considerable regional difference between governance networks in Samara and St. Petersburg.

We found many more examples of independent initiatives and variations in practices in St. Petersburg than in Samara, in the form of pilot projects, drug rehabilitation methods, and institutional set-up. As explained above, Samara has no governance networks that have been set up specifically to deal with HIV issues. Thus, when the issue is on the agenda, it is as part of governance networks that cover a much broader set of policy issues than HIV. This means that HIV is rarely on the agenda and that network members are not necessarily specialists on this particular issue. Such specialists must be invited in for special meetings. In Samara, the result of this is lack of continuity and follow-up activities.

Informants in governance networks in Samara more often complained about lack of financial and human resources in their work compared to their counterparts in St. Petersburg. Network participants in Samara were also more concerned with their inability to make changes in the legal framework thereby rendering many of their initiatives impossible to implement. It seems regional legislators in St. Petersburg paid more attention to updating their legislation to reflect current needs. Another reason why it was considered easier to implement new initiatives in St. Petersburg is the tendency for the state and civil society actors there to join their resources for common purposes instead of each defending their own domain, something which was more the case in Samara.

The larger number of organisations and institutions involved in St. Petersburg is an advantage for attracting attention towards the issue and enhances the development of horizontal networking. Historically, in St. Petersburg HIV networks were formed from the very start with the city AIDS centre as a strong and dynamic node, somewhat independent from the local authorities. In Samara, on the other hand, the regional AIDS centre, with much fewer and weaker coalition partners to lean upon, to a larger degree depends on approval from the local government before being able to implement new initiatives.

As to the differences in work between the two comparable governance network platforms, the anti-drug commissions in the two regions, in St. Petersburg they were more externally oriented in the sense that they were more likely to engage in joint cross-sectional activities or events with other platforms or actors on specific themes or issues of joint interest. One example relates to the narcotisation of youth; here the commission organised joint events with the regional youth committee, with the network of drug rehabilitation centres and with other stakeholders, followed up by joint activities.

The fact that the issue is much higher on the political agenda in St. Petersburg despite the gravity of the HIV situation being no less urgent in Samara is probably a result of differences in governance approaches between the two federal subjects. One likely reason for this is the differences in economic status, St. Petersburg being a contributor to and Samara subsidised by, the federal budget. Other possible explanations for the regional differences are the more vivid civil society landscape in St. Petersburg compared to Samara; the institutionalisation of the HIV issue in St. Petersburg, which includes a HIV strategy and a HIV coordination council; and St. Petersburg's more extensive experience of international collaboration that despite more recent setbacks has set an imprint on actors there.

3.10   Concluding Remarks

The conservative turn in Russian politics has had profound implications for the interaction between the state and civil society—and between international and domestic actors—regarding HIV prevention among drug users. Evidence-based harm reduction, which has been successful in curbing the epidemic among drug users in many countries of the world, is hardly tolerated in Russia today and has virtually disappeared from the two regions studied. Particularly damaging has been the pressure put on organisations promoting harm reduction measures such as needle exchange and distribution of condoms. The result is that those receiving funding from foreign donors are being subject not only to registration as foreign agents but are also not being invited into arenas where they can meaningfully operate.

This does not mean, however, that civil society does not have a role to play in policy. Both in declarations (such as in the draft of the new Russian HIV strategy) and in practical work, civil society is given a rather prominent role in HIV prevention. They do not have much impact on policy formulation and policy decision, but could rather be seen as the long arm of the state in providing services to hard-to-reach populations. Their considerable experience from work and contact with the target groups make them indispensable to state authorities that lack the needed trust among groups that are most at risk of catching HIV or those who have already been infected. The close relations between civil society and the drug users also puts them in a position where they can provide expert policy advice that the authorities rely on for formulation and implementation of policy. Governance networks play a significant role in structuring and informing this interaction.

Furthermore, the state is not a uniform entity, but consists of a conglomeration of institutions and individuals at different level of governance, often with diverging views on core issues. A very restrictive approach by the drug control authorities is complemented by a public health approach taken by many of the health institutions, with the regional AIDS centres being the nodes among these. Even among the responsible health institutions there are proponents of more restrictive and more liberal approaches to HIV prevention. Informal alliances can therefore develop between state and civil society actors across the, sometimes blurred, state- and non-state divide. Such alliances tend to be more of an informal than a formal nature, and the actors need to carefully assess their room of manoeuvrability within the limitations set by the network governor or other officials with a veto power. Furthermore, it is not necessarily so that NGOs take a more liberal position than state authorities in the networks. The Russian Orthodox Church, for example, with its enhanced prominence and authority also in governance networks on HIV, has in recent years tended to tilt the balance in a more conservative and restrictive direction.

The recognition that HIV and drug use prevention are complex issues that require a cross-sectoral approach has not resulted in a thorough integration of the two policies in governance networks. In fact, we found a wide institutional gap between the two issues that the governance network set-up has not contributed to solve. Networks that are oriented towards HIV and those oriented towards drug use do not recognise the importance of interaction between them, and the links between the issues are only recognised on a rhetorical level. In practice, the representatives of the AIDS centres do not understand why they are invited to the Anti-Drug Commission meetings. Likewise, representatives of FSKN/Ministry of the

Interior do not join in on meetings that are organised by HIV care providers and epidemiologists specialised on HIV.

The two policy fields (HIV and drugs) look quite different from the perspective of their level of security and institutional set-up. In the HIV sphere there is a larger and more diverse number between actors, as well as sometimes a competition between them. This sphere is also characterised by a more common practice of horizontal links, not only between agencies and sectors, but also between territorial units. This makes it easier for NGOs to manoeuvre and establish alliances with state agencies that are ready for collaboration and non-state input within this sphere. The more security type drug sphere, on the other hand, has a stricter vertical institutional set-up with much less scope for non-state initiatives. The FSKN (now Ministry of the Interior) dictates the rules and the policy themes to be prioritised. However, even in this field there is some flexibility and space for dialogue with NGOs, and even more so the further away from the 'top' levels the networks are found. Thus, considerable influence of non-state organisations can be observed in governance networks at the most local level (city districts and municipalities).

Based on our fieldwork we were able to identify a number reasons for the lack of interaction between the two issues: Firstly, the relative growth of heterosexual HIV transmission has led health authorities to focus more on this and less on prevention of HIV among drug users despite the latter continuing to be a serious challenge. Secondly, the data security law acts as a barrier to health specialists for involving other actors in policy collaboration. Thirdly, the different approach towards drug use as a medical (health sector) and a crime (drug authorities) problem hampers the quality of the interaction between the two policy fields. Health authorities tend to lean towards treatment and rehabilitation, while drug authorities are more concerned with punishing drug users. Finally, since the membership of governance networks tends to be made up of rather narrow specialists within a given field while the network composition is based on the principle that all participants should be directly relevant to the networks' tasks, constrains attention towards policy issues that are located in the intersection between two policy fields. The result of all this is that HIV prevention among drug users is largely left in a void outside the direct responsibility and attention of state agencies and governance networks. It then remains to be approached mainly by actors within the non-governmental sector which, for their part, do not have the resources or necessary authority to make the required policy impact.

NOTES

1. http://aids-centr.perm.ru/статистика/ВИЧ/СПИД-в-России (Accessed 8 February 2016).
2. http://www.avert.org/needle-and-syringe-programmes-nsps-hiv-prevention.htm.
3. http://www.demoscope.ru/weekly/2014/0599/tema03.php.
4. In a few instances the interviewees asked to turn off the recorder during parts of the interview.
5. https://www.rosminzdrav.ru/news/2016/03/22/2864-gosudarstvennaya-strategiya-protivodeystviya-rasprostraneniyu-vich-infektsii-v-rossiyskoy-feder atsii-na-period-do-2020-goda-i-dalneyshuyu-perspektivu.
6. The document can be downloaded from http://www.narcom.ru/publ/info/893 (Accessed 10 February 2016).
7. The official name is the Global Fund to Fight AIDS, Tuberculosis and Malaria.
8. The strategy can be downloaded from http://hiv-2020.ru/ (Accessed 23 November 2016).
9. http://www.kommersant.ru/doc/2840191 (Accessed 10 February 2016).
10. https://themoscowtimes.com/articles/russia-cuts-funding-for-hiv-treatment-54541.
11. http://www.aids.ru/law/law01.shtml (Russian version); also in English at http://www.hsph.harvard.edu/population/aids/russianfed.aids.95.pdf.
12. From HIV strategy, downloaded from http://hiv-2020.ru/.
13. The Leningrad District AIDS centre and the Botkin hospital are two more important institutions in St. Petersburg. There are also AIDS centres for the Federal Districts (Russia has seven), one of which is located in St. Petersburg. AIDS in prisons is dealt with through the Federal Penetary Service and not subordinated to the territorial AIDS centres. There are also specialised centres for HIV- and AIDS related statistics in the regions.
14. Since our fieldwork was conducted new self-help groups have appeared in both cities, and they are more open in the public than they used to be earlier.
15. https://gov.spb.ru/law?d&nd=822401855&prevDoc=537975650.
16. http://www.samru.ru/society/novosti_samara/83444.html.
17. According to the latest statistics (2015), in St. Petersburg 62%, and in Samara 55%, of new registered HIV cases are through sexual, predominantly heterosexual, transmission. Sources: http://www.aidsjournal.ru/statistika-po-vich-sankt-peterburg/ and https://regnum.ru/news/society/2205349.html.

REFERENCES

Aasland, Aadne, Arne Grønningsæter, and Peter Meylakhs. 2013. More are testing positive—But is everything negative? Russia and the HIV epidemic. In *Global HIV/AIDS politics, policy, and activism*, ed. Raymond A. Smith. Santa Barbara, CA: Praeger.

Aasland, Aadne, Mikkel Berg-Nordlie, and Elena Bogdanova. 2016. Encouraged but controlled: Governance networks in Russian regions. *East European Politics* 32 (2): 148–169. doi:10.1080/21599165.2016.1167042.

Aasland, Aadne, Arne Backer Grønningsæter, Peter Meylakhs, Elise Klouman, Tatiana Balaeva, Hans Blystad, and Andrei Grjibovski. 2011. The governance of HIV/AIDS prevention in North-West Russia: Description of a Joint Norwegian-Russian Project. *Human Ecology (Экология человека, Arkhangelsk)* 17 (12).

Burki, Talha. 2015. Stigmatisation undermining Russia's HIV control efforts. *The Lancet Infectious Diseases* 15 (8): 881–882. doi:10.1016/S1473-3099(15) 00163-2.

Hood, Christopher C. 1983. *The tools of government*. London: Macmillan.

Hood, Christopher C, and Helen Z. Margetts. 2007. *The tools of government in the digital age*. London: Palgrave Macmillan.

Krasnopolskaya, Irina, Yulia Skokova, and Ulla Pape. 2015. Government–nonprofit relations in Russia's regions: An exploratory analysis. *VOLUNTAS: International Journal of Voluntary and Nonprofit Organizations* 26 (6): 2238–2266.

Kuznetsova, Anna V, Anastasia Y Meylakhs, Yuri A Amirkhanian, Jeffrey A Kelly, Alexey A Yakovlev, Vladimir B Musatov, and Anastasia G Amirkhanian. 2016. Barriers and facilitators of HIV care engagement: Results of a qualitative study in St. Petersburg, Russia. *AIDS and Behavior* 2: 1–11.

Lunze, Karsten, Fatima I. Lunze, Anita Raj, and Jeffrey H. Samet. 2015. Stigma and human rights abuses against people who inject drugs in Russia—A qualitative investigation to inform policy and public health strategies. *PLoS ONE* 10 (8): e0136030.

Malakhov, Vladimir S. 2014. Russia as a new immigration country: Policy response and public debate. *Europe-Asia Studies* 66 (7): 1062–1079.

Moran, Dominique. 2004. HIV/AIDS, governance and development: The public administration factor. *Public Administration & Development* 24 (1): 7.

Moran, Dominique, and Jacob A. Jordaan. 2007. HIV/AIDS in Russia: Determinants of regional prevalence. *International Journal of Health Geographics* 6 (1): 22.

Myhre, Marthe Handå, and Mikkel Berg-Nordlie. 2016. "The state cannot help them all". Russian media discourse on the inclusion of non-state actors in governance. *East European Politics* 32 (2): 192–214.

Olisova, Olga. 2015. The role of public consultative bodies in policy-making in the social sphere in the Samara Region. Oslo: Working paper.

Owen, Catherine. 2015. "Consentful contention" in a corporate state: Human rights activists and public monitoring commissions in Russia. *East European Politics* 31 (3): 274–293.

Pape, Ulla. 2013. *The politics of HIV/AIDS in Russia.* London: Routledge.

Pates, Richard, and Diane Riley. 2012. *Harm reduction in substance use and high-risk behaviour.* New York: Wiley.

Pisani, Elizabeth, Geoff P. Garnett, Nicholas C. Grassly, Tim Brown, John Stover, Catherine Hankins, Neff Walker, and Peter D. Ghys. 2003. Back to basics in HIV prevention: Focus on exposure. *BMJ* 326 (7403): 1384–1387.

Putzel, James. 2004a. The global fight against AIDS: How adequate are the national commissions? *Journal of International Development* 16 (8): 1129–1140.

Putzel, James. 2004b. *Public policy responses to HIV/AIDS in Africa.* Geneva: United Nations.

Sakwa, Richard. 2010. The dual state in Russia. *Post-Soviet Affairs* 26 (3): 185–206.

Sidibé, Michel. 2014. *The courage to reflect, question and commit.* Moscow: UNAIDS.

UNDP. 2007. *Governance and HIV/AIDS responses: Issues and outlook.* New York: UNDP.

CHAPTER 4

Environmental Impact Assessment: Between Facilitating Public Contribution and Arbitrary Involvement of NGOs

Johannes Schuhmann and Sabine Kropp

4.1 Introduction

Russian law stipulates mandatory negotiations between business, civil society and state actors during Environmental Impact Assessments (EIA). An EIA is a legal assessment process, where companies planning a project with potential impact on the environment must evaluate the project with regards to the significance of the impact and must propose alternative options for realising the proposed project (Environment 2013). As every environmental NGO can participate in public hearings or can also act as

J. Schuhmann (✉)
Institute of German and International Party Law
and Party Research, Heinrich-Heine-University Düsseldorf,
Universitätsstr. 1, 40225 Düsseldorf, Germany
e-mail: Johannes.schuhmann@uni-duesseldorf.de

S. Kropp
Otto Suhr Institute of Political Science, Freie Universität Berlin,
Ihnestraße 22, 14195 Berlin, Germany
e-mail: sabine.kropp@fu-berlin.de

© The Author(s) 2018
S. Kropp et al. (eds.), *Governance in Russian Regions*,
DOI 10.1007/978-3-319-61702-2_4

specialists in the expert reviews of the proposed investment projects, the EIA is the key instrument for public participation in environmental policy. Due to the mandatory involvement of NGOs in each EIA, repeated forms of cooperation develop over time among the responsible local, regional and federal authorities as well as civil society actors.

The analysis of EIAs in Russia is particularly intriguing for a couple of reasons. First of all, different to the other cases of horizontal governance in this volume, interaction among state authorities, companies and NGOs is obligatory. The compulsory notion of EIAs strengthens the position of NGOs and influences the options at hand for competent authorities and business actors. Second, EIAs involve a multitude of actors from the state, civil society and the business community. This makes it necessary to conduct public hearings with often more than 60 people of very different background and interests, thus rendering cooperation more complex. Thirdly, EIAs often feature a high level of conflict.

This chapter examines how formally-prescribed collaborations during an EIA take place in practice. Particular attention is paid to the specific governance mix in EIA. This focus leads us to a few related questions: How is horizontal collaboration related to hierarchical or even coercive modes of governance? Which different mixes of governance can be found in an EIA, and which factors contribute to the divergent patterns of governance? Which societal actors are involved in horizontal collaboration? And, finally, what is the function of these networks? In order to unearth the relation between collaborative and hierarchical or even coercive modes of governance, we analysed the meta-governance tools the Russian authorities are using to govern EIAs. As described in the theoretical chapter, we follow the approach laid out by Hood and Vabo and Røiseland, paying specific attention to the application of the four tools, *Nodality, Authority, Treasure*, and *Organisation*, and distinguishing between soft and hard meta-governance tools (Hood 1983; Vabo and Røiseland 2012).

The chapter starts with presenting the main characteristics of EIAs, and then elaborating more the relevance of analysing this particular policy tool. This section is followed by a detailed description of the legal framework of EIAs. Since collaboration during an EIA is regulated in detail, one needs to have a thorough understanding of the formal institutions guiding the EIAs. The subsequent section discusses the case study design which was chosen to bring various patterns of the governance mix during EIA to the fore. The analysis is based on a qualitative design with six case studies of EIAs in the Krasnodar and Irkutsk regions. The findings are condensed into three patterns of meta-governance that constitute very different mixes of governance. In closing, there is a summary of the main features of the governance-mixes and meta-governance strategies in Russian EIAs, and this will feed into the concluding chapter of the volume.

4.2   CHARACTERISTICS OF THE POLICY TOOL

The Russian version of the EIA consists of an assessment of the environmental impact of planned business and other activities, which in Russia is usually called by its acronym '*OVOS*' and the state ecological expertise (SEE) of the EIA materials, referred to as '*ekspertiza*'.[1] When referring to both the *OVOS* and the SEE, the text uses the term EIA. The EIA is prescribed for various objects, such as project documentation of technical specifications for new equipment and technology with negative environmental impact; ecological investigations of areas/territories for giving these territories legal status of protected natural areas of federal or regional significance; projects planned to be realised on the continental shelf, in the exclusive economic zone, territorial sea and contiguous zone of the Russian Federation as well as in the protected natural areas of federal, regional or local significance; projects connected with location and neutralisation of dangerous waste. To receive a licence to operate, the EIA is a prerequisite for these businesses and other activities.

In Russia, the EIA is the only legally prescribed mechanism for realising the right of citizens to have environmental information and the right of NGOs to take part in relevant environmental decision making (Greenpeace 2015).[2] During EIAs, NGOs can publicly discuss the objects of the ecological expert assessment.[3] They can carry out a public ecological assessment[4] and send to the federal executive authorities and their territorial organs suggestions concerning ecological aspects of the planned business or other activities.[5] As every environmental NGO can participate in the public hearings for the *OVOS*, act as specialists in the state ecological assessment of the proposed investment projects and conduct a public ecological assessment, the EIA is the key instrument used for public participation in environmental policy (Greenpeace 2015). Since EIAs are mandatory, they tend to end up in blockages caused by actors who seek to promote their own interests by refusing to collaborate.[6]

Apart from NGOs and local communities, various federal, regional and local authorities as well as business actors are involved during an EIA. Being in charge of selecting the land on which the project is planned and of conducting public hearings during OVOS, local authorities are always involved in the EIA process. The involvement of either regional or federal authorities, which are responsible for preparing the state ecological assessment, depends on whether the legal documents or project documentation under consideration falls within the jurisdiction of the regional or federal level. In order to avoid conflicts, the allocation of responsibilities between the two levels is clearly outlined in the law on the ecological expertise.[7] On the regional level, the EIA is conducted by the Departments of Natural Resources and Ecology of the regional administrations. Between 2004 and 2007, the responsible authorities on the federal level were the Federal Service for Ecologic, Technical and Atomic Supervision (*Rostekhnadzor*), in addition to the Federal Service for the Supervision of Natural Resource Usage (*Rosprirodnadzor*), a subdivision of the Russian Ministry of Natural Resources and Environmental Protection. While the first organisation was in charge of the ecologic assessment in order to prevent negative impact on natural resources, the second was responsible for preventing negative impact on the environment (Begak et al. 2009: 19). As a result, companies in Russia had to deal with various state actors simultaneously, which did not coordinate their activities. Later on *Rosprirodnazor* was stripped of its responsibilities for carrying out EIA in Russia. In addition to these actors, other federal sectoral services such as *Rossemkadastr* and *Rospotrebnadzor* are involved in order to deal with specific questions (Begak et al. 2009: 19).

As Russian law prescribes EIAs only for a limited group of investment projects which usually have a major environmental and economic impact, they are often marked by a high level of conflict between various stakeholders. Thus not only are opposing economic interests at stake; participants also clash over opposing ideologies since some of them subscribe to an anthropocentric and others to an eco-centric worldview with different understandings of how much harm can be done to the environment (Schuhmann 2012). Conflicts are exacerbated by the fact that decisions taken during an EIA are irreversible and in some situations also contain risks for human health (Beck 1992). The way conflicts are dealt with depends not only on the question at stake, but also on the idiosyncratic features of the participating actors.

Agakhanjanz categorised NGOs and companies according to their approach to each other and the authorities. NGOs can either have a radical, moderate or professional approach (Agakhanjanz 2006). Radical as well as professional NGOs are rather suspicious towards the state and businesses. They regard representatives from the state and businesses as corrupt and blame them for not complying with their professional roles. It is therefore the duty of society to control them. Because of this, their interaction with the state and businesses is portrayed rather more like a battle. While radical NGOs have a confrontational approach, professional NGOs do also cooperate with them. First, they do not regard all representatives from the state and businesses as corrupt, and, secondly, they believe that they can promote more effectively their interests by cooperating with the authorities and businesses. Moderate NGOs, instead, do not accuse the authorities and companies of being corrupt. Rather they blame the lack of financial and human resources for non-compliance with EIA laws and regulations and usually tend to avoid open conflict with the authorities and businesses. Their approach is purely cooperative.

Similarly, Agakhanjanz distinguishes between moderate and conflict-oriented entrepreneurs. Moderate entrepreneurs regard themselves as socially and environmentally responsible businessmen who have to comply not only with Russian law, but also with international environmental standards (Agakhanjanz 2006: 89). By following international stakeholder engagement standards, they seek cooperation with NGOs in order to reduce conflicts. In contrast to the moderate entrepreneurs, the conflict-oriented ones oppose active public participation since they regard the public as being against economic development. They consider most NGOs and local communities as either egoistic, short-minded or not having the relevant expertise to take part in EIAs. The conflict oriented entrepreneurs, however, do believe that companies have to comply with Russian law (Agakhanjanz 2006: 88–89).

It is worth noting that these features are specific to the policy tool (EIA), but not specific to Russia. Also in Western European countries such as in Germany, EIAs are mandatory, involve a multitude of actors from the state, companies, NGOs and local communities, and often feature a high level of conflict. The analysis in Sect. 4.5 will pay particular attention to how meta-governance tools are applied in Russia to ensure the proper conduct of the EIA, to solve blockades by one or several actors, to coordinate the multitude of actors and to deal with conflicts between stakeholders.

4.3   Laws and Regulations in the Field of Environmental Impact Assessment

Similar to Western Europe, EIAs in Russia involve hard and soft meta-governance tools. Following Vabo and Røiseland (2012: 938), we include discussion, persuasion, and encouragement in the realm of soft meta-governance. However, unlike Vabo and Røiseland we do not necessarily associate hard meta-governance with coercion, but rather with *any* form of command by the state which does not allow for bargaining and compromises. A command by the state may come in the form of coercion or hierarchy. Whereas hierarchy is understood here as being based on formal powers and law equally applied to all subjects, coercion implies the use of arbitrary threats or even violence outside of legally prescribed administrative channels. The distinction between hierarchy and coercion becomes relevant when comparing the actual performance of EIA in practice with the formal laws and regulations.

In Russia, a variety of binding federal and regional laws and regulations apply for EIAs (see OECD 2006; Kovalev et al. 2007; Begak et al. 2009; Schuhmann 2012).[8] Issuing binding regulations together with controlling and sanctioning compliance, represent *authority* as a meta-governance tool in its hard version. The soft version of authority, instead, would consist of issuing non-binding regulations such as guidelines (Vabo and Røiseland 2012: 938). According to Russian law, the EIA starts with the declaration of intent. In this phase, the investor prepares a declaration of intent which is sent to either the federal or regional authorities, depending on the jurisdiction under which the legal documents or project documentation fall. This declaration provides all the necessary project information as well as an initial impact assessment. After preliminary approval by the relevant federal or regional authorities, the local administration prepares the land site selection act, leading to a preliminary approval of the project's location.

Assessing the environmental impact of projects requires expertise and information spread among various actors. Companies dispose information on technologies and techniques which shall be used in the installations, and they know the inputs and outputs of their activities. The authorities have to ensure compliance of a project under laws and regulations in various environmental subfields such as air, water and soil protection as well as ensuring the safe-guarding of fauna and flora. They monitor the accumulated emissions of all industrial sites and the state of the environment in a certain area and have to set up plans to manage negative environmental impact. Together with affected local communities environmental NGOs can provide additional information about specific local environmental and social conditions as well as presenting the potential impact of investment projects on the local communities and the environment. Some NGOs in Russia also dispose well-trained and experienced staff in technological and legal matters (Henry 2010).

As laid out in the first chapter, one's position in a network to access and provide information (Hood and Margetts 2007: 5–11), is a powerful meta-governance tool: *nodality* allows actors to argue and persuade other network members (Vedung 1998: 33). When authorities have a monopoly on spreading information, its *nodality* is regarded to be hard. Instead, *nodality* comes in its soft version if governments represent only one of many sources of information (Vabo and Røiseland 2012: 937). When it comes to EIA, *nodality* of the environmental control agencies and com-panies is limited by law since they have to share information and must, therefore, not misuse their monopoly on information. In order to spread and exchange information among stakeholders, a plan for public consul-tation is set up as soon as local authorities have preliminarily approved the project's location. This plan and the preliminary content of the EIA materials are then sent to all EIA participants and made accessible to the public during the entire EIA. In addition, the company has to inform the public in federal, regional and local official newspapers about the proposed project and the upcoming public hearings. Comments sent in by the public need to be taken into account and need to be discussed in the final version of the project materials. As necessary information is dispersed among stakeholders, *nodality* does not apply to EIA in its hard version.

The main consultation with the public takes place during the subsequent public hearings where the affected community and NGOS are invited to participate. With exception of the administrative fee for conducting the EIA and the costs for preparing the project documents, both paid by the project sponsor, participation in EIAs does not entail any expenses for participants at public hearings. As indicated in Chap. 2 economic incentives such as participation fees (Hood and Margetts 2007: 5–11) can be used for meta-governance (*treasure*). In its hard version *treasure* makes network members fully dependent on state funding, so that 'receivers cannot 'escape' from the financial support offered by the local government' (Vabo and Røiseland 2012: 938). Free participation of stakeholders, however, results in a soft version of *treasure*, since it facilitates broad public involvement. Participants of public hearings may include societal actors receiving funding from companies or the state as well as representatives from grass roots movements and NGOs, which may lack own financial resources. Publication of information on public hearings and free participation formally ensures that all relevant actors can contribute their expertise and information and influence the outcome of the EIA.

During the public hearings, the authorities can either take a more passive role by steering and coordinating the process, or actively participate in the EIA in the attempt to influence the outcome. Formally, the local authorities are only responsible for registering the participants of public hearings, conducting public hearings and providing the protocol. However, they can also take part as speakers during public hearings, trying to convince stakeholders of their assessment. Since *organisation* as a meta-governance tool differs in the degree the authorities engage in networks with their own resources, e.g. participating directly in the network or indirectly through intermediaries (Vabo and Røiseland 2012: 938), the authorities in Russia can potentially apply *organisation* as a tool of meta-governance, both in its soft or hard version.

The results of public hearings and the revised materials of the EIA are presented to the 'state ecological assessment'. Companies in Russia are obliged to provide the same amount and depth of documents no matter what is the expected impact of the project, thus requiring a usually large amount of information from the companies. Among other things, the revised materials contain information on various options for realising the project, including the option of not realising the project at all. It also must contain a description of the impact on the environment by these various options, environmental risk management activities, a reasoning for selecting a specific option as well as all materials from the public hearings. The documents must remain open to the public until a decision on the project is made. If the project sponsor does not account for the suggestions put forward by the public, he or she is obliged to explain the reasons for this decision. These challenging requirements for providing information again reduce the *nodality* of companies during EIAs.

The environmental control agencies (*Rosprirodnadzor* and temporarily also *Rostekhnadzor*) constitute the expert committee which has to evaluate the project and therefore they are free to decide whether or not to apply their own *organisational* resources in order to influence collaboration. They can select the experts for the state ecological assessment either from their own staff or from the public. Mechanisms for public participation in the state ecological assessment are controversial. On the one hand, only the secretary of the expert commission has to be a representative of the environmental control agencies. Other experts and even the chair of the expert commission can be external, non-state experts from academia, NGOs or local communities. Requirements for external, non-state experts are comparatively low in Russia, a fact which allows involving public representatives not accredited by the state. Experts only need to be sufficiently independent from the project owner and are required to have a suitable education and at least 5 years of working experience. There is no need to register as a certified expert. The option to withdraw almost completely from the state ecological expertise and leave it to the public and the low requirements for public experts, allows for very soft meta-governance by the environmental control agencies.

On the other hand, in order to be involved in EIAs, NGOs need to state their general intent of participation in EIAs when they register their organisation (Nußberger and Carmen 2007). Registration as a NGO in Russia comes with heightened state control (Crotty et al. 2014). Moreover, when selecting experts, the authorities may certainly want to rely on those NGOs which are known to be cooperative. Due to the government's policy to provide many NGOs with state funding and its intent to control them more tightly, NGOs have moved closer to the state in order to pursue their activities, maintaining strong and resource-dependent relationships (Fröhlich 2012; Mamonova and Visser 2014). In many cases, a 'constructive cooperation' between loyal civil society organisations and the state (Henry 2010: 764; Ljubownikow et al. 2013) has thus been formed. In addition to increased control, public experts also meet procedural difficulties rendering their participation difficult. Since the duration of the state ecological expertise (between 30 and 120 days depending on the complexity of the project) is very short, real involvement of members of the public, except from highly specialised experts, is rather impossible. Non-professional ecologists usually do not have the knowledge to assess the complex matters in such a short time. The public, however, is also allowed to conduct a public ecological assessment so that all types of NGOs can take part not only during public hearings but also in the review of the revised EIA materials.

Finally, the project sponsor, representatives of the involved local, regional and federal administrations, and civil society representatives are invited to the expert committee's final session. There, the public has a right to debate but is not permitted to cast a vote unless they are members of the expert group. If a two-thirds majority of the expert committee agrees on the assessment report, it will be legally binding although opposing opinions must be included in the final report. If the vote does not meet the two-thirds threshold, it then has to be revised. If the expert committee continues to refuse to accept the assessment report, the procedure has to be prolonged and/or the expert committee has to be reformed.

Concluding, one can say that the formal legal framework of EIA in Russia involves softer meta-governance tools than in many Western European countries such as Germany. EIAs in Russia, as in Germany, see the application of *authority* in its hard version. Compared to Germany, the Russian system applies its *organisational* tools in a rather soft version. While in Germany the final decision remains with the state official, in Russia the decision is taken in the collective decision-making body of the expert commission by majority vote with participation of non-state experts. The Russian environmental control agencies are allowed to withdraw much of their *organisational* resources from conducting an EIA and transferring relevant duties to non-state experts from academia, NGOs or civil society. *Treasure* and *nodality* are confined by law. In contrast to the West, companies in Russia are required to provide the same amount and depth of documents no matter what is the expected impact of the project, thereby usually requiring a high degree of information from the companies. By law, this information has to be shared with the public. However, in order to assess how these formal laws are implemented in practice, one needs to analyse specific cases of EIA, as is done in the next paragraphs.

4.4   CASE AND DATA SELECTION

The exploratory analysis is based on a qualitative design with in-depth case studies of EIAs in Russia. Six case studies addressing controversial projects proposed by energy or large infrastructure companies were analysed between 2007 and 2010.[9] The empirical work was performed in the two regions of Krasnodar and Irkutsk. The Krasnodar region is located in the Northern Caucasus on the Black Sea and was recently well-known for holding the 2014 Olympic Games in Sochi. The Irkutsk region is situated in Eastern Siberia adjacent to Lake Baikal. While Irkutsk is dominated by extractive industry, Krasnodar has developed a more diversified economic structure comprising logistics, agriculture, consumer goods and services. The economic structure of Krasnodar results in more diverse regional actor constellations which has been seen to increase the chances for non-state actors to form alliances with other state and business actors (Schuhmann 2012: 27). The selected case studies represent the economic structures of the two regions. In the Krasnodar region, the case studies involve an off-shore drilling rig for oil exploration in the ecologically fragile Sea of Azov, several docks for shipping oil, gas and chemicals in the tourist region Taman' between the Black and the Azov Sea, the state development plan for several ski resorts and a spa in Krasnaya Polyana, and the construction plans for a ski resort in the same area. By contrast, the discussion of EIAs in the Irkutsk region focuses on the construction of an international centre for uranium enrichment in Angarsk, about 50 km from Irkutsk city.

Methodologically, the chapter builds on an analysis of newspaper articles and legal and policy documents, participation in public hearings, as well as 44 semi-structured interviews with environmental protection authorities, local and regional parliamentarians, academics, journalists, environmental NGOs and companies. Interviewees were selected according to the 'snowball-technique', starting with those actors which have been identified as key figures in the selected EIAs. We were then introduced to further relevant authorities, companies and NGOs by the key figures. The interviews were coded with MAXQDA and made anonymous. It should be noted that we could not cover all possible participants in the EIAs. The recorded opinions, therefore, cannot be regarded as being completely representative, particularly since NGOs, which are not bound by hierarchies and which are eager to spread their word, were more willing to share information. The project team also attended public hearings and analysed regional and national legal documents, as well as perusing newsletters from state and non-state actors.

4.5   CASE STUDIES: IMPLEMENTATION OF EIA REGULATION

Formally, the Russian state uses a mix of hard and soft governance-tools to govern EIA. While the state makes ample use of its authority to bindingly regulate the EIA process, *nodality*, *treasure* and *organisation* are used in their soft version. In practice, however, the use of *authority*, *nodality*, *treasure* and *organisation* differs considerably. The empirical findings from the six case studies revealed three patterns which vary significantly in the way the state applied the meta-governance tools (see also Kovalev et al. 2007).

4.5.1   *Cooperation in the Shadow of Authority: Soft Meta-Governance of EIA*

In two cases, the authorities did not need to make much use of their hard meta-governance tools. One company took the initiative to cooperate with local stakeholders even before the start of the actual EIA. The other was eager to find a compromise with authorities, NGOs and local communities during the EIA.

In the first case, the Angarsk electrolytic chemical plant 'AECHK JSC' planned the creation of an international centre for uranium enrichment in Angarsk in the Irkutsk region, thus expanding their chemical and nuclear production facilities. In order to discuss the project with the public, the company had already facilitated a public discussion and organised site visits for NGOs, media representatives and local deputies in 2005. By engaging in public discourse with academics and societal actors long before the start of the EIA, the company wanted to get information about the public's concern in order to win over their consent of the project.[10] From the beginning of the early discussion until the end of the EIA, a variety of environmental NGOs took part in the dialogue, including the grassroots 'Baikal Movement', the state affiliated NGO 'VOOP Irkutsk' and the professional NGOs 'Baikal Wave' and Greenpeace.[11] ENGOs criticised that the project would be a serious threat to the ecological safety of the nature protection zone Lake Baikal, as well as to the regional capital city

Irkutsk, both located only 45–90 km to the east of Angarsk. In case of emergency, the contaminated area could reach both zones. They were also concerned that the plant operates in the vicinity of an airport and in a seismic zone, thus increasing the risk of incidents. Due to these concerns, environmental NGOs urged the cancellation of the project.[12] The public hearings for the international centre for uranium enrichment took place in June 2009.[13] On this occasion, NGOs positively noted the openness of the project sponsor to provide information and to publicly discuss their concerns. They also mentioned that the project sponsor took some of their initial apprehensions into account when elaborating on the project materials. During the public hearing, the ENGOs suggested further changes to the project which were included into the project materials for the State Ecological Expert evaluations.[14]

In 2009, several environmental NGOs, including the two professional NGOs 'Baikal Wave' and Greenpeace, in cooperation with representatives of the Russian Academy of Sciences and the University of Irkutsk, conducted a public ecological assessment of the proposed project.[15] On this occasion, ENGOs, academics and representatives of local communities were able to study the project materials in depth. They submitted further suggestions to tighten the ecological control of the project, and recommended to the State Ecological assessment group that the project be prohibited unless these deficits in the project materials were properly addressed. While NGOs initially protested the realisation of the project, they changed their approach during the public discussion. Instead of blocking the realisation of the project, they became eager to increase its environmental safety.[16] NGOs learnt from the project sponsor's readiness to share all relevant information and to address their concern seriously.[17] NGOs and local communities could also rely on professional expertise from the Russian Academy of Sciences and Greenpeace. Both the project's openness and the expertise of NGOs helped to create trust among participants of the EIA. Interaction between the company, NGOs and regional and local state authorities lasted, therefore, for more than four years.

The second company, the regional *Rosneft* subsidiary '*JSC Priazovneft*' planned to construct an offshore oil exploration drilling rig in the environmentally fragile Sea of Azov. Different to AECHK, the company did not take the initiative to consult with the wider public before the start of the hearings. A coalition of NGOs, local communities and local deputies called 'Save Taman', first protested the realisation of the project.[18] Among the coalition of societal actors which took part in the public hearings in

December 2007 and February 2008 and also negotiated with the company between the public hearings, were NGOs, which can be clearly labelled as professionalised NGOs, e.g. the 'Environmental Watch of the Northern Caucasus', the 'Social-Ecologic Union' of Majkop, and WWF Krasnodar, as well as state affiliated NGOs like VOOP Krasnodar. These NGOs were supported by the international NGO 'Crude Accountability' which provided technical information along with advice on tactics. Members of the movement 'Save Taman' argued that oil drilling in that area would harm both the local fishery and the tourism industry. They tried to halt the EIA, hinting that there were formal deficits in the conducting of the public hearing and that the project materials were incomplete.[19] At the end of the public hearings local NGOs organised a vote, the result of which turned out to be almost unanimously against the project. Local deputies, however, signalled that they would accept the project if the drilling rig were to be moved further away from the shore so that it could not be seen from the beaches, and if the company would compensate for any damage done to local communities. During the public hearings a local deputy and member of 'Save Taman' stated:

> How can oil and beaches coexist? (...) What shall the entrepreneurs think, (...) who invested all their savings into minihotels, cafes, beaches, and bungalows? What shall he think [name deleted, authors' note], who invested a loan of millions of rubles into a hotel. With sorrow, he states that he will become bankrupt, as soon as the drilling rig emerges at the horizon. (...) I understand that progress can't be halted. However, it should lead in two directions! The position of *Tolliatiazot* was clear [a company, which planned the construction of a port in the same area, authors' note] (...) and which stated: For each tonne, one dollar for the region and one dollar for the local community, and as a start you also receive two lorries. Why do the other, by far not poor, investors not make such reasonable suggestions?[20]

At this stage, *Rosprirodnadzor* had to impose their *authority* resorting to hard meta-governance. They had to declare the first public hearings as invalid and asked the project sponsor to further elaborate on the project materials and provide more information to the public. At the second hearing, the company included most of the demands put forward by local deputies and local communities. *Priazovneft* moved the oil exploration platform further away from the shore (Local deputy Temryuk), and it agreed with local authorities upon several corporate social and environmental responsibility measures, e.g. modernising the local sturgeon factory and stabilising embankments at risk of erosion (Priazovneft June 23, 2006). Also, in this case NGOs understood that the company took their concerns seriously. Vice versa, *Priazovneft* did not complain about the activity of the 'Save Taman' movement. Representatives from NGOs and academia were also invited as independent experts in order to analyse the documents and elaborate on the state environmental expertise. Although interaction between the company, local and regional authorities and NGOs did not last as long as it did in the case of AECHK, they still cooperated over an extended period of at least one and a half years.

With the exception of a very brief time, when *Rosprirodnadzor* had to apply their *authority* to declare the public hearings invalid, the EIA in both cases took place without much hard meta-governance since the stakeholders for the most part had complied with their rights and duties. According to local NGOs, the CEOs of both companies understood that it was better to comply with all laws and regulations and to cooperate with local communities in order to reduce conflicts and facilitate realisation of the project.[21]

> In general, *Priazovneft* is a company which meets modern requirements and which pays much attention (to best available techniques, authors' note). However, they have a major, principal problem, since the ecosystem of the Sea of Asov is very sensitive to the project they are planning. This means, that there will be naturally a potentially huge conflict of interest. This is, why they invest into working with the community.[22]

Both CEOs, therefore, can be regarded as the moderate type of entrepreneurs according to Agakhanjanz's typology (2006). One may argue that in response to the conscientious approach of the entrepreneurs, NGOs were also ready to cooperate with the companies in order to promote their interests, following the logic of professionalised NGOs.

In both cases, local authorities and the environmental control agency *Rosprirodnadzor* did not have to make use of their *nodality* based on privileged access to environmental monitoring data and information from the company, since stakeholders shared information among themselves. Conversely, *Rosprirodnadzor* understood that they also needed the public's information for conducting the state environmental assessment. Particularly during the period of observation, the environmental authorities lacked information, expertise and manpower (Begak et al. 2009: 21;

Schuhmann 2012).[23] During the process of splitting up the responsibilities for EIA between *Rosprirodnadzor* and *Rostekhnadzor* in 2004, most experienced staff left the state authorities in charge for conducting the EIA (Begak et al. 2009: 15). The state authorities were also confronted with an overload of state ecological assessment, as the Russian EIA at this time did not foresee a screening process filtering out smaller and less relevant cases (Begak et al. 2009: 20). In 2006, for example, about 10,000 EIAs were each carried out on federal and regional level, while the regional staff of *Rostekhnadzor* amounted only to 330 officers and the *Rostekhnadzor's* federal staff of 339 officers (Begak et al. 2009: 21). As a result, the authorities had to rely on the skilled knowledge of independent experts. In the interviews, state representatives reported that they had depended on the NGOs' (both state-affiliated and professionalised) expertise because the administrative staff responsible for environmental protection had been significantly reduced in the past.[24]

> Our suggestions are, indeed, adopted. If there is no conflict of interest, then they are glad to collaborate with us [the authorities, the authors] (…), because we come up with issues, which they might not see.[25]

This illustrates that not only Western democracies, but also states with extreme hierarchies need to activate the resources provided by private actors in order to respond to policy problems (Davies 2012). Members of the state environmental protection agency as well as business actors regard collaboration with societal stakeholders as necessary in order increase the effectiveness of policy-making and to contribute to output legitimacy (see Provan and Milward 2001).

Since independent experts from all sorts of NGOs, no matter whether they were local grass roots movements, state affiliates or professionalised NGOs, were able to take part in the EIA, local authorities and the environmental control agency *Rosprirodnadzor* did not entirely rely on their *organisational* resources.

Judging from the interviews, it appears that professionalised NGOs in both regions were independent from the state when it came to funding as they relied on own financial backing from businesses, private supporters, and international grants. As they were also able to participate, local authorities and *Rosprirodnazor* did not narrow the group of participants down to those actors which they could control through means of *treasury*. Certainly, the state affiliated NGOs were less independent as they were subcontracted by the authorities e.g. for conducting research and environmental protection activities, and received funding from the state. However, these NGOs should not be confused with GONGOs (Government Organised NGOs), as they do not function as state puppets. Such organisations are usually created by companies and state authorities in order to feign public participation (Mikirova et al. 2013; Mamonova and Visser 2014). Indeed, in these cases they equally criticised the project materials during EIAs. Other studies about NGOs in Russia have accordingly shown that the collaborative approach between state authorities and resource dependent NGOs does not imply that these organisations are always predictable or completely obedient to the authorities (Chebankova 2012). Many defend the interests of their members by putting pressure on officials (Evans 2012).

In these two cases, the EIA could fulfil its genuine function. The project's compliance with environmental regulation was checked. Stakeholders were consulted in order to identify the best option to realise the project from the point of view of its environmental impact and as a result environmental conflicts were reduced. Although the state did not have to intervene excessively, one needs to consider that collaboration between the main stakeholders took place in the shadow of authority rendering policy-making in networks more effective (Héritier and Lehmkuhl 2008; Bekkers et al. 2007).

4.5.2   Unwillingness of Companies and Societal Actors to Cooperate: Enforcement of EIA Regulations by Hard Meta-governance Tools

In two other cases, however, the local authorities and *Rosprirodnadzor* had to make hard use of their *authority, nodality* and their *organisational* resources in order to ensure the proper conduct of EIA. In these two cases, the companies, *Jugneftechimtransit* and *Evro-Trans* planned to construct several docks for shipping oil, gas and chemicals on the Taman peninsula in Krasnodar region, which is also a flourishing tourist area.

When organising their public hearings in 2008, neither of the companies informed the public in the relevant official newspapers about the proposed project and the upcoming public hearings. Moreover, the preliminary content of the EIA materials had not been made accessible to the public. They also did not hold public hearings in the local communities directly affected by the projects but instead went to distant locations, hoping to avoid public opposition. The project materials, presented at the public hearings by *Evro-Trans*, only contained brief information on the environmental condition of the area, without analysing the environmental impact.[26] In contrast to the irregularities during the EIA of *Priazovneft*, which apparently had not been committed on purpose, the law infringements in these two cases were caused by the disregard of the public's opinion. In response to the question why laws and regulations of EIA had been violated, the leader of a local NGO in Krasnodar stated:

> There are various (...) reasons. Sometimes it is obvious, that the (law infringements, authors' note) take place due to lack of knowledge of some procedural norms for example, because the requirements for the EIA have appeared only recently, and the law on obligatory EIA has become stricter. (...) Now, we pay more attention to the formal requirements for public hearings. (...) Other companies, instead, are not interested in the public's opinion, because it is not to their advantage.[27]

As in the case of *Priazovneft*, 'Save Taman', a local movement consisting of an international NGO, domestic professionalised NGOs, local communities and local deputies, as well as the state affiliated NGO WOOP Krasnodar took part in the public hearings and influenced the public discussion.[28] Members of 'Save Taman' along with the state affiliated NGO, refused to sign the minutes of public hearings and recorded violations of the formal procedures.[29] Since the revised documents for the 'state ecological expertise' did not contain the valid documentation of public hearings, the authorities forced the companies to repeat them. *Evro-Trans* even had to do this twice.[30]

In these cases, *Rostekhnadzor* applied their *authority* in favour of public participation. The head of the professionalized NGO EWNC stated that he often collaborates with state actors in order to address violations of EIA regulation:

> There are also honourable people among the Russian law enforcement and environmental protection agencies. The entire Russian environmental protection system is essentially based on the enthusiasm not only of environmentalists but also of state officials (...).[31]

During further public hearings, NGOs kept blocking the realisation of the projects by organising a vote against the projects and refusing to sign the minutes of them.[32] As in the case of *Priazovneft*, they argued that the projects would harm not only the environment, but also the local fishery and tourism industry.[33] But different to the previous case, environmental NGOs and local deputies were not willing to achieve a compromise with the companies. The project sponsors complained that NGOs and local communities did not make any constructive suggestions as how to improve the projects' environmental safety. The project designer of *Jugneftechimtansit* commented on the activities of the environmental NGOs:

> In their newsletter on 10 September 2008, the activists of this organisation describe enthusiastically how they blocked the project by *Jugneftechimtransit* (...). They proudly stated that they obstructed the project and they sabotaged the public hearings. (...) In general, their information did not contain any constructive suggestion to solve the environmental conflict.[34]

Thus, the project sponsor's understanding of the public resembles the conflict-oriented entrepreneur described by Agakhanjanz (2006). Following the logic of the professional NGOs, societal actors did not switch to a cooperative approach, but instead kept fighting and blockading the project.

As a result, the authorities had to make use of their own *organisational* resources in order to ensure the proper conduct of the EIAs. As in many Western European countries, such as Germany (Hoppe and Beckmann 2012), the final conclusion concerning the EIA has to rest with the expert committee of the state ecological assessment and not with the participants of the public hearings. Therefore, *Rostekhnadzor* continued with the assessment despite the negative vote by the public hearings' participants. In both cases, NGOs had not been invited to the expert groups of the state ecological assessment due to their wish to block the projects without considering options to reduce the environmental impact of the projects. At the end of the EIAs *Jugneftechimtransit* was granted a permit to construct the port while *Evro-Trans* had to withdraw its application.

In these two cases, the EIA could only partly fulfil its actual function. The projects' compliance with environmental regulation was checked, the companies provided necessary information to the authorities and the public, and the voices of a broad range of NGOs, members of local communities and local deputies were listened to during public hearings.

Nevertheless, societal actors were not properly consulted in order to identify the best option to realise the projects with the lowest possible environmental impact, since both the companies and the public were not willing to find a compromise solution to the stalemate. Societal actors did not take part at all in the state ecological assessment. As a result, at least in the case of *Jugneftechimtransit*, environmental conflicts were reduced. In order to ensure a formally correct conduct of the EIA, the environmental permitting agencies as well as local authorities had to apply their *authority*, *nodality*, and *organisation* in their hard form. No cooperation between the companies, societal actors and the authorities took place.

4.5.3   *Mimicked Networks or Coercive Meta-Governance to Prevent Public Participation in EIAs*

While AECHK and *Priazovneft* voluntarily cooperated with societal and state actors, and the environmental control agencies enforced a minimum of interaction between stakeholders in order to conduct the EIAs of *Jugneftechimtransit* and *Evro-Trans*, the next two cases illustrate how competent authorities approved the EIAs due to pressure from above, which lack proper consultation with the public. In these cases, the project sponsors were not ready to collaborate with representatives from NGOs and local communities according to the EIA regulations and the competent authorities did not use their *authority* to ensure the proper application of EIA regulation. The authorities even applied the tools of *treasure* and *organisation* to further undermine collaboration.

The EIAs described in this paragraph concern the state development plan for several ski resorts and a spa in Krasnaya Polyana of the Krasnodar region, as well as the construction plans for a ski resort in the same area where the Winter Olympics took place in 2014. The ski resorts and Olympic infrastructure fell partly in the Sochi National Park and the UNESCO World Nature Heritage 'Western Caucasus'. Similar to *Jugneftechimtansit* and *Evro-Trans*, important parts of the project materials for the state development plan of Krasnaya Polyana were not disclosed to the wider public prior to the public hearings. Public hearings were not conducted in all the affected municipalities; and with exception of one representative, NGOs were not allowed to speak at the public hearings. Instead of drafting the reports of the public hearings for the state ecological assessment jointly with NGOs, the project sponsor fabricated them in advance without mentioning any criticism of the project. The project sponsor also refused to discuss the minutes of the public hearings with civil society representatives.[35]

A coalition of NGOs and local community representatives, however, opposed the projects as they feared harm to protected natural areas, the rising cost of living and the squeezing-out of local businesses. As in the previous cases the coalition consisted of a broad range of NGOs, such as the professionalised NGOs 'EWNS', the 'Social-Ecologic Union' of Majkop, WWF Krasnodar, and state affiliated NGOs such as VOOP Krasnodar. In addition to these NGOs, at least one GONGO also took part in the EIA, since the 'Association of Nature Protection Zones and National Parks of the Northern Caucasus' claimed to represent community interests, although it was just an organisational unit of the state administration of the Sochi National Park. At the public hearings this organisation supported the restructuring of Sochi National Park.

In the second case of this pattern, the project sponsor conducted an EIA for the construction plans for a ski resort in the Krasnaya Polyana area. In this case the project sponsor did not conduct any public hearings at all. It just presented the project materials for its ski resort during an exhibition without prior disclosure of the materials to the public. In both cases, NGOs tried to fight the infringements intensely. They filed law suits, wrote petitions to the regional governor, members of government including the president, and took to the streets. Some prosecutors, judges, the general accounting office and the regional entity of *Rosprirodnadzor* even approved or echoed their claims.[36] However, the EIAs were declared invalid.[37] According to NGOs, higher ranking political regional and federal state actors protected the projects.[38] A former *Rosprirodnadzor* official stated in an interview:

> Some projects are controlled by very powerful people. Usually the expertise had to be carried out very quickly in those cases (...) so conducting public hearings was out of the question (...). The company just says that it needs the expertise immediately (...) and addresses the issue to Moscow. Moscow can give such an instruction. The company is also able to address the issue to the regional administration because the regional administration can influence the experts' report.[39]

The plausibility of this position is supported by the fact that the Minister of Economic Development and Trade, German Gref, pushed other ministries and state agencies to speed up preparation for Sochi 2014. In the end, local authorities which were in charge of organising the public hearings did not intervene and did not enforce the binding EIA regulation so that the project sponsors succeeded in detaching societal actors from relevant information. Although the project materials did not include proper reports of public hearings, they were accepted for the state ecological assessment.[40] No independent NGOs were invited to the state ecological assessment and NGOs were not permitted to conduct the public ecologic assessment. Courts of cassation reversed prior rulings upholding the demands of NGOs.[41]

Needless to say that the EIAs in these two cases did not fulfil at all its actual function. The projects' compliance with environmental regulation were properly checked. The companies did not provide necessary information to the authorities or to the public, and the voice of real NGOs were not heard either during public hearings or at the state ecological assessment. In both cases, the state did not make use of its *authority* to enforce binding law. Instead, this pattern demonstrates how influential political actors used their *authority* in its hard, *coercive* tools to govern EIAs. They deliberately pressured local authorities and the environmental protection agencies to support the issuing of a positive conclusion to the EIA of the state development plan and the construction of the ski resorts, even though the public hearings did not comply with EIA regulations. They also pressured competent authorities to use its *nodality* to withhold relevant information and to squeeze independent NGOs out of the state and public assessment. As to *treasure*, the authorities involved at least one GONGO in the EIA in order to facilitate a positive conclusion to the EIAs (Table 4.1).

4.6   Conclusion

This analysis has revealed that the Russian authorities use a mix of hard and soft governance tools to govern EIAs. As pointed out in Sect. 4.4, the legal framework of EIAs in Russia involves relatively soft meta-governance tools in comparison to Western European countries such as Germany, since the Russian environmental control agencies can refrain from applying their *organisational* resources, and companies have to share much more information with the public, thus reducing the *nodality* of the state and companies. The empirical findings from the six case studies, however,

Table 4.1 Patterns of collaboration and meta-governance in EIAs

Type of network	Softly dominated networks	Strongly dominated networks	Mimicked networks
Pattern of meta-governance	Rather soft meta-governance	Hard meta-governance making ample use of *hierarchy* (hard version of *authority*) and *organisation*	Hard meta-governance making ample use of *coercion* (hard version of *authority*), *nodality*, *organisation* and *treasure*
Function of network	• Voice position of participants • Consultation between stakeholders • Coordination (cross-sectoral) • Conflict management • Decision making – Real collaboration between responsible authorities, business actors, NGOs and local communities	• Voice the positions of participants • Only partly consultation and coordination – Only very limited collaboration between responsible authorities, business actors, NGOs and local communities	• Formally complying with the need to conduct an EIA • Squeezing out NGOs and local communities from EIAs – No collaboration between responsible authorities, business actors, NGOs and local communities
Actors involved in the networks	• Domestic professional (critical, but consensus-oriented), state-affiliated, a grassroots movement and an international NGO • State: federal, regional and local authorities • Companies • Academics • Citizens	• Domestic professional (critical, but consensus-oriented), state-affiliated, a grassroots movement and an international NGO • State: federal, regional and local authorities • Companies • Academics • Citizens	• State: federal, regional and local authorities • Companies • GONGOs
Formalisation of networks	Formalised	Formalised	Informal

demonstrate that in practice EIAs are conducted very differently. Thus, one can identify three major patterns which differ significantly in the way the state applied meta-governance tools.

Although there are no truly self-regulated networks when it comes to EIA, one can find soft-dominated networks since the authorities did not need to make use of their hard meta-governance tools. In order to learn about the society's concerns and reduce conflicts, the companies themselves were eager to talk to NGOs and to find a consensus even before the official start of the EIA or during the actual process of public participation. However, it needs to be said that cooperation between the main stakeholders took place under the shadow of authority. Companies were most probably well aware that the authorities would enforce public participation in EIA, if the companies had not properly conducted public hearings. The authorities were equally eager to involve representatives from NGOs and local communities in order to comply with the law, receive relevant information, and source out part of the work of the EIA. In these cases, the EIA could fulfil its real role to check the project's compliance with environmental laws and regulations, discuss potential environmental conflicts, identify the best option to realise the project from the point of view of its environmental impact, and involve non-state experts in environmental decision making during the state environmental expert assessment. Since stakeholders also agreed that companies would compensate identified economic losses suffered by local communities due to the negative environmental impact, the EIA also served as a cross-sectoral coordination between stakeholders. In addition to the authorities and companies, a wide range of NGOs, academics and local communities participated in the EIAs, among them professional international and domestic NGOs, state affiliates, as well as grassroots NGOs. Since the project of *Priazovneft* was realised on the Taman peninsula where several EIAs for major projects on oil and gas exploration and transportation were conducted, and the public discussion of the project of AECHK in Angarsk already started a couple of years before the beginning of the actual EIA, cooperation between state authorities the business community, academics and NGOs evolved over one and a half to three years.

The second pattern also involved a wide range of NGOs, academics and local communities. International and domestic professional NGOs took part, along with state affiliates and grass root NGOs. In these cases, stakeholders equally interacted over an extended period. In contrast to the first pattern, the state, however, had to apply hard meta-governance tools, since companies and NGOs either did not comply with EIA regulations at all or refused to cooperate. Conversely, they tried to avoid real public involvement or block the EIA. Hence, one can hardly call this form of interaction 'real' cooperation. Local authorities and environmental control agencies had to use their *authority* to ensure proper conduct of the EIAs. The EIAs could, therefore, only partly fulfil their original role as a consultative tool to diminish the negative environmental impact of the projects. Although the authorities ensured that NGOs were able to voice their position during public hearings, they did not involve them in subsequent state or public ecological assessment.

By contrast, the third pattern consisted only of bogus collaboration, since NGOs were not able to raise their voice in public hearings. They could not suggest improvements to the projects and did not take part in decision-making during the state environmental assessment. The function of these EIAs was rather to get a positive EIA conclusion while disregarding the procedural rules. Although a wide range of NGOs, experts, academics and citizens were present at the public hearings, they were not involved in exchange of information, consultation, problem-solving or decision-making. Critical voices from state authorities were also not heard. Instead of complying with the formally prescribed rules for conducting the EIA, the responsible authorities and companies applied a variety of tactics to prevent real discussion at the public hearings and state ecological expert assessments due to informal *coercive* pressure by influential elites. Instead of disqualifying the EIA because of the legal infringements, the authorities issued a favourable conclusion to the state environmental assessment and granted a permit to go ahead with the project.

The variety in these three patterns can be largely explained by the characteristics of the policy tool. Although EIAs are mandatory, the local authorities and environmental permitting agencies are free to decide to apply their meta-governance tools in either soft or hard versions. This depends largely on the level of conflict as well as the idiosyncratic features of the participants. As described in paragraph 4.3, many actors do participate in EIAs and the level of conflict during these EIAs is often, but not always, very high. Under these circumstances conflict can easily roll out of control depending on the experience and the personality of EIA participants from the companies, authorities and civil society. Because EIAs are compulsory, some actors are tempted to block or circumvent them, in order to promote their own interests. The case studies suggest that local authorities and environmental permitting agencies apply their meta-governance tools in soft form if participants are cooperative. Vice versa, if they turn out to be hostile, the authorities utilise hard meta-governance tools to ensure that the EIA is properly conducted. While the level of conflict and idiosyncratic features of participants are necessary causes to explain the various patterns, they cannot sufficiently elucidate all of the varieties in our cases. Another factor contributing to one of the described patterns turned out to be deficiencies in the rule of law, along with corruption among some parts of the authorities and companies.

In summary, one needs to consider that the small number of cases studied does not allow any firm conclusion about the quantitative distribution of the three patterns among the entire number of EIAs conducted in Russia. Nevertheless, the cases do illustrate that a state with extreme hierarchies also needs to activate the resources provided by private actors in order to adequately respond to policy problems. They have also shown that breakdown of collaboration between the state, business actors and NGOs may be caused not only by the authorities or companies, but also by NGOs.

It is also necessary to keep in mind that the cases do not tell about the effectiveness of public participation at EIAs. Although the case studies revealed that several suggestions put forward by NGOs and local communities during public hearings were introduced into the project materials, observers doubted the effectiveness of independent experts at the state ecological assessment. Independent experts often write their evaluations after a multitude of state authorities have already corroborated their conclusion. Expressing an alternative opinion is, certainly, much more difficult when the authorities have already created a collective opinion (Begak et al. 2009: 15, 21). Moreover, conclusions by independent experts can easily be disputed at court since the normative framework lacks detailed and clear information on specific environmental parameters, upon which the experts can rely to foster their conclusions. As a result of this, independent experts are tempted to issue positive conclusions. Indeed, in the period of observation about 90% of SEEs received such a positive appraisal (Begak et al. 2009: 20).

NOTES

1. Federal Law No.174-FZ 'On Ecological Expertise'; Federal Law No.199-FZ 'On environmental protection'.
2. Art. 42 of the Russian Constitution; Art. 12, Federal law No.199-FZ 'On environmental protection'.
3. Art. 14 Federal Law No.174-FZ 'On Ecological Expertise'.
4. Federal Law No.174-FZ 'On Ecological Expertise'; Federal Law No.199-FZ 'On environmental protection'; accessed October 28, 2015.
5. Federal Law No.174-FZ 'On Ecological Expertise'.
6. The list of activities and documents subject to an EIA has been considerably reduced in Russia over the last 10 years, while at the same time most industrial countries have been increasing the coverage of EIA and public participation during EIA (Begak et al. 2009). Already in 2007, at the beginning of the period of observation the objects needing an EIA, consisting of the state ecological expertise and OVOS, has been reduced on demand of the construction lobby in the state duma (Begak et al. 2009: 15). In the following years, the EIA has been even further weakened. In 2008, still all activities which needed a license from the authorities and which may have negative impact on the environment, required an EIA. Today, merely a limited number of documents, which are listed in the law and involve activities with negative environmental impact require an EIA. The continuous reduction of the scope of the EIA was meant to reduce barriers for economic growth, as political decision makers in government and parliament as well as business representatives see the state ecological expertise, not only as a chance to enhance quality and legitimacy of environmental decision making, but they also regard it as part of the problem of weak economic growth.
7. Federal Law No.174-FZ 'On Ecological Expertise'.
8. For an overview of relevant laws and regulations for conducting the Environmental Impact Assessment (EIA), and the State Ecological Expertise of the EIA materials on the federal and regional levels; refer to: http://www.arcticcentre.org/RussianEIA/legislation.
9. The cases do not reflect the further authoritarian turn which started after the protests on Bolotnaya Square in Moscow in December 2011. Media coverage of more recent EIAs, however, suggests that our findings are still valid. Greenpeace (2013): Is Gazprom Neft preparing to drill in the Russian Arctic without an environmental review? Greenpeace News, 16 September; http://www.greenpeace.org/russia/en/news/16-09-2013_ Dolginskoe_EIA/; Greenpeace (2013): Ufa citizens still opposing Austrian formaldehyde and the local authorities. Greenpeace News, 7 November. http://www.greenpeace.org/russia/en/news/Ufa-citizens-

still-opposing-Austrian-formaldehyde—and-the-local-authorities/;   both accessed January 1, 2017.

10. Interviews with the head of an NGO and with the editor in chief of BABR. ru in Irkutsk, conducted between March and October 2008; N.N., 17.1.2008: Opyt irkutskoj oblasti po sozdaniju Obščestvennogo soveta po voprosam bezopasnogo ispol'zovanija atomnoj ėnergii zainteresoval predstavitelej obščestvennosti v drugich regionach, in: Delovoj kur'er Pribajkal'ja ot IA 'Teleinform'; http://babr.ru, accessed January 1, 2017.

11. Bel'gskaja, Ol'ga (2010): O Bajkal'skom dviženii: http://baikal.babr.ru/? ev=about, accessed January 1, 2017.

12. Mašerova, Anna, 21.02.2007: Namerenija s kommentarijami, ili komu on nužen, ėtot atom?, in Babr.ru: http://babr.ru; Kulechov, Michail, 08.06. 2009: Poluraspad proekta, ėkzperty ne verjat v real'nost' centra obogoščenija urana, in: Babr.ru: http://babr.ru, accessed January 1, 2017.

13. Pšonko, Elena, 08.06.2009: O mirnom atome pogovorili v poliklinike, in: *Oblastnaja Gazeta*: http://babr.ru; accessed January 1, 2017.

14. Jablokov, A., Richvanova, M., Čuprov, V., Korenblit, S., Veselova N., 22.10.2009: Argumentirovannye predloženija v komissiju gosudarstvennoj ėkologičeskoj ėkspertizy materialov obosnovanija licenzii na sooruženie Kompleksa razdelitel'nogo proizvodstva ZAO 'Centr po obogaščeniju urana', in: Babru.ru: http://babr.ru. Accessed January 1, 2017.

15. N.N., 04.09.2009: Ėkologi namereny provesti ėkspertizy licenzii na sooruženie kompleksa razdelitel'nogo proizvodstva ZAO 'Centr po obojaščeniju urana', in: NIA Bajkal: http://babr.ru. Accessed January 1, 2017.

16. Jablokov, A., Richvanova, M., Čuprov, V., Korenblit, S., Veselova N., 22.10.2009: Argumentirovannye predloženija v komissiju gosudarstvennoj ėkologičeskoj ėkspertizy materialov obosnovanija licenzii na sooruženie 'Kompleksa razdelitel'nogo proizvodstva ZAO 'Centr po obogaščeniju urana', in: Babru.ru: http://babr.ru. Accessed January 1, 2017.

17. Pšonko, Elena, 08.06.2009: O mirnom atome pogovorili v poliklinike, in: *Oblastnaja Gazeta*: http://babr.ru; N.N., 17.1.2008: Opyt irkutskoj oblasti po sozdaniju Obščestvennogo soveta po voprosam bezopasnogo ispol'zovanija atomnoj ėnergii zainteresoval predstavitelej obščestvennosti v drugich regionach, in: Delovoj kur'er Pribajkal'ja ot IA 'Teleinform': http://babr.ru. Accessed January 1, 2017.

18. N.N., 07.12.2007: Priazovneft' predstavila proekt po bureniju razvedočnoj skvažiny v Azovskom more, in: Novostnaja Lenta: http://www.wwf.ru/ resources/news/article/3513. Accessed January 1, 2017.

19. N.N., 19.02.2008: Deputaty Temrjuka dobyči nefti v Azovskom more, in: Ėkologičeskaja Vachta po Severnomu Kavkasu informacionnaja rassylka: http://ewnc.org/node/98. Accessed January 1, 2017.

20. N.N., 25.02.2008: Ėkologičeskaja situacija v Temrjuke 21 fevralja sosto-jalas' sessija Temrjukskogo rajonnogo soveta. Privodim fragmenty vystu-plenija deputata V. Novopašina, in: Na Taman'i: http://naTaman'i. ru/index.php?area=1&p=news&newsid=43. Not accessible on January 1, 2017, print version available from the authors of this article.
21. Interviews with the head of an NGO and editor in chief of BABR.ru in Irkutsk as well as with heads of the NGOs EWNC and WOOP in Krasnodar, conducted between March and October 2008.
22. Interview with the head of the NGO WOOP in Krasnodar, conducted between March and October 2008.
23. Interviews with the head and an employee of the NGO 'Baikal Wave' in Irkutsk', and with a former employee of Rosprirodnadzor in Krasnodar, conducted between March and October 2008.
24. Interview with former officer of Rozprirodnadzor Krasnodar, conducted between March and October 2008.
25. Interview with Head of NGO 'Baikal Wave', conducted between March and October 2008.
26. Gazarjan, Suren (2007): Burenie i dobyča nefti v Azovskom more mogut zakončit'sja tak že plačevno, kak i perevalka nefti v Kerčenskom prolive. EWNC News, 5 December 2007. http://ewnc.org/node/286. Accessed January 1, 2017.
27. Interview with the head of the NGO WOOP in Krasnodar, conducted between March and October 2008.
28. Pravda (2008): Žiteli Taman'skogo poluostrova vystupili protiv rejdovoj perevalki nefti v Kerčenskom prolive. EWNC News, 27 August 2007. http://ewnc.org/node/1290. Accessed January 1, 2017; Gipanis (2008): 'Obščestvennost' dobilas' perenosa obščestvennych slušanij, kotoriye byli organizovany s grubymi narušenijami.' Gipanis, 5 September 2008. www. gipanis.ru/?level=349&type=page&lid=359. Accessed January 29, 2017.
29. Pyčka, Aleksej (2008): EWNC – mif i real'nost. Epos, 09., http://eposk. biz/news/ekomyth.htm. Accessed January 29, 2017.
30. N.N., 27.08.2008: Žiteli Temrjukskogo rajona i ėkologičeskie organizacii vystupili protiv rejdovoj perevalki nefti v Kerčenskom prolive, in: Ėkologičeskaja Vachta po Severnomu Kavkasu Life Journal: http://ewnc. livejournal.com/46310.html; N.N., 28.08.2008: Žiteli Taman'skogo poluostrova vystupili protiv rejdovoj perevalki nefti v Kerčenskom prolive. EWNC News, 27 August 2007. http://ewnc.org/node/1290. Accessed January 1, 2017.
31. Interview with the head of the NGO EWNC in Krasnodar, conducted between March and October 2008.
32. N.N., 05.09.2009: Obščestvennost' dobilas' perenosa obščestvennych slušanij, kotoriye byli organizovany s grubymi narušenijami, in: Gipanis:

www.gipanis.ru/?level=349&type=page&lid=359;   N.N.,   08.2008:
Rejdovaja perevalka sery v Kerčenskom prolive nadopustima! *Gipanis*:
www.gipanis.ru/?level=358&type=page&lid=359. Accessed January 1,
2017.

33. WWF (2007): Priazovneft' predstavila proekt po bureniju razvedočnoj
    skvažiny v Azovskom more. *Novostnaja Lenta*, 7 December 2007. http://
    www.wwf.ru/resources/news/article/3513. Accessed January 1, 2015.

34. Pyčka, Aleksej (2008): EWNC – mif i real'nost. *Epos* 09, http://eposk.biz/
    news/ekomyth.htm. Accessed January 29, 2017.

35. EWNC (2005): Ėkologičeskaja i naučnaja obščestvennost' predstavila
    osoboe mnenie po genplanu razvitija Krasnoj Poljany. *EWNC News*, 5 May
    2005. http://ewnc.org/node/410. Accessed January 29, 2017.

36. Brinnich, Valerij (2007): Zajavlenie sopredsedatelja soveta MSOĖS V.A.
    Brinicha v svjazi s prinjatiem Majkopskim gorodskim sudom v 1-j instancii
    rešenija o priznanii nezakonnym izmenenija funkzional'nogo zonirovanija
    Sočinskogo nacional'nogo parka. *EWNC News*, 3 November 2007.
    http://www.ewnc.org/node/265;   EWNC   (2008):   Prokuror
    Krasnodarskogo Kraja provel soveščanie s obščestvennymi organizacijami
    po voprosam obespečenija ėkologičeskoj bezopasnosti pri stroitel'stve
    olimijskich ob'ektov; *EWNC News*, 20 November 2008. http://ewnc.
    org/node/1668. Accessed January 29, 2017.

37. Rudomacha, Andrej (2006): Olimpiada-2014 trebuet vse novych 'žertv'.
    EWNC News, 27 December 2006. http://ewnc.org/node/324. Accessed
    January 29, 2017.

38. Interview with the head of the NGO EWNC in Krasnodar, conducted
    between March and October 2008; see also: Rudomacha, Andrej (2007):
    Sud'ja Vladimir Tkačenko rešil spasti olimpiadu v Soči i reputaciju
    Rosprirodnadzora. *EWNC News*, 9 November 2007. http://www.ewnc.
    org/node/266; Lysenko, Tat'jana (2006): Adygejskaja 'demokratija'
    protiv zaščity rossijskogo lesa. *EWNC News*, 17 December 2006. http://
    ewnc.org/node/342. Accessed January 29, 2017.

39. Interview with a former employee Rosprirodnadzor, conducted between
    March and October 2008.

40. EWNC (2008): Gazprom zavralsja. *EWNC News*, 4 October 2008. www.
    ewnc.org/node/1540. Accessed January 29, 2017.

41. Rudomacha, Andrej (2007): Sud'ja Vladimir Tkačenko rešil spasti olim-
    piadu v Soči i reputaciju Rosprirodnadzora. *EWNC News*, 9 November
    2007. http://www.ewnc.org/node/266; Lysenko, Tat'jana (2006):
    Adygejskaja 'demokratija' protiv zaščity rossijskogo lesa. *EWNC News*, 17
    December 2006. http://ewnc.org/node/342. Accessed January 29,
    2017.

REFERENCES

Agakhanjanz, P. 2006. Prinjatie ėkologicheski znachimych reshenij i rossijskaja obshchestvennost': Pozicii uchastnikov processa (po materialam intervju). *Ėkologicheskoe planirovanie i upravlenie* 1: 81–90.

Beck, Ulrich. 1992. *Risk Society: Towards a New Modernity*. London: Sage.

Begak, Michail, Valerij Kulibaba, Juhan Ruut, and Yana Molchanova. 2009. *Preventivnye mechanism ochrany okruzhajushchey sredy v Rossii Evropeiskom Sojuse. Perspektivy Garmonizacii*. Moscow: IurInfor-Press Publ.

Bekkers, Viktor, Geske Dijkstra, Arthur Edwards, and Menno Fenger. 2007. *Governance and the Democratic Deficit*. Hampshire: Ashgate.

Chebankova, Elena. 2012. State-sponsored Civic Associations in Russia: Systemic Integration or the 'War of Position'? *East European Politics* 28 (4): 390–408.

Crotty, Jo, Sarah Marie Hall, and Sergej Ljubonwnikow. 2014. Post-Soviet Civil Society Development in the Russian Federation: The Impact of the NGO Law. *Europe-Asia Studies* 66 (8): 1253–1269.

Davies, Jonathan S. 2012. Network Governance Theory: A Gramscian Critique. *Environment and Planning* 44 (11): 2687–2704.

Evans, Alfred. 2012. Protests and Civil Society in Russia: The Struggle for the Khimki Forest. *Communist and Post-Communist Studies* 45: 233–242.

Fröhlich, Christian. 2012. Civil Society and the State Intertwined: The case of Disability NGOs in Russia. *East European Politics* 28 (4): 371–389.

Greenpeace. 2015. *Chinovniki snova pokushajutsja na ekologicheskuju ekspertizu*. http://www.greenpeace.org/russia/ru/news/2015/27-07-ecologicheskaya-ekspertiza-pokushenie-2/. Accessed 29 Jan 2017.

Henry, Laura A. 2010. Between Transnationalism and State Power: The Development of Russia's Post-Soviet Environmental Movement. *Environmental Politics* 19: 756–781.

Heritiér, Adrienne, and Dirk Lehmkuhl. 2008. The Shadow of Hierarchy and New Modes of Governance. *Journal of Public Policy* 28: 1–17.

Hood, C. 1983. *The Tools of Government*. London: Macmillan.

Hood, C., and H.Z. Margetts. 2007. *The tools of government in the digital age*. Basingstoke: Palgrave Macmillan.

Hoppe, Werner, and Martin Beckmann (eds). 2012. *UVPG-Gesetz über die Umweltverträglichkeitsprüfung. Kommentar*, 4th ed. Köln: Carl Heymanns.

Kovalev, Nicole, Johann Köppel, and Eckhard Dittrich. 2007. *Demokratie und Umwelt in Russland*. Berlin: Lit.

Ljubownikow, Sergej, Jo Crotty, and Peter W. Rodgers. 2013. The State and Civil Society in Post-Soviet Russia: The Development of a Russian-style Civil Society. *Progress in Development Studies* 13 (2): 153–166.

Mamonova, Natalia, and Oane Visser. 2014. State Marionettes, Phantom Organisations or Genuine Movements? The Paradoxical Emergence of Rural Social Movements in Post-socialist Russia. *The Journal of Peasant Studies* 41: 491–516.

Mikirova, Karina, Kathrin Mueller, and Johannes Schuhmann. 2013. The Influence of Civil Society Activism on Regional Governance Structures in the Russian Federation: Cross-Regional and Policy Comparison. In *Civil Society Activism under Authoritarian Rule: A comparative Perspective*, ed. Fracesco Cavartorta, 111–134. New York: Routledge.

Milward, H. Brinton. 2001. Do Networks Really Work? A Framework for Evaluating Public-Sector Organizational Networks. *Public Administration Review* 61: 414–423.

Nußberger, Angelika, and Carmen Schmidt. 2007. Vereinsleben auf Russisch oder Don Quichote und die russische Bürokratie. *Russlandanalysen* 138: 2–6.

OECD. 2006. *Environmental Policy and Regulation in Russia: The Implementation Challenge*. http://inece.org/oecdtmp/cd/en/docs/regional/environmental_policy_challenge_russia_en.pdf.

Schuhmann, Johannes. 2012. *Governance-Strukturen in der regionalen Umweltpolitik Russlands: Verhandlungen zwischen Staat, Wirtschaft und Zivilgesellschaft*. Wiesbaden: Springer VS.

Vabo, Signy Irene, and Asbjørn Røiseland. 2012. Conceptualizing the Tools of Government in Urban Network Governance. *International Journal of Public Administration* 35 (14): 934–946.

Vedung, Evert Oskar. 1998. Policy Instruments: Typologies and theories. In *Carrots, sticks & sermons. Policy instruments & their evaluation*, eds M.-L. Bemelmans-Videc, R.C. Rist and E. Vedung, 21–58. New Brunswick: Transaction Publishers.

CHAPTER 5

Climate Change Adaptation: Governance in a Fragmented and Unsettled Policy Area

Jørn Holm-Hansen and Mikkel Berg-Nordlie

5.1 Introduction

Fourty Russian cities with more than 250,000 inhabitants experience flooding annually. Among these are the two cities studied in this chapter, Arkhangelsk and Saint Petersburg. As the results of global climate change are becoming more and more visible, the problems connected with flooding in Russia are becoming worse, and have resulted in a need for new adaptive measures and expansion of the ones already in use.

Some adaptive measures are 'win-win' such as the establishment of green spaces to absorb rain water but others, for example putting a ban on construction of residential buildings in attractive zones, may be controversial. Others are complex and require a combination of policy tools and cut across

J. Holm-Hansen (✉)
Department for International Studies and Migration,
Norwegian Institute for Urban and Regional Research NIBR-HiOA,
0166 Oslo, Norway
e-mail: jorn.holm-hansen@nibr.hioa.no

M. Berg-Nordlie
Department for International Studies and Migration,
NIBR Institute of Oslo and Akershus University College,
0166 Oslo, Norway
e-mail: Mikkel.berg-nordlie@nibr.hioa.no

© The Author(s) 2018
S. Kropp et al. (eds.), *Governance in Russian Regions*,
DOI 10.1007/978-3-319-61702-2_5

various policy sectors. In the literature on adaptation to climate change, an analytical distinction is being made between incremental adaptation on the one hand and transition to a more fundamental change that requires involvement and input from a broad spectrum of actors on the other (Heltberg et al. 2009; Hallegatte 2009; Bukeley 2013; Pelling 2011). The incremental adaptation amounts to no-regret and win-win solutions, i.e. measures that are likely to be considered favourable even by decision-makers and citizens who are not alarmed by climate change. Among this type of adaptive measures, we find the modernising of water pipes or the laying out of new parks to absorb the increasing amounts of rainwater. They can easily be implemented without horizontal, network-like tools of governance.

However, climate change adaptation, and more specifically urban climate risk governance, is too complex only to be met with mere incremental measures. It is a fragmented policy area with a large number of actors dispersed across sectors involving different levels of government. Knowledge is needed about risk, vulnerability and adaptation options. City authorities, even when they are aware of climate change challenges, may lack mandated capacity and financial resources and are thus dependent upon allies in civil society and a pro-active business sector.

The theoretical core of network governance is that the increasing complexity of contemporary policy issues, and the increasing understanding of them as being complex and 'wicked', necessitate a non-hierarchical and qualitatively new type of close interaction between state authorities, non-state actors and business (see Berg-Nordlie, Holm-Hansen and Kropp, Chap. 2). Climate change mitigation and adaptation is highly interconnected to other policy areas and the factors to solve the problems are interdependent. Climate change adaptation, therefore, can be seen as belonging to the category of 'wicked problems' and, according to network governance theory, requires new and more collaborative approaches on the part of state authorities. State, regional and local institutions need to interact closely and harmonise their policies. In the field of climate change adaptation, the policy sectors of planning and construction, waste water and sewage, emergency situations, housing and communal infrastructure, hydro-meteorology and environmental protection all have a share in climate adaptation. In addition to inter-sectoral cooperation, the resources of non-state actors may be of use. The involvement of developers, the construction branch, and insurance companies in the development of adaptation measures and policies is particularly relevant. The inclusion of civic groups of concerned citizens, environmental organisations, and neighbourhood initiatives may be helpful in raising general awareness about the challenges resulting from climate change and also in identifying legitimate adaptive measures.

This chapter identifies elements of network governance in five subcases (three in Arkhangelsk and two in Saint Petersburg) and analyses them as part of the mix of governance modes applied in addressing climate change adaptation in the two cities. What mechanisms are created to ensure that inhabitants of Russian cities are safe from climate-related threats? To what extent do local authorities, civil society and private interests coordinate to solve this complex problem—and how do different levels of the public authorities coordinate with each other? How does international cooperation affect local climate change adaption? Will we find patterns of organisation that correspond to the notion of 'network governance' as a tool to solve complex problems, e.g. through affected parties taking part in decision-making or through the delivery of adaptive measures?

When we set out to peruse the literature we soon found that there had been next to nothing written on climate change adaptation in Russia at the city level. At least at first sight, looking for network governance in Russia may be likened to trying to find the proverbial needle in the haystack. Neither is climate change a salient subject. Whereas referring to 'extreme weather phenomena' is uncontroversial in Russia, bringing in the concept of 'climate change' may result in some dispute. In the scholarly literature, climate change adaptation has been mainly an issue relegated to remote regions of Russia's north, and to a large extent linked to the impacts on small-numbered and vulnerable indigenous peoples; and very little of it was initiated by Russian researchers or authorities. While conducting the case studies, we entered unploughed ground and much of the work has been explorative. Urban climate change is a clear case of a policy field that has not yet been established in Russia. Instead, urban climate change is just a policy issue (cf. Chap. 2), with a low level of institutionalisation and no strong actors that are specifically oriented towards the subject of climate change.

5.2 DATA AND METHODOLOGY

The chapter is based on 15 interviews with authorities, scholars and civic groups. Interviewees were offered confidentiality. Document analysis, comprising official policy documents and environmental NGO publications, was also conducted. The various bodies with a share in local climate change adaptations have websites that have served as a rich source in this respect. The study also included a media analysis (the regional newspaper for Arkhangelsk, *Pravda Severa* and the Saint Petersburg papers *Peterburgskiy Dnevnik, Vechernyi Peterburg, Saint-Petersburg Times* and web-based *fontanka.ru*). In addition, observation and participation at three network building conferences were made. Our data sources on local climate change adaptation, therefore, are triangulated. Data come from what has been written in official documents and press, from what actors told us when asked to describe and reflect over current policies, and also from how relevant actors talk about problems and policies in public forums.

The two cities of Saint Petersburg and Arkhangelsk were selected because they both, unlike most other Russian cities, have had projects related to climate change adaptation for a while. Moreover, they are both vulnerable to hydrological factors and due to their geographical position they are involved in international environmental cooperation.

This chapter forms part of the research project *RUSSBYKLIM* (Climate change, governance and planning in Russia) under the Norwegian Institute for Urban and Regional Research's Strategic Institute Programme, *Challenges for Governance and Planning in Cities and Municipalities* (ES466326). The programme was financed by the Research Council of Norway.

5.3   THE PROBLEM AND THE POLICY AREA

Since 1996 the frequency of extreme weather situations has increased. In Russia as a whole between 1976 and 2015, annual rainfall grew by 0.2% per year; spring rainfalls increased by 0.58% per year. Between 1976 and 2012 the average warming in Russia was 0.43 degrees Celsius whereas on a global level it was 0.17 degrees. 2015 was the warmest year in Russia since 1936. On the coast of the Arctic Ocean the warming was 0.8 degrees annually. During summer, however, the areas of Western Russia south of the 55th latitude had the most warming (0.8 degrees). In the northern parts of the Russian Far East and Southern Siberia the climate change resulted in colder winters (Roffey 2014: 21). In other words, there is a need for developing different measures to adjust to the impacts of climate change in different regions of Russia.

Rosgidromet—the federal agency for hydro-meteorology and environmental monitoring—concluded that 2012 was a record year for extreme weather. For instance, that year Saint Petersburg received 861 millimetres of rain. This record was then surpassed in 2016 (863 millimetres). Most of the disasters in Russia are technological incidents such as breakdowns in the power supply systems. In all, 30% of disasters are natural ones: fires, floods, etc. In the north, permafrost thaw causes damage to buildings and pipelines. Many Russian towns and cities face challenges caused by weather fluctuations. Cities located on the coast or at the banks of large rivers are particularly exposed. River flooding, sea level rises and surface water (caused by heavy rainfall) are the main problems. Russia's water management programme (2012–2020) refers to the fact that no less than 746 out of a total 1030 Russian cities and towns experience annual floods or inundations (*Dolgosrochnaia tselevaia programma* 2012), among them Saint Petersburg and Arkhangelsk.

Climate Change Challenges in Arkhangelsk

Since 1996, the annual average temperature has increased from zero degrees Celsius to almost 1.5 degrees, mainly due to higher winter temperatures. Precipitation, too, is on the rise (Grishchenko 2011: 9–10). Arkhangelsk city is situated where the river Northern Dvina widens before it forms its delta at the White Sea. Thus, the spring onrush of water spreads, easily reducing the risk of floods. The landscape in which Arkhangelsk finds itself is flat and marshy which means that a rising water level soon will have an impact on the soil mechanics. The city is also vulnerable to changes in sea level. Being situated in a delta, Arkhangelsk is exposed to storm surges (*vetrovoi nagon*). The most serious occurrences of these were in 1957 and 1985 with a water rise of 297 and 284 centimetres respectively. In 2010 the water level rose 257 centimetres (Skripnik 2013). For two consecutive years (2015–2016), the Arkhangelsk region experienced record warm winters and snow-melt floods almost reached the level of 'danger', although only for areas considerably upstream of Arkhangelsk city (Dvinsko-Pechorskoe BVU 2016: 113, 119).

The breaking up of ice involves huge masses of ice and water and then a two-day inundation follows, often at locations where the rivers bend. Buildings and drinking water may be affected. The northern city districts of Maimaksa and Solombala are the most vulnerable areas. However, even smaller rises of the water level may cause problems for the sewage system. The drainage system is to a large extent dilapidated and the older parts of the city centre still have a combined drain system in where surface water and sewage water are not separated (*Dolgosrochnaia tselevaia programma* 2012).

Climate Change Challenges in Saint Petersburg

Saint Petersburg was planned into existence—established by Czar Peter I as a 'Window to the West' on newly claimed land. It soon became evident to the city's planners that local conditions presented Russia's new capital with challenges precipitated by flooding. In fact, only three months after the city's foundation, the water rose by two metres. All over inner Saint Petersburg historical tide-gauges (*'futshtok'*) indicate extreme water levels from various floods that have occurred ever since.

The so-called 'Baltic Surge' occurs when cyclonic low-pressure fronts from the North Atlantic draw large volumes of water into the Baltic Sea. This results in long, low-frequency waves that grow in height as soon as they reach the shallow waters outside Saint Petersburg. The water from the west 'crashes' with the water from the Neva River, thus trapping the river water in the bay and further intensifying the flood. Even today large parts of the city lie lower than four meters above sea level. Since the founding of Saint Petersburg, there have been more than three hundred floods of varying degrees of intensity—some of them catastrophic.

The floods not only damage infrastructure and wash away land (the shores of the city and surroundings retreat by 50 centimetres a year), but also pollute ground water, hence constituting an epidemiological risk. In addition to the Baltic Surge, this is also the case with surface water flooding (as a result of increasingly heavy rainfall) which furthermore leads to an overload on the sewage system that is intended to wash pollutants out. But floods do not only happen during Baltic surges and rainfall, even if these are the main contributors. The increased moisturisation of the soil also makes sub-surface water more likely to penetrate to the surface, creating problems for urban infrastructure. Even before the onset of flooding, subsurface water penetrating to the surface is a problem in Saint Petersburg.

Furthermore, the global temperature change also delays the formation of a stable ice cover in the Bay of Finland. This again leads to a longer flood season and more intense flooding because the ice would otherwise inhibit the surge, not allowing the winter winds to push the water into the Bay of Finland. Finally, the rising sea level may in itself threaten Saint Petersburg and could, at even a pessimistic estimate, cause the city to lose 1300 hectares of land.

Between 1752 and 2010 the average winter temperature of Saint Petersburg increased by 3.4 degree Celsius (Menshova 2012). Various models show that the mean annual temperature in the area around the Gulf of Finland could rise by 7 degrees Celsius by 2100 and the average annual precipitation could increase by 40%. For the same time span, the expected rise of the sea level varies between 21 and 81 centimetres. For the city of Saint Petersburg where the post glacial land uplift is only between 0 and 1 mm/year this may have dramatic consequences because it is built on a flat and swampy delta plain. Increased riverside erosion also occurs as a result of of the rising temperatures.

The increased urbanisation of the Neva Bay area has not only led to a clustering of vulnerable infrastructure in a location where flooding is endemic, but it has also worsened the potential for flooding. Firstly, the already shallow Neva River becomes increasingly shallower due to dumping of waste in the river and sea. Secondly, in addition to the general global warming, Saint Petersburg as a densely populated area suffers from a 'heat island' effect which makes the temperature rise particularly noticeable. This effect also makes it difficult to determine how much of the local change is related to the global climate change—and how much is just due to the 'local warming'. Whatever the reason—global or local or both—the urban area and its surroundings are warming up, resulting in worsening soil conditions and flooding.

5.4   THE LEGAL FRAMEWORK, FORMAL INSTITUTIONS AND STATE POLICY

How is climate being put on the agenda—and by whom? The perception of climate change and its causes may prove to have an influence on what measures are taken to adapt to them. In Russia the so-called 'climate sceptical' position is relatively strongly represented and what in other European countries is called 'climatic change' is usually termed 'undesirable weather phenomena'. Rowe (2009) points to the fact that, despite Russia's ratification of the Kyoto Protocol, highly positioned decision-makers express doubts about anthropogenic climate changes. Often the argument is that changes will not necessarily be dramatic and are just as likely to have positive as negative effects (Yamineva 2013: 554; Vatsanever and Korppoo 2012).

Our interviews in Saint Petersburg and Arkhangelsk with actors within policy sectors relevant for climate change adaptation show that the discourse on man-made climate change is being actively challenged by a discussion on cyclical changes; in addition, there is a marked discourse defusing the problems of climate change in general. All this could be related to Russia's dependence upon oil and gas for income as well as the economy's high energy consumption which is due both to the cold climate and the fact that much of Russia's industries and heating systems are antiquated and consume a vast amount of energy. As argued by, among others, Rowe (2013: 95), Russia's economic interests and power aspirations count more than internationally produced scientific knowledge.

Nonetheless, Russia has a strong tradition for climatological research. *Rosgidromet* is the federal body managing government services in hydrometeorology and related areas, and monitoring the environment and environmental pollution. Between 1993 and 2009 the head of *Rosgidromet* was Aleksandr Bedritskij. He was also chairman of the World Meteorological Organisation (WMO) between 2003 and 2011. Since 2009 he has been presidential advisor and representative on climate issues. The large conference on *Problems of Adaptation to Climate Change* which took place in Moscow in November 2011 was hosted by *Rosgidromet*. Since 2009 *Rosgidromet* has issued a bulletin called Climate Change (*Izmenenie klimata*) in which research data along with measures taken by the authorities and NGO activities are presented. *Rosgidromet* also has a Climate Change Centre. The fact that the WMO was led by a prominent Russian scientist in the years when climate change was fully put on the agenda is probably one of the reasons why Russia has been closer to the scientific consensus in international forums than it is in the domestic spheres.

New approaches to adaptation and preventive measures were recommended in the Russian Climate Doctrine of 2009. Despite having a strong basis to build on, climate change adaptation is not a salient problem area in Russia and the follow-up of the 2009 Climate Doctrine has been slow despite the multi-sectoral plan for the Realisation of the Climate Doctrine (*Rosgidromet* 2011). The aforementioned plan has the status of resolution (*'rasporiazhenie'*), i.e. it is issued by the government to solve a specific problem within a certain time limit but has a lower status than orders (*'postanovlenie'*). As a policy area, climate change adaptation in Russia is characterised by not having been defined as such and there is no public agency responsible for coordinating efforts.

However, as a follow-up of the Climate Doctrine, the Federal Ministry of Economic Development was charged with the task of incorporating climate change adaptation into the federal socio-economic development plan (that has the status of resolution). The multi-sectoral plan assigns several ministries and agencies specific tasks in the field of climate adaptation. *Rosgidromet* has to incorporate adaptation into its research on weather and climate and develop scenarios for adaptation to increased rainfall, sea level rise and hurricanes. The Ministry of Natural Resources and Environmental Protection was given the task of preparing handbooks for relevant policy sectors on how to assess risks and potential losses due to climate change to be used in adaptation plans for relevant policy sectors and agencies as well as for regional and local authorities. The Ministry of Regional Development's task in this regard is to assess the vulnerability of buildings and infrastructure to climate change and develop scenarios for adaptation to permafrost changes. The Federal Ministry of Health and Social Protection was assigned the task of developing a strategy for adaptation to increased risks for infectious and parasitic diseases. The forestry agency *Rosleskhoz* has to develop adaption scenarios for forest and peat-bogs. Finally, the Ministry of Agriculture shall develop measures and stimulate the agricultural sector's adjustment to climate change.

Risk and catastrophe management is well-developed in Russia but is not included in the multi-sectoral plan. The Ministry of Emergency Situations (*MChS*) is the core institution for its eponymous conditions. *MChS* has regional offices and cooperate closely with municipalities. It pays attention to preventing and mitigating climate issues to an increasing degree but it is still its preparation and response which receives most of the attention. At the local level, flood commissions are appointed every year to supervise evacuations and secure the supply of drinking water, if needed. The hydro-meteorological services are also well-developed.

Nonetheless, the economic losses from extreme weather and climate change are palpable. It has been calculated that the annual costs amount to between 30 and 60 billion roubles annually. In response to these costs, early in 2017 the Ministry of Construction, the Ministry of Economic Development, the Ministry of Energy Resources, and the Ministry of Natural Resources and Environmental Protection started up a process together with regional authorities to follow up the Climate Doctrine with a methodology to identify risks and to assess costs resulting from climate change. On the basis of the findings, concrete measures are to be developed for the adaptation of buildings, transport and other infrastructure.[1]

5.5   REGIONAL STAKEHOLDERS, GOVERNANCE NETWORKS AND THE POLICY PROCESS

The authors have made in-depth studies of the legal and administrative set-ups for climate change adaptation in the two cities Archangelsk and Saint Petersburg. A general finding was that the issue was not explicitly put on the agenda and that, just as at federal level, no specific agency was pinpointed as being responsible for this concern. In Arkhangelsk we first identified the institutions with an actual or possible role in policy issues relevant to climate change adaptation. Then we followed up by identifying networks of actors that might have a potential role in city-level adaptation. These were networks on health, floods and waste water and sewage. In our study of Saint Petersburg, we looked into the Saint Petersburg Dam (opened in 2011) and the attempts at preparing a climate change adaptation plan for the city.

The study soon revealed that the two cities differed as to how much adaptation was singled out as an explicit policy problem. In Arkhangelsk emerging networks relating to climate change modification could be explored. In Saint Petersburg we unearthed concrete measures, although very different from those identified in Arkhangelsk, to cope with climate change. Overall then, the subcases from Arkhangelsk are loosely defined networks that deal with issues related (or relatable) to climate change whereas in Saint Petersburg there were more formalised and issue-targeted networks. The following sections describe these networks and the findings are linked to the basic ideas of meta-governance in the final section.

5.5.1   Arkhangelsk

In Arkhangelsk we identified the main actors concerning this issue as being the disaster management authorities (*MChS*), the water basin management agency, the hydro-meteorological services, and the authorities responsible for environmental protection, public health, and spatial planning respectively. Since many of the climate-related challenges in the city are connected to water, a central role is played by the water supply and waste water company, *Vodokanal*. Another key actor in the field of communal and municipal infrastructure are the housing and utilities companies. None of these institutions or policy areas have, or have taken on, any formal, leading role in shaping climate change adaptation as a comprehensive policy area. The most actively engaged institution, however, has been the Emergency

Ministry's regional department. Every winter the *MChS* at the regional level prepares a Regional Integrated Plan, in which responsibilities for adaptation are divided among various agencies. The plan mainly addresses flooding defence. Among the municipal bodies and enterprises, *Vodokanal* has been the most actively involved in these plans.

The current strategy for socio-economic development of the Arkhangelsk region contains merely general formulations on climate change and points to its positive effects on shipping traffic and access to natural resources. Among the negative effects of climate change, the strategy mentions floods and permafrost thaw (*Administratsiia* 2008). The city's strategy for social and economic development does not address the climate issue at all (*Mèr goroda* 2008).

In this setting, would it be possible to discover occurrences of network governance-like interaction between governmental bodies and civic groups? What we found, in fact, were networks with relevance—or at least potential relevance—for climate change adaptation, but they were all vaguely delimited and defined. In the case studies, a flood risk network, a climate and health network, and a waste water and sewage network could finally be identified.

The Flood Risk Network

The Emergency Ministry (*MChS*) is the nodal actor within the loosely organised flood risk network. During the period when the river ice is breaking up the network is fixed into an operative group that meets at least once a week. In addition to the *MChS*, the participants are the service for supervision in the use of natural resources, the firefighting and civic defence agency, *Rosmorport* (responsible for the ice-breakers), and the river transport authorities, road authorities, the Dvina-Pechora authorities, and the regional *Rosgidromet* services for hydro-meteorology (contributing with data on weather and climate). Also at local (*raion*) level, *MChS* has partners in the integrated standby service (*edinaia dezhurnaia sluzhba*).

The network cuts across several policy sectors and does not include non-governmental actors. The Arkhangelsk regional department of *MChC* has a special role in taking precautions against problems occurring from the breaking-up of ice during spring. One of the measures appropriated is to cut (using ice-breakers, among other methods) and dynamite the ice in advance in order to avoid floods and inundation. As a preventive measure, the deepening of the rivers at critical points is also suggested. *MChS* works according to established procedures to counter an annual, recurring problem rather than just seeing the problem as being 'new' and resulting from climate change. Earlier, all construction projects had to be approved by the *MChS* but currently only larger projects need to be sanctioned. At times the city authorities contact *MChS* for information about the advisability of building in certain areas. In such cases, *Rosgidromet* may also be involved and makes a preliminary monitoring.

The inter-sectoral cooperation includes *Dvina Region VodKhoz*, which is the regional department of the federal state water management institution under the Dvina-Pechora river basin authority. These institutions fall under the Ministry of Natural Resources and Environmental Protection. *Dvina Region VodKhoz* is responsible for shoreline protection. The Water Code of 2006 deprived the federal state water management institutions of their authority in questions of building permits, which would have been an important tool to avoid construction on plots vulnerable to floods or other water related risks.

In addition, the regional department of the service for supervision in the use of natural resources (*Rosprirodnadzor*) carries out inspections of water protection zones, protection belts along the riversides and 'floodable' (*zatoplivaemye*) areas as a part of the annual preparation for the breaking-up of the ice. The inspections are made to avoid pollution and other harm from waste illegally placed in the protected areas. They are conducted in cooperation with the large industrial enterprises and their heads of environmental protection along with agencies and services for technical inspections, water management, forestry, fisheries, consumer rights and local municipalities. These institutions come together for working meetings. Likewise, *Rosprirodnadzor* cooperates in a nodal position with heads of municipalities, who are charged with the task of ensuring protected zones are cleared of rubbish and waste and also to check the state of dams and water reservoirs before expected spring floods. The absence of non-state actors makes this network not fulfil the criteria for a true 'governance network' as established in Chap. 2, but rather becomes an internally institution-transcending network established to effectively coordinate, make and implement decisions and implement (cf. Chaps. 2 and 9).

The Health and Climate Network

The health and climate network was a foreign-funded project. Whereas the general climate change discourse in Russia tends to play down the gravity of the challenges, there was one exception in Arkhangelsk. The Science Centre for Polar Medicine of the Northern State Medical University carried out a project that, among other stratagems, consisted in developing a regional strategy for the health sector's management of the effects of climate change (*MinZdrav-Sots* 2012).

The climate and health network resulted from a project funded by WHO and the German Ministry for environment and security. Studies show that Russia lags behind other nations regarding climate adaptation and health (Lesnikowski et al. 2013). The network involved environmental scholars and state-based actors at the regional level. Thus the Arkhangelsk Medical University served as the node of the network that included the region's ministry for health and social protection, the regional department of the federal Service for Surveillance on Consumer Rights Protection and Human Wellbeing (*Rospotrebnadzor*), the centre for hygiene and epidemiology, and the regional agency for natural resources and nature protection. This network was clearly organised on the basis of a climate change adaptation discourse and the project was approved and supported at the top political level with the governor's administration. It may be worth noting that this network, basing itself explicitly on a climate change discourse, is financed from abroad. The strategy that came out of the project resulted in the production of a joint publication by the regional Ministry of Health and the medical university. It consisted of a study and a recommendation of a set of measures to better deal with the adaptation of climate change, although was allocated no formal status beyond a request by the ministry that their employees make themselves familiar with its contents. Just like the flood network presented above, the health and climate network did not include non-state actors but the nodal role played by the Medical University points at the possibility of governance networks being driven by institutions not being authorities. Moreover, by leaving funding to foreign institutions, the authorities refrained from controlling the network through 'treasure' (see Chap. 2).

The Waste Water and Sewage Network

Since 2011, a series of conferences on climate change have been arranged in Arkhangelsk. The conferences were formulated and funded jointly by the Nordic Council of Ministers and the regional authorities. The first conference—*Climate Change and Water Management—Meeting the Challenges in the Barents Region*—was prepared in summer 2011. The theme partly mirrored the fact that Finland had the chairmanship in the Nordic Council and had chosen climate change as a focus area. Between 2013 and 2015, the Barents Euro-Arctic Council operated with an Action Plan on Climate Change covering a wide range of issues. For urban climate change adaptation, it was comprised of measures in the field of water resources management.

The event was followed up by a conference in 2012 as a start-up of a new project called *Water Management and Climate Change—Common Challenges, Common Decisions*. The participants in the project were a groups of specialists in the field of water supply and waste water management and was aimed at upgrading and modernising infrastructure to make it able to cope with the increase in surface water. The loosely connected network, mainly facilitated by the conferences, consisted of specialists within environmental and hydro-meteorological surveillance, municipal infrastructure, and scientific staff from local universities. The main partner from Arkhangelsk was the Agency for Natural Resources and Environmental Protection. The NGO sector took part through the umbrella organisation *Garant*. Several Nordic organisations also participated, among them municipalities and research institutions.

At the local level, the upgrading of waste water and sewage pipes is one of the most urgent needs resulting from climate change. More than 20% of the pipes are classified as dilapidated. Little has been done in this respect during the last 25 years. Therefore, the development of financing mechanisms were at the heart of the network's attention. The Arkhangelsk-based water supply and sewage company *Vodokanal* is the most active partner in this network. However, it does not frame its activities as climate change adaptation but simply as ones replacing old pipes with new and wider ones. Some international funding was in sight through the Nordic financing mechanism, the Nordic Environment Finance Corporation (NEFCO). Then infrastructural upgrading was designated as climate change adaptation. NEFCO is an international finance institution established in 1990 by the five Nordic countries. Very little came out of Arkhangelsk region's municipalities trying to get loans for this purpose. Arkhangelsk city's waste water and sewage company carries on trying to acquire funding for upgrading of pipes but now it is done without reference to climate change. This network was classifiable as a 'true' governance network as it transcended the state-/non-state divide. Its main focus was to facilitate access to financing mechanisms. For the Arkhangelsk regional authorities, then, sharing the nodal position and also 'treasure' with a foreign institution was fit for purpose and including non-state organisations was part of the game. The non-state organisation played a minor role as compared to the role played by the Medical University in the health and climate network.

5.5.2   Saint Petersburg

In Saint Petersburg climate change adaptation took place in two main fields. Firstly, there was the Saint Petersburg Dam, and secondly, there were endeavours to prepare a climate change adaptation plan for Saint Petersburg as a whole.

The Saint Petersburg Dam

The seasonal storm floods have been a constant destructive force in the history of Saint Petersburg, and therefore the idea of building a giant 'shield' to protect the Neva Bay area is not new and, having first been suggested in 1727, it has long predated the global realisation that the climate is worsening.

The decision to build the dam complex was made in 1979 by the USSR Council of Ministers and the Central Committee of the Communist Party of the Soviet Union. This decision to construct the dam was made, not in expectation of a worsening situation, but from the realisation that the situation was already grave enough, a belief still very much in line with the dominating view in Russia today. The project appears neither to have been widely discussed as a climate change adaption measure, nor does it tend to be discussed as such in legal and project documents.

As has been stated above, the need for a protection facility has long appeared to decision makers as something already being substantial enough to warrant the investment. There is also the matter that this is a 'prestige project' signalling the ability of Russia to construct large defence mechanisms and undertake impressive projects—in stark contrast to the 1990s which saw the dam programme halted for economic reasons. Some commentators also point to the fact that the project was picked up again at the federal level immediately following the ascension of Saint Petersburg native

Vladimir V. Putin to the 'throne' of Russian politics. Indeed, the dam complex is sometimes jokingly—or perhaps seriously—referred to as the '*Damba imeni Putina*', the 'Putin Dam', a moniker which may not be entirely undeserved.

As has been seen, though, local concerns have been voiced over worsened water quality caused by water from the Neva not being allowed to move as freely into the Bay of Finland, even when the dam was open. At times, the conflicts over this matter have been substantial—with local authorities also being critical, despite their definitive interest in the protective nature of the construction project. As a response to this concern and to address this problem, however, thirty purification centres for cleaning up the outgoing water before it reaches the gulf have been installed around the complex. It is of note also that the Saint Petersburg Master Plan, which by its nature was a strongly locally anchored project, had already in 2005 presupposed the construction of the dam. At this point even Vladimir Putin himself, as he admitted during the opening ceremony in August 2011, had doubts as to whether or not the dam could be completed.

The complex is built as a series of stations along a new ring road on bridges connecting the northwest shore of Saint Petersburg with the southwest shore via Kotlin island on which is situated the city of Kronshtadt. The dam has a length of 25.4 kilometres, is 30 metre wide and stands eight metres above sea level. It consists of 11 stone and earth dams with two locks for ship passage and six water passage constructions. A complex algorithm decides when weather conditions deem it necessary to close the gates between the stations, effectively shutting out the surge, while river water from the Neva Bay is pumped out into the Bay of Finland in order to prevent the river from backing up and flooding the urban infrastructure.

Due to its dimensions, the dam project has been anchored in Moscow since day one as a federal project. It still remains very much a federal-level structure, and as such is not deeply integrated with local authorities and perhaps therefore not as accessible for local civil society. Seen from the local grass roots level, the federal placement in Moscow of the project may have made it more difficult for it to have an impact. As we have seen though, local concerns have been voiced over worsened water quality as a result of water from the Neva not being allowed to move as freely into the Bay of Finland even when the dam was open.

The Saint Petersburg Committee for Nature Usage, Environmental Protection and Safeguarding of Environmental Security (*KPOOS*) has called the dam the only climate change adaption measure featured in the city's Master Plan, and it has already spared the city from a flood. At 8 metres high, the dam will be able to protect Saint Petersburg from the Baltic Surge. There is also, however, now an increased risk for flooding in areas finding themselves on the immediate periphery of the dam. While nowhere near as densely populated as the metropolis itself, these peripheral areas also have settlements, some of which are considered to have a high recreational value.

The completion of the Saint Petersburg dam is an example of Russia's recovery after the difficulties that cropped up in the post-Soviet 1990s. At the same time, it also provides an example of a top-down undertaking that, albeit generally beneficial, does not address the issues of more fine-tuned, but also more controversial, adaptation measures such as banning development projects for residential areas on the city's sea front. As such, it is a purely old-school incremental measure, and one not characterised by network mode of governance. It is included here because of its centrality as a relevant climate change adaption measure. What should be highlighted, however, is its adherence to a hierarchal mode of governance.

The Climate Change Adaption Strategy for Saint Petersburg City

We will now at last turn to the only federally state-based political project we have found in Saint Petersburg explicitly centred on the idea of climate change: the climate change adaption strategy for Saint Petersburg. Despite the fact that the federal-level doctrine calls for regional climate adaptation, only Saint Petersburg has followed up with a climate strategy, one that was adopted as recently as 2016 (*KPOOS* 2016). The work with the strategy started up in 2013 and was presented in the autumn 2015 at the Civic Environmental Council that gives advice to the city government.

The strategy gives priority to shoreline protection along the Gulf of Finland and protection of water bodies in the city, as well as integrating the adaptive measures into city planning and economic planning documents. The next step envisaged is to strengthen the adaptive capacities of the city through education and improvement of the administrative functions. The strategy also foresees an assessment of the economic, environmental and health-related losses due to climate change.

So far, the Strategy of Climate Adaptation in Saint Petersburg is the only regional level climate adaptation one in Russia. It was developed as the result of an international project through the initiative of the city's environmental authorities, the Saint Petersburg Committee for nature use, and the protection of the environment and ecological safety—*KPOOS*. This committee's designated focus on environmental issues as security issues makes an adaptive approach a logical conclusion.

Notably, there was no official decision in Saint Petersburg to create a climate change adaption strategy. Technically, it was the goodwill of the governor that allowed *KPOOS* to follow up on the idea of developing a strategy. In the end, the strategy was indeed not adopted by the city government, allegedly due to legal obstacles. Instead, *KPOOS* has tried to have the strategy's basic propositions included in the city's General Plan 2018–2043 and, in line with the 2011 multi-sectoral plan and the Saint Petersburg's Environmental Policy Plan of 2013 (*Pravitel'stvo* 2013), into the Strategy for Economic and Social Development to 2030 as well (*Pravitel'stvo* 2014). As of the moment of writing, the current environmental policy plan contains a section on climate adaptation, pointing at the need for adaptation, melioration and hydro-technical installations among other needs. The socio-economic plan does not mention adaptation at all.

A 'plot twist' in this otherwise straightforward story of Russian political 'verticalness' is the strong involvement of an international cooperation in the project to create an adaption strategy in Saint Petersburg—the project Climate Proof Living Environment (CliPLivE). It is very revealing for the weakness of the climate change discourse in Russia that the follow-up of the federal doctrine had to be channelled into an international project, a practice which is more common for developing countries in the global south than for a country like Russia. CliPLivE was co-funded by the Russian Federation (20%), Finland (20%), the EU (40%) and partner organisations (20%) and started up in December 2011. The project formed part of the framework of South-East Finland-Russia ENPI (European Neighbourhood and Partnership Instrument). Among its goals is to promote experience transfers and develop new tools and methodologies for risk assessment and management of environmental and geological risks in different planning levels. A part of this involved learning from Finland's National Strategy for Adaption to Climate Change from 2005, the world's first of its kind. CliPLiVe began in December 2011.

The lead partner on the Russian side was *Mineral*, a unitary state company owned by the Saint Petersburg Government. *Mineral* monitors different environmental and geological factors of importance to the city and originated as a small official company operating from the city district (*raion*) Kolpino but was upgraded after the city had become more in need of their services. Today the company numbers more than 100 permanent employees. In the Saint Petersburg administrative vertical, *Mineral* is located under the authority of *KPOOS*.

Other partners in CliPLivE included *KPOOS*, the Karpinsky Geological Research Institute *VSEGEI* (a federal state unitary company under the Natural Resource and Ecology Ministry's Agency of Mineral Resources), the Geological Survey of Finland, the Helsinki Region Environmental Services Authority, and the Finnish regional councils of Uusimaa and Kymenlaakso. The city of Turku's Department of Environment and City Planning was an associated partner. The application writing process necessitated five international meetings a year but after that international meetings became less frequent. As for contact between the Russian partners, all actors we have talked to have described this as ongoing on an ad hoc basis. *KPOOS* underscored that there are rules for when official bodies are to be in contact with each other and with other actors, and that these rules were followed. When contact is necessary, it runs smoothly between the Russian actors.

According to *KPOOS,* no institution can 'prepare such a document alone', inter-disciplinarity is important with input from relevant authorities, scientific communities and also civil society. Yet, the picture painted so far is of a project group which involves partners from the state hierarchies, mainly at the local level. Public hearings were organised during 2013 to provide input from the civil society sector. Regarding municipalities, *KPOOS* stated that it would be difficult to involve all Saint Petersburg's 111 city district municipalities in all hearings. Interestingly, public hearings are to be conducted at the level of intra-city municipality. Politically, these micro-municipalities are weak, but they are designed precisely for the purpose of bringing up local concerns. Studying how the public hearings are carried out in practice was not a part of the study providing the empirical data for this article and needs more close-up investigation of real-life practices to conclude whether or not climatic phenomena are being addressed.

It must be noted that CliPLivE is hence not a typical case: finding international funding for climate change related projects is generally difficult. According to the international financing institution NEFCO, this type of projects is seen as 'negative service'—paying to prevent something rather than paying for something to happen—and it also does not generate any measurable cash flow, making it challenging for such projects to find support when market-based forms of rationality dominate. In addition, Russian local authorities and their subunits are generally not very credit worthy. The result is that the system works against international projects to finance climate change adaption in Russian local contexts (NEFCO, EBRD). Notably, though, when it comes to local authority poverty, Saint Petersburg is an exception. According to EBRD even subunits of Saint Petersburg such as the city's '*Vodokanal*' water-supply and wastewater-disposal company are credit worthy in their own right and can hence easily take part in internationally financed projects.

Several actors point to *KPOOS* as the initiative-taker in CliPLive—and *KPOOS* again refers to their getting responsibilities for the subject 'environmental security' and the signals from the federal Climate Doctrine as the catalyst events. Their decision to go with an international cooperation is rooted in Russia's modest national experience with climate change adaption strategies. The international experience of making adaption strategies is hence seen as a highly beneficial tool for shaping Saint Petersburg's own route in this direction. *KPOOS*, through CliPLivE, studies the international experiences, particularly experiences from Helsinki, which is also a major city on the shores of the Gulf of Finland. Experiences from other Baltic cities, Germany and Denmark have also been studied. Tallinn, for instance, has even worse problems with the ice cover. At times, information from these cities is more accessible to *KPOOS* than it is from the Russian cities.

In addition to the CliPLivE funding, *KPOOS* in the beginning of 2012 procured two positions to work with climate change issues. Both formed part of the same effort to create activities aimed at a climate change adaption strategy. *KPOOS* targeted giving the document a status that would bind other documents to take climate aspects into account: a legal document explaining to authorities and citizens what climate change concretely means to Saint Petersburg by identifying the worst risks and elaborating strategies to overcome or avoid them. According to *KPOOS*, 'we must look particularly at what areas may be hardest hit, and what it means for the construction sector in particular'. The result of this effort is a document underpinned by scientific mapping. The actual use of this document to initiate comprehensive climate adaptation is still pending. The international network described here has only feeble characteristics of network governance as defined in Chap. 2, due to the weak inclusion of non-state actors. The intended function of the network can be summed up as being advisory. The Russian state agency that participated in it had the intention of utilising the network to prepare a strategy on the decision-making authorities could decide. CliPLive itself was intended as a coordinative effort to facilitate experience transfer and know-how. It also had an advisory ambition through its goal of creating knowledge and tools for state authorities.

5.6 Concluding Discussion: Limited Networks and Weak Nodality

Throughout the sub-cases we have been looking for elements of 'network' governance, where representatives of public, private and civic institutions—as well as local, regional and federal bodies—come together to solve issues in a relatively non-hierarchical way. According to the literature on network governance, a highly complex issue such as climate adaptation would be particularly prone to be addressed by this mode of government. Nonetheless, we found little in terms of emerging network governance.

As shown in this study, the case of urban adaptation to climate change in Russia is more a case of authorities being hesitant to address the issue to the full and of non-state actors not pushing the situation rather than a case of top-down steering of governance networks. The networks we have identified are weakly defined and in general do not even understand themselves as being involved in climate change adaptation. Rather they are framed as engaged in preparations for the annual floods or forest fires. Climate change adaptation plans and strategies have been developed mainly as a result of projects implemented thanks to foreign funding and to a large extent also to foreign initiative. The reliance on foreign cooperation has remained strong despite the fact that federal policy documents call for regional follow-up on climate adaptation and regional initiatives therefore could have been expected. One could also have expected institutionally strong actors struggling with the effects of climate change in Russia to take the lead, such as the emergency services (*MChS*) and enterprises responsible for municipal infrastructure, notably the water companies.

The project-generated networks identified in the sub-cases can hardly be classified as true governance networks. Instead they have been inter-sectoral, to a large extent involving regional departments of federal structure and to a lesser degree municipal agencies and enterprises. In some cases, networks are international, encompassing working groups of agencies and /or specialists. The outcomes of the network activities have been relatively insignificant. The health and climate strategy developed in Arkhangelsk has been merely symbolic, and the climate strategy in Saint Petersburg ultimately failed to get approval by the city authorities. The ad hoc waste water and sewage network in Arkhangelsk did not result in loans to finance a much needed upgrading of infrastructure.

The study in this chapter found that there have been attempts at developing networks to deal with adaptation to climate change, but despite the fact that several bodies are involved, there were no coordinating bodies or common networking arenas utilised explicitly for the issue of climate change adaptation. The NGO sector is almost absent, but the business sector is involved to a certain extent. The NATO-model of nodality-authority-treasure-organisation referred to in Chap. 2 may be of some use to explain why climate change adaptation has not established itself as a policy area.

Possible information networks and social networks have not struck roots, in part because they have lacked a helper with institutional muscles to take the position as a node for urban climate adaptation networks. The federal and regional authorities have been reluctant to undertake the task to engage deeply other agencies and non-state actors and have left this to different sector agencies that have proved unable or unwilling to act as nodes, except for during narrower assignments related to flood prevention or the implementation of international projects. The calls from federal authorities for local and regional climate adaptation have been interpreted as being half-hearted and only confirmed by the reception of, for example, the strategies developed by some of the networks studied in this chapter. As has been shown here, climate adaptation networks exist but they are ad hoc and organised around delimited tasks and projects. In other words, 'nodality' is not necessarily only a tool used to steer from above but also one to get governance networks started. This is in line with findings referred to in Chap. 2, where civil society actors report that they prefer networks where the authorities are distinctly present.

The use of 'authority'—legal authority to make decisions—has either not taken place, as in the sub-cases of the water network and the emergency network, or it has been used to shelve the product of the network's endeavours as in the example of the health and climate strategy in Arkhangelsk. It has also been used to stop such endeavours completely, as was the situation with the climate adaptation strategy in Saint Petersburg.

The impression of half-heartedness is reinforced by the authorities failing to provide sufficient 'treasure' and 'organisation', i.e. economic and human or material resources. Some of the sub-cases show that organisation has been left with foreign actors—the Nordic Council of Ministers of the

EU for example. In contemporary Russia this in practice enables the networks to grab a foothold but not to reach their goal (Table 5.1).

Climate adaptation in Russia is a case of a policy issue struggling to get institutionalised. Networks do not seem to be the drivers for converting the awareness of 'unfortunate climate phenomena' into 'climate change adaptation' with a need for comprehensive approaches. Networks are either very formal, ad hoc, dominated by regional departments of federal ministries and agencies and focused on narrow aspects of climate and environmental risks, or they are linked to international projects, meaning that they are short-term and full of problems in the attempt to link up with domestic policy processes. The weakness of local climate adaptation as a policy area is reflected in the table above, showing that in most cases relevant authorities refrain from making use of the meta-governance tools to steer the networks while they are working. Instead, as in the case of the health and climate strategy in Arkhangelsk and the adaptation plan in Saint Petersburg, regional authorities make use of 'authority' ex post.

NOTE

1. '*V Rossii otseniat ushcherb ot budushchei nepogody*', *Kommersant*, 7 February 2017.

Table 5.1 Meta-governance tools and the climate adaptation networks

	Flood risk	Health	Waste water and sewage	Dam	Climate adaptation strategy
Nodality	Dispersed	Shared; regional / international	Shared; regional/ international	Federal	Shared; regional/ international
Authority	Diffuse	Regional authorities	Regional authorities	Federal	Regional authorities
Treasure	Federal and regional	Shared; regional/international	Shared; regional/ international	Federal	Shared; regional/ international
Organisation	Mainly regional; emergency ministry	Shared; university, regional authorities, Nordic council	Shared; regional authorities, Nordic council	Federal	*KPOOS*

REFERENCES

Administratsiia Arkhangel'skoi oblasti. 2008. *Strategiia sotsial'no-ėkonomocheskogo razvitiia Arkhangel'skoi oblasti do 2030 goda*. Archangelsk.

Bukeley, H. 2013. *Cities and Climate Change*. New York: Routledge.

Dolgosrochnaia tselevaia programma Arkhangel'skoi oblasti. 2012. *Razvitie vodokhoziaistvennogo kompleksa Arkhangel'skoi oblasti na 2012–2020 gody*. Postanovlenie ot 11 okiabria 2011 goda, no 361-PP, Archangelsk.

Dvinsko-Pechorskoe BVU. 2016. *Otchët o prokhozhdenii polovod'ia i pavodkov po zone deiatel'nosti Dvinsko-Pechorskogo BVU v 2016 godu*. http://dpbvu.ru/images/docs/pavodok/pavodok_2016.pdf (retrieved May 2017).

Grishchenko, Irina V. 2011. *Opasnye iavleniia pogody v usloviiakh izmeneniia klimata na territorii Arkhangel'skoi oblasti i Nenetskogo Avtonomnogo Okruga*. Sankt-Peterburg: Glavnaia geofizicheskaia observatoriia A. I. Voeikova.

Hallegatte, S. 2009. Strategies to Adapt to an Uncertain Climate Change. *Global Environmental. Change—Human Policy Dimens.* 19 (2): 240–247.

Heltberg, R., P. Siegel, and S. Jorgensen. 2009. Addressing Human Vulnerability to Climate Change: Toward a 'No-Regrets' Approach. *Global Environmetal. Change—Human Policy Dimens* 19 (1): 89–99.

KPOOS. 2016. *Strategiia klimaticheskoi adaptatsii Sankt-Peterburga do 2030, Saint Petersburg: SPB Committee for nature use, protection of the environment and ecological safety—KPOOS*. Sankt Peterburg.

Lesnikowski, Aleksandra, James D. Ford, Lea Berrang-Ford, Magdalena Barrera, Peter Berry, Jim Henderson, and Jody Heymann. 2013. National-Level Factors Affecting Planned, Public Adaptation to Health Impacts of Climate Change. *Global Environmental Change* 23 (5): 1153–1163.

Menshova, Y. A. 2012. Climate Change Adaptation Policy of Saint Petersburg. Presentation at Seminar on Climate Change Adaptation in the Gulf of Finland in Espoo 09.10.2012 [available on CLIPLIVE's website] http://cliplive.infoeco.ru/dl/sem1/MenshovaYulia_CEP.pdf (retrieved 10 May 2017).

Mèr goroda Arkhangel'sk. 2008. *Strategiia sotsial'no-ėkonomocheskogo razvitiia munitsipal'nogo obrazovaniia Arkhangel'sk do 2020 goda*. Archangelsk.

MinZdravSots Arkhangel'skoi oblasti, Severnyi Gosudarstvennyi Meditsinskii Universitet, and MinZdravSots RF. 2012. *Strategiia adaptacii k vozdeistviiu izmeneniia klimata na zdorov'e naselenia dlia Arkhangel'skou oblasti i Nenetskogo avtonomnogo okruga Rossiiskoi Federatsii*. Archangelsk.

Pelling, M. 2011. *Adaptation to Climate Change: From Resilience to Transformation*. London: Routledge.

Pravitel'stvo Sankt-Peterburga. 2013. *Postanovlenie o 'Ėkologicheskoi politiki Sankt-Peterburga na period do 2030 goda'*. Sankt Peterburg.

Pravitel'stvo. 2014. *Postanovlenie o 'Strategii ėkonomicheskogo i sotsial'nogo razvitiia Sankt-Peterburga do 2030 goda'*. Sankt Peterburg.

Roffey, Roger. 2014. *Climate Change and Natural Disasters—A Challenge for Russian Policy-Makers.* Stockholm: FOI.

Rosgidromet. 2011. *Kompleksnyi plan realizatsii Klimaticheskoi doktriny Rossiiskoi federatsii na period do 2020 goda.* Moskva.

Rowe, Elana W. 2009. Who is to Blame? Agency, Causality, Responsibility and the Role of Experts in Russian Framings of Global Climate Change. *Europe-Asia Studies* 61(4): 593–619.

Rowe, Elana W. 2013. *Russian Climate Politics—When Science Meets Policies.* Basingstoke: Palgrave Macmillan.

Skripnik, Elena N. 2013. *Vetrovye nagony vody v ust'iakh rek.* Sevmeteo.ru «Obzory», http://sevmeteo.polarpost.ru/articles/9/534.shtml.html (retrieved 10 May 2017).

Vatsanever, Adnan, and Anna Korppoo. 2012. *A Climate Vision for Russia from Rhetoric to Action. Policy Outlook.* Washington, D.C.: Carnegie Endowment.

Yamineva, Yulia. 2013. Climate Law and Policy in Russia—A Peasant Needs Thunder to Cross Himself and Wonder. In *Climate Change and the Law,* ed. Erkki J. Hollo, Kati Kulovesi, and Michael Mehling, 551–566. New York: Springer.

CHAPTER 6

Child Welfare Policies in Russia—Civil Society Contributions Without Return?

Jørn Holm-Hansen

6.1 Introduction

Based on studies of Russia's child welfare and child right policies, this chapter examines the assumption that *network governance* theory may help to gain a more accurate picture of how policies are developed and implemented in a (semi)-authoritarian, 'hybrid' regime. The concept of 'network governance' was originally developed to account for an assumedly non-hierarchical and qualitatively new type of close interaction between state authorities, non-state actors and business in advanced democracies. Our assumption is that non-democratic regimes as well may prefer incentives and collaborative practices over direct intervention, because they may believe policy problems to be too complex for mere top-down government modes to be efficient (Davies et al. 2016). This—and the possibility that governance networks may be used by existing power structures to reinforce themselves—allows us to take network governance 'out of area' and ask: Why does a semi-authoritarian (or outright authoritarian) regime set up platforms and financing mechanisms for interaction with non-state actors?

J. Holm-Hansen (✉)
Department for International Studies and Migration,
Norwegian Institute for Urban and Regional Research
NIBR-HiOA, 0166 Oslo, Norway
e-mail: jorn.holm-hansen@nibr.hioa.no

© The Author(s) 2018
S. Kropp et al. (eds.), *Governance in Russian Regions*,
DOI 10.1007/978-3-319-61702-2_6

In this chapter we will discuss this question in the light of the literature on network governance. The policy area of child welfare is well-suited for our purpose for several reasons. Child welfare is given high priority in Russia, not only because it is a huge social problem but also because it belongs to part of the policies to strengthen the country's demography. The policy area has relatively many non-state organisations, voluntary initiatives and funds which are mainly involved in charitable work and the development of more modern methods and approaches (in Russia called 'social technologies'). However, the involvement of non-state actors is not purely charitable. In addition, the policy area of child welfare is fraught with controversies that relate to larger ideological debates on the role of the family and the individual. Conservative religious groups have mobilised civil society and others in parental groups fighting 'juvenile justice', a concept used as a collective term for treating children as individuals with rights.

Identifying and analysing possible governance networks on child welfare and child rights in Russia, therefore, has to take into consideration the fact that the issue is politically delicate. A tug-of-war is going on between a child rights lobby and a family rights lobby. This touchy issue makes the increasingly authoritarian Russia seem an unlikely location for loosening up hierarchies and the introducing of horizontal relations among state, civil society and business. The theoretical core of network governance, however, is not primarily about a regime's degree of political authoritarianism but rather about the factors that make network governance 'necessary'. Here, we may find similarities between Russia and the West. The theoretical underpinning of network governance is that it is a response to an increasingly complex contemporary policy issues. A shift from hierarchies is linked to the interpretation of problems as being 'wicked'. The complexity of the problems requires a broader basis of actors taking the responsibility of solving them. In the case of child welfare, this would imply that not only state authorities for child protection and social prevention should be involved but also civil society in the form of foster parent associations, groups of concerned specialists, charity foundations and—one would believe—advocacy groups for example introducing innovative working methods.

Also, the increasing 'volume' of the problems to be solved—and the ensuing budgetary implications—form another backdrop of network governance. According to the theoretical assumptions of network governance, co-financing and shared responsibilities are needed. In the following we will discuss whether inviting domestic NGOs—*NKOs*—in as partners is a strategy pursued by Russian authorities to deal with the type of problems described above.[1] In doing this, we will ask to what extent resources in the hands of Russian *NKOs* make authorities invite them into network governance-like settings. Relevant types of resources *NKOs* can contribute are funding, man hours, access to target groups, legitimacy and innovative methods and approaches.

6.2 Data and Methodology

This chapter is based on data from two projects. The majority of data are from the project 'Network governance: A tool for understanding Russian policy-making?' funded by the Research Council of Norway (Project number 220615). Data from an evaluation of an international NGO that wanted to remain anonymous is included. Research was carried out between 2013 and 2016.

The chapter builds on data from different sources, i.e. analysis of newspapers and legal and policy documents, as well as around 15 semi-structured interviews with leaders and specialists of relevant *NKOs* and NGOs. More than 40 officials in the sphere of child protection on local and regional levels of government have been interviewed. Several family centres and orphanages were visited. Also, some data were drawn from observations of formal meetings between authorities and Russian *NKOs*. Concrete projects where *NKOs* provided services to children and parents were visited. Interviews and on-site visits were carried out in four regions in Northwest Russia, one region in the Volga federal district and Moscow. In all, nine towns and cities were covered. The regions differ as to economic resources, political climate and density of *NKOs*. Some of the interviews with Russian authorities were conducted by our Russian partners because of their reluctance to meet with foreign researchers.

6.3 The Problem and the Policy Field

Since the early 1990s in Russia, there has been a clear correlation between the number of children in a household and poverty. Child welfare policies in Russia, therefore, form part of the overall welfare policies of the country aiming to reduce the number of inhabitants falling under the poverty line. Moreover, Russian child policies are integrated in the country's policies as a way to solve the demographic crisis (Golenkova 2016: 80–84) which is considered a threat to Russia's future economic growth and stability, and even survival (Ovcharova et al. 2007). The authorities are alarmed by the low birth rate as well as the fact that a relatively large number of children grow up under conditions that may reduce their ability to be active and 'positive citizens' and create social stability in the future. This way, Russia's child and family polices obtain an additional pillar by being 'securitised' and 'economised' which means it gains leverage and is not solely dependent upon a pro-social political climate.

Moreover, child welfare shapes part of the overall Russian welfare system that undergoes reform. One major motive behind welfare reform is to 'de-budgetise', i.e. lessening the financial burden on public budgets by leaving more of the responsibilities and costs to the population. Foster families encouraged, trained and defended by *NKOs* is one way of doing this. One example from the Komi Republic: The costs of keeping a child in an orphanage may be 78,000 roubles a month whereas a foster family is remunerated with 8000 roubles. Adoptive families receive a lump sum of 200,000 roubles (250,000 roubles if the child is disabled).[2]

However, the issue of child welfare becomes controversial as soon as it moves towards child *rights*. Russia has signed the UN Convention on the Rights of the Child (CRC), but the conservative twist in Russia's cultural and lifestyle policies during the last decade has made issues such as family violence, child participation, and juvenile justice highly controversial. The culturally conservative climate in the country gives priority to maintaining organic units like family and nation intact over the rights of the individual. Giving children individual rights infringes upon the unity of the family and its inner hierarchy. The campaign against 'juvenile justice' is illustrative in this respect.

Juvenile justice reforms have been carried out all over Russia but the federal subjects (regions) have chosen different models in approaching this. Some have set up youth courts, others have based themselves on preventive measures such as counselling, awareness-raising, and youth clinics (Hakvåg 2009: 61–72). A law package on juvenile justice was turned down by the state *Duma* in 2010 after massive protests from a plethora of right-wing civil society grassroots groups. In Russia, the concept of 'juvenile justice' is used as a common term for measures to not only deal with young offenders according to the two principles of prevention and restorative justice but also to consider the concerns of child rights. Höjdestrand (2016) argues that 'juvenile justice' serves as 'a convenient all-purpose category for a variety of supposedly Western-originated policies, practices, people, and sociocultural trends that are expected to erode parental authority over children and/or infringe on the integrity of the family vis-à-vis the state'. The resistance to bestowing individual rights to children is based on an understanding of the child as being in the making and not yet developed as moral subjects. Their rights are not given to participation but to becoming moral subjects. Without the hierarchy-God-man, male-female, adult-child-morality will not develop, so the argument goes. In line with this, and as a last resort, parents must be allowed to use corporal punishment to instruct children.

On their side, the child rights' lobby did rally around the demand for child rights ombudspersons in the regions and at the federal level and the appliance to the CRC. The ombudspersons are in place and the first federal ombudsperson Aleksei Golovan (in office 8 September–December 2009) is still a leading figure on the child rights' side. His successors have been conservative. The ombudsperson in St. Petersburg clearly belongs to the child rights' camp.

The population at large is divided on the issues pertaining to child rights as illustrated by the general attitude to physical violence against children but is growing more conservative. The high quality and independent Levada Centre carried out a survey asking the following question: 'Should parents of 13–14 year old children be allowed to punish them physically?' In 2000, 8% answered 'yes, definitely' as compared to 7% in 2015. In 2000 19% answered 'somewhat yes,' while in 2015 it decreased to 15%. In the same survey years, 'somewhat no' was given by 37% of those surveyed (in 2000) as compared to 33% (in 2015). Thirty-seven percent said 'definitely no' in 2000 and that answer dropped to 20% in 2015. In other words, the population is divided but is growing more conservative.[3]

In addition to being a symbolic issue dividing culturally conservative from culturally progressive tendencies within the country, child rights have been drawn into the geopolitical rivalries between Russia and 'the West'. In 2012, mass media gave much attention to a case where a Russian child adopted by US citizens died from overheating after having been left alone for hours in a car. As a response, Russia introduced a law 'On measures against persons involved in violations of fundamental human rights and freedoms, rights and freedoms of citizens of Russian Federation', (the "Dima Yakovlev Law") that imposed a ban on adoptions of Russian orphans by US citizens. Foreign adoption was controversial at the outset because it may be perceived as a demonstration of Russia's inability to take care of its own children, thus directly triggering the biologically-oriented mind set of the right wing where the nation is a body with reference made to the Motherland, the sons of the nation, etc. Similar mechanisms are triggered in the cases of placement of children with a Russian family background residing abroad.

As a controversial rallying point for conservatives who want to fight against the concept, child rights is a potential danger zone for civil society organisations. As we will see in this chapter, they are welcomed in as service-providers and partners in a wide variety of consultative bodies but as soon as they touch upon child rights or enter into cooperation with foreign groups or funders they have to be careful not to provoke.

6.3.1   Terminology

'Social orphanhood' is one of the relatively uncontroversial issues within child welfare, and a wide variety of non-commercial organisations (Russian NGOs), charitable foundations and foster parent associations are involved. The issue is high on the political agenda in Russia but is often framed in a sentimentalised way by charitable funds as well as by businesses and politicians.

In the Russian system of child welfare, a distinction is made between biological—often called 'ordinary'/*obyknovennyi*—orphans and 'social orphans'. The latter are categorised as 'children left without parental care'; '*deti, ostavshiiesia bez popecheniia roditelei*', as the Russian expression goes, because their parents were not able to take care of them for (broadly defined) social reasons. These families are called 'unfortunate families' ('*neblagopoluchnye sem'i*'). The English expression 'unfit family' does not have a Russian equivalent (Rockhill 2010: 42).

Between 80 and 95% of children living in residential care or in foster families are social orphans. '*Beznadzornye*' are unsupervised children living in their original household and '*bezprizornye*' are street children. These are children whose parents have not been deprived of parental rights but due to alcoholism, drug use and infantilism do not fulfil their rights according to the Family Code, as one official put it in an interview. These households are targets for preventive work.

6.3.2   The Scope

Throughout the 1990s the number of social orphans in institutional care grew dramatically despite policies at federal and regional levels to promote prophylactic work before placement as well as providing alternative placement in various forms of foster families. In other words, institution-alised care is not only a Soviet, but also a post-Soviet, legacy. Between 1990 and 2005 the share of children (from birth to 18 years old) taken from their biological parents increased by 2.5 times. Since around 2005, however, the number of placements out of home has decreased (Biriukova et al. 2014).

In 2015, 60,000 children in all were placed out of home as compared to 94,000 in 2010 and 133,000 in 2005. Also the number of children whose parents have been deprived of their parental rights has decreased from 74,500 (2008) to 40,000 (2015) and their share of all children 0–17 years old have decreased from 0.28% (2008) to 0.14% (2015) according to statistics from *Rosstat*.[4] In 2016, placement in orphanages were defined as an intermediary solution until the children could be adopted or placed in families, i.e. guardianship with relatives (often grandparents, unpaid) and paid foster families and patron families.

Among the 60,000 children who were placed out of their parental homes in 2015, 10,000 were placed in institutions (educational, medical and social), of which only 30 were consigned to private institutions. 21,000 were placed in intermediate arrangements, almost all of them in families (guardians or foster parents). In all, 33,000 were assigned out of home, two thirds of which were unpaid arrangements with relatives (guardians) and one third of which were placed with paid foster or patron parents. The latter placement form is mainly used in cases where the legal status of the child has not yet been determined. In all, 2600 children were adopted. By the end of 2015, a total of 410,000 orphans were placed in families and 60,000 in institutions.[5]

6.4   The Legal Framework, Formal Institutions and State Policy

6.4.1   *Legal Framework*

In 1990 Russia became one of the first countries to ratify the CRC. The rights of the child are regulated in the Family Code's (2005) Chap. 8 Law number 120 from 1999 regulated the preventive work on unsupervised children and juvenile criminality. In 2014 the law on the framework for social services was passed and confirmed the principle of assisting the families in their homes and a greater role for *NKOs* as providers of social services. Also in 2014 a by-law was introduced on the principle of ensuring family-like accommodation of children in institutions. The main policy goals are outlined in the National Children's Strategy 2012–2017.

6.4.2   Institutions Involved

The Ministry of Education and Science is the core ministry for child rights. The educational sector is responsible for the major part of the orphanages and the reforms within them. This sector also answers for preventive measures against social orphanage. In most municipalities the 'organs of guardianship and care' (the child protection authorities) belong to the educational sector but may also be a part of the social sector.

Handicapped children often end up as social orphans. The Ministry of Health develops preventive measures aimed at helping parents cope with difficulties emanating from the fact that they have a child in need of extra care. This ministry also answers for the youngest orphans (up to three years old).

According to the Family Code (1995) 'family rights' falls under the domain of the Ministry of Labour and Social Protection. This means that it is the sector of social protection that is the master of most of the tools that may help households over the worst situations, and thus avoiding having to resort to social orphanage.

Street children are placed in temporary centres called police collection and distribution departments. These centres are mostly found in big cities and are under the auspices of the Ministry of the Interior.

The responsible bodies for revealing and placing abandoned children are called *organs of guardianship* (*organy opeki i popechitel'stvo*). They belong under the Ministry of Education and their tasks are decentralised down to the municipal level. In general it has been the educational sector—more precisely the municipal educational committees' departments of child rights' protection—that is responsible for the care of minor orphans. The specialists working in these departments cover a wide range of issues related to children. In each municipality the child inspector is the main official responsible for placement of children.

However, should the child be defined by the court as disabled or only partly able-bodied, he or she becomes the responsibility of the health care bodies. Likewise, if the child is able-bodied but in need of care because of health problems, the child is to be taken care of by the social work sector. When the organs of guardianship are unable to place a child in a family or under family-like conditions, children will be settled in an institution. Traditionally these have been divided in two according to children's age. Infants under four years old are placed in a baby's home (*dom rebënka*). For those between five and 17 there are children's homes (*detskii dom* or *internat*). Some of the schools known as corrective schools are intended for children with special needs. Street children are placed in temporary centres called police collection and distribution departments. These centres are under the Ministry of the Interior as are the committees for work with minors.

The *commission on minors and their rights* aim at preventing child neglect, 'anti-social behavior', and juvenile delinquency. The commissions are composed of representatives from different branches of public authority such as police, health, education and social protection.

The *child and family centres* that belong to the social services and exist in most cities are vital in providing preventive measures and follow-ups of households and families in difficult situations. As one interviewee put it, they can be likened to 'social polyclinics'. Each social worker may have to follow-up a total of 40–60 individual cases at the same time.

The *psychological-medical-pedagogical commission* carry out diagnosis of the child's physical and mental capacities and recommend the type of educational institution needed for any particular child. Most of the time parents decide where the child should be sent but in the case of orphans the organs of guardianship make the decision.

In the everyday child welfare policies, priority is given to developing family care and family-like care. The authorities have set up federal programmes which are then followed up in regional programmes. Child and family centres are established and often run by the city administration to provide services that prevent social orphanhood. There has been an increasing focus on preventive measures. New professions such as social pedagogues and specialists in social work have been introduced since the early 1990's.

6.4.3   Policies

In May 2006, President Vladimir Putin made an important speech to the Federal Assembly where he launched a set of actions to strengthen maternal health and children's well-being as measures to improve the demographic situation. One year later the Concept Note on Demographic Policies was introduced. It is a well-documented fact that having children in Russia enhances the risk of being or becoming poor. Therefore, the Concept Note's measures to encourage child birth focus on the targets groups' private economy. Childcare benefits were increased, expenditures for pre-school attendance were compensated and material support to guardians and foster parents was raised. The most spectacular improvement, however, was the introduction of the Maternity Capital Programme, under which mothers are entitled to 250,000 roubles when they give birth to or when they adopt a second or third child. The sum is to be paid only once and must be used for housing, education or pension. The sum, which is considerable for many households, is adjusted annually for inflation. Also, in 2007 the federal programme 'Russia's Children' was introduced and concretised in regional programmes.

In November 2010 the Annual Address of President Dmitry Medvedev to the Federal Assembly was also of importance. The crucial mechanism of child rights protection highlighted by the president was the recent introduction of the Child Rights Ombudsperson Institution under the auspices of the president of the Russian Federation. In his address the president urged all Russian regions to establish their own regional-scale *Child Rights Ombudsperson Institutions* in their territories.

Today, 80 out of the Russian Federation's 85 constituent regions have a child rights ombudsperson. So far, however, there has been no federal legislation concerning the ombudspersons, thus resulting in a wide variety of institutional set-ups in the regions. Some child rights ombudspersons are part of the Human Rights Institute while others are from independent offices; however they are accountable either to the regional assemblies or are subordinate to the regional governors. The Russian National Children's Strategy 2012–2017 aims, *inter alia*, at strengthening the institution of the child rights ombudsperson.

This group operates with ambitious goals within the following fields: family policy of childhood protection, accessibility of quality education and upbringing, cultural development and child informational safety, child-friendly healthcare and healthy lifestyle, a child rights protection system, and child-friendly justice and child participation. The Strategy has focused on enhancing financial state support to large families and parents who adopt children, curbing violence against children, preventing social orphanhood and providing support for children with disabilities. The Strategy contains elements that bear traces of the pro-child 'lobby', by prescribing non-violent interaction between parents and children, among other measures. The general policy in the national strategy has been concretised in regional programmes where *NKOs* have taken part in preparations and are assigned a role in the implementation.

6.4.4   *The Non-commercial Organisations (NKOs)*

The Putinist concept from 2005 of 'sovereign democracy' does not leave much leeway for foreign-funded *NKOs* to pursue a political agenda. At the core of the concept is the idea that Russia shall develop its own regime type and policies without external interference.

Working conditions for child rights organisations and being linked up to foreign partners or funders have further deteriorated during Vladimir Putin's third term as president (2012–) but still foreign cooperation and funding is allowed in, e.g. for the training of foster parents or training in responsible parenthood. Foreign-funded advocacy aimed at revising Russian legislation or practice is another matter and legal provisions have been introduced to prevent this. Child welfare organisations thus operate in a less hostile environment than *NKOs* in the field of human rights or in election monitoring. Nonetheless, advocacy work such as pushing the CRC child participation issue, constitutes a risk for the NGOs doing it.

The scholarly and journalistic literature on recent Russian developments has dealt extensively with the restrictive legal provisions. However, less attention has been directed towards the fate of domestically-driven *NKOs,* as well as whether Russian authorities mainly fear foreign influence—or whether they seek to ward off any kind of alternative input, e.g. in the field of child welfare.

The clampdown on externally funded *NKOs* is clearly an attempt to reduce foreign influence on organised civil society in Russia, putting an end to what Jakobson and Sanovich (2010) refer to as 'import substitution'. Whether it is also an attempt at curbing *NKO* influence as such is less clear. In general, the authorities divide *NKOs* into 'allies' or 'adversaries' of the state (Lyytikäinen 2014; Sundstrom 2006; Hemment 2012). The allies are helpers of the state, combining a strong commitment to their ideal with supporting the state in carrying out services that the state itself cannot provide. The adversaries are groups financed from abroad and pursuing agendas not in line with the priorities of the Russian authorities.

The restrictive trends co-exist with an officially recognised need to find practicable solutions to the current child-welfare challenges in Russia. Joint projects involving Russian child welfare authorities, police or medical personnel and foreign professionals, NGOs and/or funders have played an important role in the development of innovative methods and new, more child-friendly approaches. Much of this has been appreciated by sector authorities at all levels of government.

This picture is one of political tightening for 'negative' *NKOs* on the one hand, and an invitation for 'positive' *NKOs* on the other. This is a reflection of the dual needs facing the Russian authorities—to control, but also to modernise. Civil society organisations are expected to serve the overall interests of Russia, *inter alia* by pressing for modernisation but not necessarily pushing for democratisation (Bindman 2015). Thus, the non-state actors find themselves caught in the regime's balancing act between hierarchical control and modernisation. To complicate the picture, *NKOs* are called upon to do 'public control' of the authorities' work on orphans and foster parents among other responsibilities. For instance, in 2012 President Putin presented a bill to the State *Duma* on public control of orphanages, a bill that got strong support from veteran child right activist Boris Altshuler but which so far has not been passed.

As seen from the top of the 'power vertical', *NKOs* are a potential nuisance but they also have valuable resources to offer—as the authorities know. The *NKOs* find themselves in-between restricting and enabling factors. The restricting factors relate mainly to the new *NKO* legislation, whereas the enabling ones concern policies on 'socially oriented *NKOs* and 'public control'.

To pave the way for an *NKO* sector that is primarily financed by Russian funds and operating according to an agenda set in Russia and not abroad, the authorities have introduced legislation and policies in three main areas. Firstly, they have initiated financing mechanisms of funds and grants for *NKOs*. In his address to the Federal Assembly in 2009, President Medvedev proposed the establishment of a new category of 'societally oriented *NGOs*'. This was then included in the April 2010 Law 7-FZ 'On Non-Commercial Organisations' (Chebankova 2013: 105). In July 2009 came a state doctrine on 'On the support of charitable work'. The document was drafted with inputs from the Ministry of Economic Development and the Public Chamber, the two main sources of domestic funding for *NKOs*'. Big business supports charitable organisations to show loyalty to the state and to consolidate its political position.

The federal law 'On the Foundations of Providing Social Services to Citizens in the Russian Federation' that entered into force in 2014 paved the way for commercial as well as non-profit (*NKO*) providers in the welfare sector. Individual entrepreneurs, small businesses, large commercial companies and non-profit organisations may all apply to become social service providers.

Although providers are to be paid under the budget, the idea is that they will produce added value that will help to 'de-budgetise' the social welfare sector. To boost this development, a zero income tax has been introduced for both commercial and non-profit providers. Corporate Social Responsibility was an established practice for large enterprises during Soviet times, but that was largely ended with the demise of the USSR. Modern CSR has been on the rise in recent years, but the economic crisis may have negative repercussions here. Nonetheless, banks have their own programme activities such as those concerning financial literacy for children. As for the NGOs, special rosters will be established in the regions. Russian *NKOs* are making use of these opportunities; many of them already have experience in providing social services which have been commissioned by local authorities.

Today, Russian 'socially-oriented *NKOs* (so-called *SONKOs*) have access—through competition—to a wide range of funding sources: presidential grants, ministerial grants, huge grants from the Ministry of Economic Development and the Public Chamber. Each policy area has its own grant operator, and the annual sums distributed have been increasing.

Early 2017, an amendment to the *NKO* Law was made to introduce the concept of '*NKOs* performing services useful for the society'. These are socially oriented *NKOs* that carry out one or more of a fixed set of 20 'useful services', among them follow-ups of families having children with health problems, of orphans, and of families in difficult life situations. As soon as a socially-oriented *NKO* achieves this status and gets a contract for delivering services, it has access to stable funding for two subsequent years. They also have access to training for staff and volunteers. The explicit purpose of facilitating this type of *NKOs* is to 'give state institutions competition', according to the minister of economic development whose ministry is in charge of support to the socially-oriented *NKOs*. The minister claims there 140,000 organisations (40% more than five years ago) of this type in Russia having 900,000 employees and 2.5 million volunteers.[6] In 2015, a total of 38 *SONKOs* won the competition over grants, amounting to a sum of 240 million roubles.[7]

In the field of children's rights, the Foundation for Children in Difficult Life Situations plays an important role in funding projects. The international NGO operating with partners in Russia included in this study has cooperated with the Foundation since the mid-2000s and has an open and transparent dialogue with its leadership. The Foundation sees the NGO as a guarantor for quality. If the NGO's partners seek funding from this grant scheme, and the Foundation knows that the NGO will train them and states that they are trustworthy and expresses this in a letter of support, then funding will be granted.

Presidential grants have grown from 600 million roubles (17.3 million euros) in 2006 to 2.7 billion roubles (56.7 million euros) in 2014.[8]

Secondly, the authorities promote 'public control' carried out by domestic *NKOs*. An elaborate system of consultation mechanisms has been set up, with public chambers (*obshchestvennye palaty*) at federal and regional level and public councils (*sovety*) being the most prominent. Child-oriented welfare organisations take part in these chambers and councils. The civic chambers were established in 2005 to serve as organs for public control of the authorities. Their members—prominent personalities, normally leaders of *NKOs* and other types of organised civic groups—are partly selected by the president, and partly through co-opting mechanisms. One of their tasks is to carry out 'civic impact assessment' (*obshchestvennaia èkspertiza*) of draft legislation. The activities of the civic chambers thus—in a heavily institutionalised way—cover many of the same functions as the consultative rounds and consultative statements in other European countries.

Thirdly, new opportunities to provide welfare services have been opened up for *NKOs*. The 2014 law 'On the foundation of public control in Russian Federation' defines the role of non-state actors in monitoring the performance of the authorities. Although drawing on earlier Soviet practices, the concept of 'public control' may give *NKOs*, civil activists, and professional experts additional leverage in Russia today. Also, the Public Chambers have been assigned a central role in performing 'public control'.

6.4.5   Provision of Welfare Services

The overall Russian welfare system is under reform. Despite the official rhetoric on 'sovereign democracy', 'Russia following its own way' and the like, reforms bear the clear stamp of international inspiration. Greater market provision and less public provision form part of these welfare reforms, and these tendencies have gained speed since the turn of the millennium (Cook 2013: 3; Tarasenko 2015). Encouraging *NKOs* to 'produce value added' sparked off by grants is one way whereby the authorities invite *NKOs* in.

6.5   REGIONAL STAKEHOLDERS, GOVERNANCE NETWORKS AND THE POLICY PROCESS

Child welfare is a fairly decentralised policy area in Russia as the organs of guardianship form part of the municipal administration. The overall guidelines, however, are given in regional programmes. Russia's 85 regions each organise child welfare in slightly different ways. The training and follow-up of foster parents, for instance, may differ as to how much it is emphasised and how it is done. The degree to which *NKOs* are involved differ significantly both as a result of the actual existence of these organisations and the willingness of the regional authorities to draw on them. The regional child ombudspersons partly were established through a campaign from the child rights lobby and often work closely with child rights groups. These groups tend to be very low key in their promotion of child rights. They work together with like-minded leaders and specialists in the welfare service bodies at city district and regional levels and authorities looking for innovative methods in the field of social protection and child welfare. Meeting places then become areas for training, round tables, workshops and sometimes even international conferences organised by the *NKO* in cooperation with the authorities. These are platforms for exchange of information and development of mutual trust. In this kind of cooperation, authorities tend to distinguish between '*obshch-estvenniki*' and 'professionals', the former referring to *NKOs* of users and clients such as foster family groups or parents of disabled children. In St. Petersburg parents of disabled children have come together to set up the city-wide association of more than 85 civic groups of disabled children's parents, the *NKO GAOORDI*. The city's target programme for this category of children was elaborated with the *NKO* actively taking part. They are also being consulted by the St. Petersburg city council's commission on social issues in other relevant matters. A third category of Russian *NKOs* is represented by the activist groups, usually those which are either child rights or family rights oriented.

In addition to networks of likeminded groups (child rights versus family rights) and their allies in the state, regional and local public administration, there are formal platforms where authorities meet civic groups (*NKOs*) and individual civic leaders and professionals. These are mainly in the civic chambers at federal and regional levels and in the civic councils at the local level. In addition, federal and regional ministries have the civic council as a vehicle for communicating with society. For instance, since 2013 the

Ministry of Education has had a Council on the protection of child rights and legal interests of orphans where representatives of relevant public bodies and *NKOs* are members.

In addition, orphanages, schools and other institutions for children have public councils. In some cities, *NKOs* carry out so-called 'supervisions of the work of guardianship organs' and family and child centres where representatives of *NKOs* and the relevant public bodies meet to discuss concrete cases. As one *NKO* representative said in one of our interviews: 'Here we work together with the authorities, side by side. We raise each other's level of professionalism of each other.'

One *NKO* in a big city has the prevention of social orphanhood as its core activity and is a service-providing *NKO* of activists. It receives funds from the city's committee for social policies and has official agreements with three city district (*raion*) administrations. These city district administrations hand over to the *NKO* a list of families in need and then the *NKO* follows up in cooperation with the local city district centres for assistance to these particular children and families. Among the services offered by the *NKO* and commissioned by the city districts are: to provide assistance to children graduating from orphanages to find a flat and a job, to acquire the necessary documents and fill in forms, to assist families with many children to find a suitable flat, and to arrange excursions.

Most of the *NKO's* links with local authorities are based on personal acquaintances often established at roundtables and other intra-sector meetings. A special fund organises seminars and '*superviziia*' (a kind of roundtable consultation) for those working in non-commercial organisations in the city.

What values does this *NKO* add? In its own eyes it contributes to their ability to follow up on families over time as well as providing non-material support while the city district administration are busy sticking to formal criteria for the distribution of living areas (flats), food, space, clothing etc. The *NKO* has its own fund-raising department trying to get monies from businesses in addition to the commissioned work for city districts. One company offers non-monetary support by sending employees with language skills over to the centre to assist children from 'difficult' families to learn English. The *NKO* does not take part in discussions with authorities on difficult issues on a regular basis, but the director has taken part for a while in some meetings on the controversial issue of juvenile delinquency.

Another *NKO* is actively involved in child welfare in the same city. It is a typically profession-based *NKO* and designs projects that they bring to the city's committee for social policies and city districts at an early stage in order to allow for later adjustments. In 2006 the *NKO* had already set up a 'social hotel for minors', i.e. a shelter for one of the city districts. At that time they had a foreign donor and could propose a model in which the city district provided the premises, the *NKO* refurbished it, and hired and trained staff. The profile of the shelter was to be developed jointly by the *NKO* and the city district. The head of the department for social protection and the vice-head of the city district are the two main counterparts for socially oriented *NKOs* at the local level. The *NKO* funded the shelter for two years. After that the city district assumed the financial burden and included the centre in its day-to-day work. The resources brought in by the *NKO* are mainly the competence to fill the centres for children and families with innovative models, ideas and to provide 'extra-budgetary' funds. This *NKO* is capable of taking the initiative of working groups on specific issues with the committee for social protection as was the case on children and migration. Such groups usually are inter-sectoral and may have from ten to 30 members.

In one regional capital an *NKO* with a low profile (doing handicraft with children and distributing hygiene articles for children) but also with an ability to engage in controversial issues such as the closing down of a boarding-school for disabled children takes part in the societal council of the regional ministry of social protection, demography and family affairs and also in the civic council of the city *Duma*. In the civic council charitable organisations and social institutions such as orphanages and boarding-schools also participate. The NKO in question received funds (50,000 RUR) from an international donor and registered in *Rosfinmonitoring* that they had obtained these funds from abroad.

This charitable NKO does voluntary work in orphanages and boarding-schools and has established a school of volunteers. It joins in civic councils where issues on the agenda may be mainly charitable such as the preparations of summer camps for children but also the involvement in more political issues—a recent revision of the regional adoption law for example. The establishment of a school of volunteers came as a result of one of these meetings. The school is a joint project of four institutions participating in the council: the *NKO* itself, the regional *Duma*, the regional university, and the city's department of education. The *NKO* was offered premises for its activities in the regional house of youth organisations. The same *NKO* has absolutely no relations with the regional ministry of education after it several years ago had actively fought a decision to close down a boarding-school for disabled children. 'Here everything depends on the human factor' as the leaders of the *NKO* said, adding the accusation that representation in the Civic Chamber was 'for sale'. Being a member of the regional Civic Chamber would help getting in contact with officials on a higher level, those 'on whom depends decisions on concrete issues, and that otherwise are difficult for us to get in touch with. They are too good at isolating themselves from society', as one NKO representative said. 'It is not easy to tell whether the invitation to cooperation is a real wish to cooperate or just motivated by the need to make it look as if there is cooperation'.

The civic council of the city *Duma* operates 'in a liberal atmosphere and representatives from regional ministries are invited and engage in dialogue and open discussion, even quarrels, and listen to suggestions from representatives of society', another local NKO leader said. Taking part in the council helps to arrange separate meetings, e.g. with vice-ministers at regional level to discuss concrete issues—in the case of this *NKO*, a project to establish a centre for follow-up of young people who have stayed in orphanages or boarding-schools until they became 18. This is an issue that has high priority politically and the *NKO* offered to set up this centre where they would serve as 'social parents' for the young people in need of assistance for coping with practical life, for instance in how to deal with money issues. 'We can assist the regional ministry in improving statistics on criminality', the *NKO* leader said in an interview.

Another *NKO* used to be the Russian branch of an international *NGO* but changed its status into a Russian *NKO* to avoid problems with the foreign agent law. In 2014 nonetheless, 65% of its funding came from international sources. From having worked directly with parents and children the *NKO* changed into working together with city district authorities in a bigger city and the city's Committee on Social Protection. This strengthened the sustainability of activities and results, the interviewee from the organisation said. 'We develop innovative methods, plan them, describe them, evaluate their effectiveness and hand over the 'product''. Such innovative methods have to avoid incurring significant extra costs and they must fit easily into the existing framework within which the local agencies of child protection and social affairs operate. Otherwise they will be rejected. This *NKO* often initiates inter-sectoral meeting on concrete issues, e.g. on the problems of one individual family, where the NGO works together with specialists from, among others, the organ of guardianship and department on social affairs.

The *NKO* helps parents with disabilities to cope with everyday life by taking care of the children for shorter periods of time, among providing other services. Also, short term placements of children in trained foster families is among this *NKOs* activities. In other words, the *NKO* is engaged in preventive measures against social orphanhood. The *NKO* tried to initiate a typical child rights project on letting children themselves have a say in cases of out-of-home placement. The project was to be run in cooperation with the organs of guardianship and the courts and was in accordance with the law but concrete mechanisms to let this happen have not been developed. The project initiative was never realised, probably because it was too child rights oriented.

Our research on one international NGO operating with partners in Russia shows that it chose to maintain a low profile on individual child rights in the CRC sense. Direct advocacy for child rights is hampered, particularly as regards to the aim of getting children and young people to be active participants in societal life defending their own rights. Today, the NGO's and partners' activities among young people have become mainly restricted to leisure pursuits. Awareness-raising and capacity-building aiming at making the children and youth familiar within the UN CRC convention form part of these activities although quite toned down in order not to provoke. The organisation is careful to avoid doing anything that might be labelled 'political'. However, it takes part in national public hearings when invited.

The present conditions in Russia make partnership selection a sensitive issue for international NGOs. Current *NKO* legislation makes it difficult to have local *NKOs* as partners. Transferring money to them would entail the risk of making them qualify as 'foreign agents'. Partners must be able to cooperate within the existing system and link up with current policies, but should also be able to add something more. For the international NGO in question, the solution has been to work with local and regional governmental organisations as well as Child Rights Ombudspersons. Although the 'natural reflexes' of the international NGOs is to work with 'civil society' and the fact that they are working with the authorities at times is presented as an 'emergency solution', the model has resulted in child rights approaches being strengthened in the public agencies and institutions that provide services. This has enabled the NGO to reach out and achieve results to scale in ways it would have been hardly able to through 'civil society' only. Government institutions are duty-bearers with permanent responsibilities in the policy areas they cover.

Having good relations with child rights-oriented ombudspersons allows the NGO to be linked to a wider range of key child rights actors and to conduct some indirect ('silent') lobbying. At project level the NGO seeks to avoid challenging norms and methods in the child welfare sector. Instead, it links up with ongoing initiatives and frameworks, e.g. on strengthening the family institution by introducing innovative methods such as techniques to help parents avoid violence against their children. This entails a balancing act between provocation detrimental to the NGO and activities of little significance.

6.6   CONCLUSIONS

The real-life child welfare governance networks identified above do not measure up to the somewhat idealistic imagine of network governance. In the case of Russian child welfare policy, implementation and public service delivery are not moving away from direct top-down formal government to processes and practices where public, semi-public and private resources and actors come together on equal terms on horizontal platforms. Nonetheless, they come together and not everything they do is top-down. To a certain extent there is a 'common' purpose. Goals, knowledge, and resources are being shared on many issues such as family-like placement of orphans and the prevention of family problems. *NKO* activities come in the form of well-intentioned advice to the authorities and policy positions are framed to conform to current policies. If there is contention within the networks *NKOs* make sure it is 'consentful' and not 'dissentful', to use the dichotomy terms put forward by Cheskin and March (2015: 266) and presented in this book's Chap. 2.

Applying the taxonomy of nodality, authority, treasure, and organisation introduced in Chap. 2 unsurprisingly shows that the Russian authorities on all levels of government have a firm grasp of all four resources, with highly formalised public chambers and councils being the most important platforms on which actors meet. In some cases, however, mainly at local level, *NKOs* are able to take up a nodal position and initiate workshops, supervisions, conferences and even working groups. Doing this, they—although on a small scale—are able to set the agenda in discussions on 'social technologies'. By and large, the *NKO's* function as conveyors of innovative working methods is appreciated by the authorities. In some cases the *NKOs* are nodal by having a privileged access to target groups such as foster parents who may trust trainers and specialists from these organisations more than they trust social workers or municipal agencies.

Authority has been used to prevent unwanted forms of action, notably governance networks developing that were partly influenced by agendas set abroad by foreign funders. The foreign agent law from 2012 significantly influenced the working style and contents of the networks. Outspoken child rights approaches suffered and family rights approaches gained the upper hand. The conservative turn in Russia's cultural policies from the mid-2000s also contributed to this. On the other hand outspoken child rights defenders still take part on the governance network platforms.

Treasure is made use of for control. *NKO* projects are more likely to be funded if they for example refer to strengthening the family to avoid social orphanage than if they aim at strengthening children's right to participation. The fact that foreign funding still is allowed in the field of child rights makes treasure less of a resource than it could have been but the ban on activities that seeks to change current policies keeps the authorities in control.

Organisation is certainly in the hands of the authorities as they provide the major platforms for governance networks. There are, as mentioned above on nodality, platforms that are initiated and organised by *NKOs*. A certain division of labour takes place where the more general platforms are formed by the authorities and platforms on operational and methodological issues may be left to *NKO* to organise.

The issue of nodality, authority, treasure and organisation is not problematised by the child welfare *NKOs* except for the ban on foreign funding. They tend to expect the authorities to have the initiative and see the platforms as opportunities to meet the authorities—not to compete with them.

On the basis of our research it is possible to draw some conclusions. Firstly, Russian state authorities have a clear strategy on how to draw on the resources of domestic *NKOs*. *NKOs* are being perceived as important actors within the various 'adjusting mechanisms' that have been set up: the public chambers, systems of public control and the like. These mechanisms lie parallel to the elected, representative organs which are assigned a weak role under the present, increasingly authoritarian regime. With this parallelism, the Russian governance networks have features in common with the actual governance networks elsewhere in Europe.

The adjustive/corrective function of *NKOs* is closely related to their role in adding legitimacy to the authorities. By being able to show that they work closely with concerned doctors or parents of disabled children for example, authorities try to gain legitimacy.

Although geopolitical rivalries have made official Russia assume a 'sovereignist', partly anti-Western rhetoric, the country's welfare reforms are emulating reforms in the Western world (privatisation, individualisation, monetisation, and decentralisation). Non-state actors (business but also *NKOs*) are invited in as service-providers. *NKOs* had already been providing services for municipalities for many years. The idea is that this will 'de-budgetise' the welfare sector.

The *NKO* role as 'agents of change' and channels of innovation has been reduced as a result of the withdrawal of foreign funds. At times Russian *NKOs* cooperating with advanced milieux in the West used to be conveyors of new methods and approaches, often more efficient and humane than those already in place. Sometimes the *NKO* projects funded from abroad were poorly rooted in the real-life welfare structures and professions but at best they resulted in the incorporation of innovative methods in the every-day running of the sector. The current, domestic Russian funding mechanisms for *NKOs* do not seem to be opening up for a revitalisation of the links to outside practices. *NKOs* still receiving foreign funding fear accusations of 'political activity'. Although to a lesser degree, similar fears affect domestically-funded *NKOs*. To avoid problems foreign-funded and domestically funded *NKOs* alike impose restrictions on what methods and approaches they promote. If they are too innovative it may be interpreted as an indirect criticism of current policies—in other words, a political activity. Thus *NKO*-initiated innovation from inside Russia has been made less likely to happen due to ongoing political tightening.

How do the Russian child welfare *NKOs* manoeuvre under the current conditions? Broadly, on the basis of our analysis we can conclude that *NKOs* have adapted to the 'nationalisation' of funding. Keeping in touch with foreign funders may attract the attention of state regulatory bodies in unwanted ways, thus leading to excessive reporting requirements. In addition, in the current geo-political climate, receiving foreign funds may negatively affect the reputation of the *NKO*. In a landscape of informal cooperation and contact, having a positive reputation is a very important resource for *NKOs*.

Advocacy work is being made unassertively and mainly by linking up to ongoing reforms. The National Children's Strategy of 2012–2017 operates with objectives that enable this approach, which to some extent balances out the effects of the policies discouraging activities that may be classified as 'political'. For the *NKOs* to be included in federal, regional or city-level child welfare programmes is highly desirable. Having a project incorporated into one of these programmes means a secure status and funding. Therefore, from the very beginning of planning and designing a project or service, the *NKO* tends to link up with the relevant authorities to harmonise it with their objectives.

Our research has found that the Russian regime's combining authoritarianism with technocratic development is in need of an *NKO* sector. The *NKO* itself has to manoeuvre between the regime's need for explicit control on the one hand and input on the other.

NOTES

1. In the following we will use the Russian acronym *NKO* (*ne-kommercheskaia organizaciya* = non-commercial organisation) for Russian civil society organisations, and NGOs for foreign organisations.
2. Source: radio station *Ekho Moskvy* 17 February 2017.
3. Source: '*Deti: prava, dopustimost' roditel'skogo i gosudarstvennogo kontrolia, Levada Tsentr*, 30.05.2015.
4. Source: '*Chislennost' detei, roditeli kotorykh lisheny roditel'skikh prav*'. http://www.gks.ru/wps/wcm/connect/rosstat_main/rosstat/ru/statistics/population/motherhood/#.
5. Source: '*Svedeniia o vyiavlenii i ustroistve detei-sirot i detei, ostavshikhsia bez popecheniia roditelei za 2015 g.*', *Federal'noe statisticheskoe nabliudenie, Rosstat Rossii.*
6. 'Evgeniy Elin: *Neobkhodimye mery podderzhki nekommercheskikh organizatsii budut ustanovleny do kon'tsa* goda', 24.11.16, http://economy.gov.ru/minec/press/news/2016241102# and 'Regionam ukazali na sotsial'no *orientirovannye NKO*', 07.09.2016: http://economy.gov.ru/minec/about/structure/depIno/20160906. Both references from the website of the Ministry of Economic Development.
7. *Rezul'taty konkursnogo otbora sotsial'no orientirovannykh nekommercheskikh organizatsii* 2015 *goda*, 7 October 2015, Ministry's website: http://economy.gov.ru/minec/activity/sections/socorientnoncomorg/2015100702.
8. Website of the Foundation of Civil Society Development cited by Tarasenko (2015).

REFERENCES

Bindman, Eleanor. 2015. The State, Civil Society and Social Rights in Contemporary Russia. *East European Politics* 31 (3): 342–360.

Biriukova, S., M. Varlamova, and O. Siniavskaia. 2014. "Sirotsvo v Rossii". Demoskop Weekly, No. 609–610.

Chebankova, Elena. 2013. *Civil Society in Putin's Russia*. London: Routledge.

Cheskin, Ammon, and Luke March. 2015. State–Society Relations in Contemporary Russia: New Forms of Political and Social Contention. *East European Politics* 31 (3): 261–273.

Cook, Linda J. 2013. *Postcommunist Welfare States: Reform Politics in Russia and Eastern Europe*. Ithaca, NY: Cornell University Press.

Davies, Jonathan S., Jørn Holm-Hansen, Vadim Kononenko, and Asbjørn Røiseland. 2016. Network Governance in Russia: An Analytical Framework. *East European Politics* 32 (2): 131–142.

Golenkova, Z.T. 2016. *Sotsial'naia politika v Rossii i Kitae*. Moskva: Novyi Khronograf.

Hakvåg, Una K. 2009. *Juvenile Justice in the Russian Federation*. Master's Thesis, European and American Studies. Oslo: University of Oslo.

Hemment, Julie. 2012. Nashi, Youth Voluntarism, and Potëmkin NGO's—Making Sense of Civil Society in Post-Soviet Russia. *Slavic Review* 71 (2): 234–260.

Höjdestrand, Tova. 2016. Social Welfare or Moral Warfare? Popular Resistance Against Children's Rights and Juvenile Justice in Contemporary Russia. *International Journal of Children's Rights* 24 (4): 826–850.

Jakobson, Lev, and Sergey Sanovich. 2010. The Changing Models of the Russian Third Sector—Import Substitution Phase. *Journal of Civil Society* 6 (3): 279–300.

Lyytikäinen, Laura. 2014. Performing Political Opposition in Russia—The Case of the Youth Movement Oborona. Ph.D. dissertation, Department of Social Sciences. Helsinki: University of Helsinki.

Ovcharova, L.N., A.I. Pishniak, and D.O. Popova. 2007. *New Measures Supporting Families with Children: Improving Living Standards and Raising Birth Rates*. Moscow: Independent Institute for Social Policy/UNICEF.

Rockhill, Elena Khlinovskaya. 2010. *Lost to the State: Family Discontinuity, Social Orphanhood and Residential Care in the Russian Far East*. Oxford, New York: Berghahn Books.

Sundstrom, Lisa McIntosh. 2006. *Funding Civil Society—Foreign Assistance and NGO Development in Russia*. Stanford: Stanford University Press.

Tarasenko, Anna. 2015. Russian Welfare Reform and Social NGOs—Strategies for Claim-making and Service Provision in the Case of St. Petersburg. *East European Politics* 31 (3): 294–313.

CHAPTER 7

Imitation and Enforced Cooperation: State and Civil Society in Ethnic Conflict Management

Sabine Kropp and Johannes Schuhmann

We are very grateful to Karina Mikirova for conducting and analysing the semi-structured interviews and contributing to this chapter with thoughtful ideas and comments. Karina Mikirova was an invaluable part of the project team which was generously funded by the Metro-Foundation. More detailed results on the investigated 'ethnic' platforms are published in her dissertation on regional ethnic policy (Mikirova 2016). Whenever possible, we refer to her work in the following sections.

S. Kropp (✉)
Otto Suhr Institute of Political Science, Freie Universität Berlin,
Ihnestraße 22, 14195 Berlin, Germany
e-mail: sabine.kropp@fu-berlin.de

J. Schuhmann
Institute of German and International Party Law and Party Research,
Heinrich-Heine-University Düsseldorf, Universitätsstr. 1,
40225 Düsseldorf, Germany
e-mail: Johannes.schuhmann@uni-duesseldorf.de

7.1   Ethnic Conflict Management
as Network-Enforcing Policy Issue?

Ethnic policy has always been of paramount importance for the Russian Empire and the Soviet Union and since 1990 has also ranked high on the Russian political agenda. The collapse of the Soviet Union in 1990 left Russia with an ethnic patchwork. In 2010, 193[1] ethnic groups were officially registered in the country. Until the present time, managing interethnic consent and peace in the regions has remained a high priority for the Russian federal government because the issue is regarded as a key prerequisite for the political, social and economic development of the entire country.[2] Very often are normative acts related to security aspects (see Chap. 8) because the topic is directly linked to racially motivated violence, extremism and terrorist attacks (Mikirova 2016: 106). Correspondingly, federal security agencies and regional administrations address considerable attention towards ethnic conflicts.

Since the Soviet era, the federation has been built along a combination of administrative-territorial and ethnic-territorial principles. Russia has inherited this structure and is still divided into different types of 'federal subjects' featuring striking political and economic asymmetries. Within the regions, ethnic policy often takes shape of a 'nested game', since Russians and non-Russians do not appear as compact ethnic communities. Today, a lot of Russian federal subjects provide a combustible ethnic mix, sometimes comprising even more than 130 ethnic groups.[3] Although the situation has somewhat calmed down since 2000, at least 290 xenophobic attacks were counted in 2008 alone. It is especially alarming that youth groups and youth movements appear particularly aggressive (see Savva 2008; Mikirova 2016).

Due to the high level of conflict and the salience of the issue, ethnic policy seems particularly suited to studying how different modes of governance are intertwined. Ethnic conflict management is a policy field which requires multi-dimensional coordination. It cuts across various sectoral policies such as health, education, culture, demographic and labour market policy, security, and migration. Besides, the study of ethnic issues is crucial for unravelling federal relations in Russia. Any successful management of ethnic tensions requires the collaboration of state authorities with local and regional representatives of ethnic groups. In general, hierarchy and coercion are not appropriate means to pacify ethnic conflict but, on the contrary, may instead become counterproductive. Responsibilities centralised at the federal level would probably fuel existing conflicts because this centralisation disregards the specific regional and local socio-economic conditions. Government regulation is, of course, the most conventional tool for solving problems, but standardised top-down approaches work properly only if they cope with policy issues which can be managed by rather unadorned policy instruments. Such tools regularly fail when it comes to ethnic conflicts. Therefore, regional authorities need some leeway to deviate from this 'average' in order to tailor solutions to specific local conditions. All these arguments make governance networks located at the subnational levels an obvious approach to managing ethnic policy issues.

This chapter focuses on governance networks in ethnic policy, placing special emphasis on bodies coping with interethnic peace and youth policy. In the following, a clear-cut and institutionalised element of ethnic policy is investigated: the so-called 'platforms', i.e. bodies designed to mediate and prevent ethnic conflicts at subnational level. In these entities, NGOs and other non-state actors, among them experts and academics, interact with regional authorities on a more or less regular basis. As regional and federal authorities need to devote considerable attention to ethnic issues, this chapter also shows which tools of 'meta-governance' state actors apply to manage the platforms (see Berg-Nordlie et al., Chap. 2) and it therefore elaborates interferences into network-like interactions.

7.2   Case Selection and Methodology

Between 2007 and 2010, four case studies examining the 'negotiation platforms' in ethnic policy were conducted in the regions of Stavropol' and Krasnodar. For the purposes of the following study, each platform is treated as a single case (see Table 7.1). The North Caucasus, where both so-called 'Russian' regions are located, has remained an ethnic hotbed featuring overlapping socio-economic and ethnic tensions. Krasnodar and Stavropol' *krai* represent rather similar cases with respect to their ethnic composition.[4] Economically, the ethnic republics neighbouring Krasnodar *krai* and Stavropol' *krai* are reckoned to be among the most underdeveloped regions in Russia. The both 'Russian' regions, in contrast, perform considerably better, even though Stavropol's economic performance has been inferior to that of Krasnodar. Due to high unemployment rates in the

Table 7.1 Platforms for state-civil society collaboration in ethnic policy

Case	Issue	Basic interests of state and private actors	Composition of platform	Mode of governance
'Advisory body for interethnic affairs' Stavropol' (S1)	Established in 1993 to mediate conflicts; reorganisations in 1997 and 2005	*State actors*: receiving legitimacy and information, reputation for the governor; state dominance, realised by hierarchy and control *Private actors*: access to state support; Slavic NGOs not willing to interact with other ethnic NGOs	Mainly state actors; invitation of handpicked private actors, critical NGOs excluded; GONGOs, platform headed by the governor	Clearly state-dominated, paternalistic features, state actors aim at getting some consultation; imitation of collaborations between state actors and handpicked loyal non-state actors; platform remained ineffective during conflicts
'Youth advisory body for interethnic affairs' Stavropol' (S2)	Established after massive conflicts between ethnic youth groups in 2007	*State actors*: interested in receiving information; but state dominance, realised by hierarchy and control *Private actors*: mainly information, access to state support	Mainly non-state actors, invitation of selected private actors, critical NGOs excluded; GONGOs, platform headed by head of 'Committee for Youth Affairs' in the regional administration	Clearly state-dominated, tendency to paternalism, state actors aim at getting some consultation; dialogue between state actors and selected loyal non-state actors; partial imitation, vertical control; platform remained largely ineffective

(continued)

Table 7.1 (continued)

Case	Issue	Basic interests of state and private actors	Composition of platform	Mode of governance
'Advisory body for ethnic issues' Krasnodar (K1)	Already established in 1992 to fill gaps in legislation on ethnic issues, but regular reorganisations; conflict resolution, organisation of events and conferences, informing citizens	*State actors*: interested in gaining access to resources of NGOs (mainly legitimacy, information and expertise) *Private actors*: some access to decision-making	Private actors and state actors as experts; NGOs appoint representatives; platform initiated by NGOs, headed by the head of the centre of ethnic NGOs in the region	Horizontal, collaboration of state actors and loyal as well as critical non-state actors, coordination, consultation (decision-making)
'Advisory body for socially important issues' Krasnodar (K2)	Established in 2003 as a permanent body to solve problems and resolve conflicts; educating people in using tolerance	*State actors*: access to resources of NGOs (see above) *Private actors*: some access to decision-making	Private actors, state actors with expert status; NGOs appoint representatives; platform initiated by Dept. of Federal Interior Ministry in Krasnodar, headed by expert and head of an ethnic NGO	Horizontal, collaboration of state actors and loyal as well as critical non-state actors, coordination, consultation (decision-making)

Source Data collected by Mikirova (2016)

bordering ethnic republics, mainly poorly qualified workers migrate to the wealthier 'Russian' regions. Impoverished Caucasians as well as ethnic Russians fled the 'ethnic republics' in the North Caucasus due to the Chechen wars in the 1990s and early 2000s and the breakdown of the Soviet Union; this widespread migration resulted in a continuously decreasing share of the Russian population ('de-russification') and a general growth of population. In Stavropol' *krai*, which borders not only Chechnya but several other ethnic republics in the North Caucasus and thus has been the first place of refuge for many migrants, the non-Russian population even doubled between 1989 and 2010 because of this large-scale in-migration (Foxall 2015: 154). The migrant population moving to Stavropol' was also poorer on average than in Krasnodar and settled as compact populations in some districts, thereby changing the proportion of Russians to non-Russians (Light 2016: 122). The mass migration resulted in fierce competition for the labour and housing markets and led to increasing social pressure and a changing regional ethnic composition. Today, both regions suffer from migrant phobia, blatant *kavkazofobiya* (resentments against people from the Caucasus) and ethnic conflicts. Although Krasnodar is the wealthier region and could have better provided for migrants, it is striking that the regional government followed a more aggressive course against ethnic minorities and migrants than the regional government in Stavropol' *krai* did in the 1990s and 2000s (Light 2016: 115–148).

In both regions the federal government exercised different regional economic development strategies. Since the early 2000s, Krasnodar has been considered a region with high investment potential and gradually improved in investment rankings, while Stavropol' lagged behind (Mikirova 2016: 76). Most importantly, Krasnodar hosted the Winter Olympics in Sochi in 2014, an event which the Kremlin regarded as particularly relevant for Russia's international reputation and the country's national self-esteem (Richmond 2013: 205–207). After the International Olympic Committee had made its decision in favour of Sochi in 2007, the Russian federal government initiated programs to develop the region economically and to attract international investments.[5] The mediation of interethnic and religious conflicts[6] was put on the political agenda, since the federal government aimed at diminishing the pervasive threat of terrorist attacks and at stabilising the fragile region. Responding to these objectives, in 2010 the federal government also decided not to integrate Krasnodar into the newly created North Caucasian Federal District because it feared (amongst other reasons) that potential investors could be scared off by ethnic tensions. A similarly strong interest in improving the precipitous situation in Stavropol' did not exist. Nevertheless, Stavropol' was also of particular importance for the federal government because it has always been an outpost for the Russian government in the North Caucasus. In 2009, when the Southern Federal District comprising all Northern Caucasian regions was split into two parts by President Medvedev, Stavropol' became the only region in the newly created North Caucasus Federal District which featured a Russian majority population.[7] As most money flowing in and out the ethnic republics is channelled through Stravropol' *krai*, the region has also become a financial centre for North Caucasus (Foxall 2013: 164).

As regards the functioning of the platforms established to manage ethnic issues, our cases reveal a different outcome in both regions. Whereas the platforms in Krasnodar were used as an opportunity fostering collaboration between state and non-state actors, the authorities in Stavropol' more or less feigned partnership and cooperative relations between state authorities and ethnic NGOs. This finding seems to be somewhat paradoxical since the regional government of Stavropol' had widely refrained from exploiting migration and playing the ethnic card for populist strategies, whereas the governors in Krasnodar '...indulged in fiery denunciations of migrants, usually on an ethnic basis, and emphasized the threat they pose to the... (region's) security...' (Light 2016: 124). Considering the federal government's development strategy in Krasnodar, the 'similar-cases-different-outcome' research design underlying this chapter (see Gerring 2008) suggests an important role of the federal authorities in promoting collaborative forms of governance in the regions. This, however, is not to say that the federal-regional relations investigated in our case studies are exclusively shaped top-down; one can instead observe an intricate interplay between the centre and the federal subjects on the one hand and state and non-state actors at regional level on the other.

This chapter is based on a case study design which allows for contextualising the research question (see Yin 2014). Two platforms in each region dealing with ethnic issues were selected for empirical investigation (see Table 7.1). They represent prominent examples coping with (youth) ethnic issues (Mikirova 2016: 77); however, they cannot cover the whole spectrum of networks in both regions and therefore allow just for preliminary conclusions. The data were analysed by using method triangulation. A primary technique for data collection was semi-structured face-to-face interviews. Finally, a total of more than 50 interviews with representatives of ethnic NGOs covering nearly all relevant groups, deputies of local parliaments, officials of regional administrations and of regional departments of federal ministries, experts and representatives of local businesses was realised (see Mikirova 2016: 213–216). Even though it was impossible to cover all participants in each platform, Karina Mikirova, the interviewer, was able to talk to many actors. Most interviews could be taped. Besides, the interviewer also attended meetings and round tables so that supplementary notes could be made. In addition, regional and national legal documents as well as local and national media and newsletters of state and non-state actors were analysed (see Mikirova 2016). For ethic reasons, all interviews are made anonymous in the following. For citations in this chapter we only refer to region and category of respondent.

7.3   FORMAL INSTITUTIONS AND LEGAL FRAMEWORK

All federal states need a minimum of vertical integration in order to prevent separation and to avoid falling apart. Accordingly, researchers emphasise that strong regional parties and intertwined subnational networks are a peril for the cohesion of decentralised, ethnically divided federations (Wolff 2011; Brancati 2009). During the Yeltsin era, most governors and the ethnic republics' presidents were not members of federalised parties but rested their power on regional voter bases and informal regional networks. Regional leaders controlled economic, financial, and legal resources, established subnational authoritarian regimes and monopolised national-subnational linkages—most apparently financial flows (Deryugin and Kurlandskaya 2007). Since 2000, in order to resolve the struggle between the ethno-territorial units and the federal government, much power has been shifted to the federal level. With 'United Russia' (*Edinaya Rossiya*), a hegemonic party loyal to the president was created at all territorial levels in order to re-establish vertical integration and to tame regional elites who had gained far-reaching self-sufficiency under Yeltsin (see Smyth et al. 2007; Reuter 2010). After a couple of years, most local, regional, and business elites had been co-opted from above into the recentralised party-based regime

(Gel'man 2010: 10; Ross 2010).[8] Today, the governors are not only accountable to their regional publics (despite electoral manipulation), but also expected to act as agents of the Kremlin. The federal government expects regional and local political elites to prevent protest, ensure mass loyalty, solve policy problems and guarantee election results favourable for the Kremlin (Gel'man and Ryzhenkov 2011: 456). Securing interethnic stability and peace is also part of these expectations.

The term 'power vertical' commonly used to describe the core of the federal-regional relations tends to obscure the fact that the links between the centre and the regions are shaped by interdependencies, albeit with a predominating centre. Overall, the federal government acts pragmatically with regional authorities rather than dogmatically (DeBardeleben and Zherebtsov 2010: 99). Within their territories, the governors have preserved leeway for shaping various governance styles (Sharafutdinova 2009; Reisinger 2013). Governance networks can be brought to life most differently in the regions.

As regards ethnic and youth issues, the federal subjects possess relevant powers for creating their own problem-solving strategies. Despite the remarkable recentralisation Russia has witnessed since the early 2000s, in this policy area the distribution of responsibilities was not considerably altered. Studies confirm a noteworthy passivity of the Kremlin allowing for various regional approaches. Moreover, as long as there is no corresponding federal law, the federal subjects can pass their own regulations. In explaining the various regional outcomes of migration policy—an issue closely related to interethnic peace and security issues—a recent study concluded that the 'final layer of causality...itself depends on regional policies' (Light 2016: 140).

At the federal level, the department of interethnic affairs within the Ministry for Regional Development is responsible for developing ethnic policy strategies. The Ministry of Interethnic Affairs which had existed in the 1990s was integrated into this department. At the regional level, almost every federal subject has established a specialised body reporting to the corresponding regional administrative unit. However, there is no formal subordination between the federal and regional administrative bodies. Critical statements therefore highlight that a coherent ethnic policy 'all of a piece' does not exist in Russia (Mikirova 2016: 106–108). Since the 1990s, interethnic relations and discourses have been strongly 'securitised' (Popov and Kuznetsov 2008: 228). Accordingly, a considerable number of state bodies are concerned with ethnic issues, particularly law enforcement units:

'...if there are ethnic conflicts, the law enforcement bodies start by going to the leaders of *EthNGOs* for help...'.[9] Not coincidentally, the regional branches of the Federal Interior Ministry and the Federal Security Service (*FSB*) took actively part in ethnic processes in Krasnodar and Stavropol' (Mikirova 2016: 149).

Since ethnic policy comprises various sectoralised policies, the legal basis resembles a patchwork consisting of numerous laws, directives, and other normative acts. For a long time, no federal law on nationalities policy had been issued or amended. A concept bill for the 'State Ethnic Policy of the Russian Federation' was adopted in 1996. However, it was not even a law but just a compilation of recommendations and directives. This main document has now become outdated. Since 2006, some reforms regulating migration policy have been put into place (Light 2016: 148–166). In June 2012, Putin also created the so-called 'Presidential Council for Interethnic Relations'.[10] In December 2012, he signed a decree 'On the National Ethnic Policy Strategy of the Russian Federation through 2025',[11] which replaced the 1996 policy on nationalities. According to the document, the main issues which require special attention of the state and municipal authorities are the preservation and development of cultures and languages of the peoples in Russia. It is also stipulated that the rights of indigenous groups and national minorities are to be protected. Ethnic policy in the North Caucasus is especially emphasised.

In line with the general objective to create a 'managed' civil society (Cheskin and March 2015), the new strategy regards cooperation with civil society organisations as being an important mechanism. Collaboration between state and non-state actors is considered as a priority which needs to be enhanced in order to join forces. Correspondingly, scholars observed considerable efforts to improve local civil society building and conflict management in the North Caucasian regions (Savva and Tishkov 2012). In accordance with the overall objectives of the Russian government, the plan of action to implement this strategy provides resources for capacity building among civil society organisations.[12] Moreover, the government intensified its relations with Muslim organisations in 2007 by creating the 'Fund to Support Islamic Culture, Science and Education' and establishing a privileged relationship with Russia's Council of Muftis. This included the coordination of work on the regional level (Braginskaya 2012).

The basic idea of cultural autonomy grants the right of cultural self-determination to ethnic minorities. In the eyes of the Russian population, Russians have only a weak ability for ethnic mobilisation (Foxall

2010: 693, 2015). State assistance and organisational support are guaranteed to minority groups but, to the Russian majority's discontent, not to Russian NGOs: '...they (ethnic minorities) are coming here and have the right to be financed. They establish ECAs [ethnic cultural autonomies, the authors]....If we got money, we would finance the propaganda of Slavic culture'.[13] Federal law no. 74 'On national cultural autonomies', which was adopted in 1996 and amended several times, guarantees NGOs defining themselves as ECAs some particular rights, such as the right to obtain education in their own language, the protection of their respective language, or the opportunity to get access to media. Based on their particular status, ECAs (or national cultural autonomies) have become the most common type of ethnic NGOs (see also Osipov 2013).[14] Moreover, the mentioned law provided the fundamentals for regional and local administrations to establish public councils on ethnic cultural autonomies' affairs. Mikirova (2016: 117) regards these bodies as prototypes for the establishment of the platforms.

In addition to and for further substantiating federal laws, the federal subjects adopt their own legislative acts regulating ethnic issues.[15] In Krasnodar and Stavropol', resolutions of the governor and target programmes represented the main documents in this sphere.[16] Markedly, the corresponding law in Krasnodar emphasised the development of interactions and collaboration between state actors and different types of NGOs as a main goal of regional ethnic policy. It also mentioned that state actors lack information and coordination as resources essential to resolve conflicts and organise interethnic relations. In both regions, the legal documents aim at supporting ethnic NGOs, at initiating cooperative relations between state and non-state actors, and at preventing extremism and ethnic conflicts. In the first target program which was adopted in Stravropol' in 2006, no financial support was budgeted for realising the objectives. In the successor programme of 2010, however, about 10 million roubles were provided; in Krasnodar, the target program stipulated that 3.5 million roubles had to be spent every year (Mikirova 2016: 142). Therefore, some legal and financial preconditions for establishing platforms dealing with ethnic issues were given in both regions.

Most notably, interactions between state and non-state actors were officially regarded as an indispensable consequence of mutual resource dependence, even though not all state actors made the same efforts to establish collaborations with NGOs. To mediate, diminish and prevent inter-ethnic conflicts, numerous 'platforms' incorporating ethnic NGOs, experts and other private actors have been established. In 2007, 62 out of 84 regions had already founded such advisory bodies which were mostly initiated top-down by state actors (Mikirova 2016: 118). Regional and local executives can shape the platforms to their own purposes (Richter 2009a: 15). Correspondingly, these bodies differ significantly with respect to their objectives, composition, and organisation. Regional administrations established corresponding departments responsible for coordinating state and civil society activities. It needs to be mentioned that the platforms in ethnic policy should not be confused with the public chambers. While the regional public chambers, which are modelled on the 'Public Chamber of the Russian Federation',[17] were created to coordinate state and societal actors in all relevant policies (Richter 2009a, b, cf. Chap. 2), the platforms studied in this chapter focus on a single policy, i.e. ethnic issues.

The regional and local platforms were not formed in order to enable private actors to control regional administrations. Rather they were initiated to make policy-making more efficient by involving resource-rich non-state actors, which can deliver information and expertise, enhance legitimacy, or contribute to the coordination of various types of actors, into the policy process. These bodies should also not just be assessed as a government tool for getting societal interests under control. They were instead designed as an instrument for civil society actors participating in policy-making (Evans 2008). Their most relevant, non-exclusive, and sometimes overlapping functions are consultancy, coordination, conflict management, and, to a lesser degree, involvement into implementation (see Kropp and Aasland, Chap. 9). They were created to '…become a formal structure for interactions between state and non-state actors, promote transparency in the state's work…, increase the effectiveness of feedback…[and] the potential expertise of public authorities by attracting NGOs…' (Mikirova 2016: 92). However, their responsibilities are limited insofar as platforms cannot make binding decisions but can only be recommended for implementation; just a few laws mention that state bodies have to at least respond to these recommendations in written form (Mikirova 2016: 97). As the following section reveals, non-state actors gained considerable strength in some cases (see below). The case studies also show whether or not (and why) ethnic NGOs could effectively influence decisions or whether and why some networks just gained symbolic value.

Compared to other types of NGOs, ethnic NGOs involved in this study share some distinct features. Nearly all ethnic NGOs (except GONGOs) are established bottom-up, based on the principle of ethnic affiliation. They usually comprise a dozen to as many as a hundred officially registered members, but informally also include family members. Moreover, they '... possess idiosyncratic resources, which consist of the...popularity and authority of the head of EthNGO in the ethnic group and in the regional population' (Mikirova 2016: 158). In fact, the organisation is usually headed by a prominent representative of the respective ethnic group, someone such as a scientist or a businessman. Different from Russian NGOs, ethnic NGOs representing minorities can get financial aid through the state budgets. Altogether, ethnic NGOs usually rely on mixed funding which comes from membership dues and from contributions of ethnic businessmen with the latter being the most important financial source (Mikirova 2016: 114). In addition, though, the funding is supplemented by financial resources generated from the ethnic mother countries and provided by international grants. With the 'Foreign Agents Law' adopted in 2012 (FZ-121, 20 July 2012), however, external funding has become more complicated since organisations receiving money from abroad have to register and declare themselves as 'foreign agents'.

7.4   Empirical Findings

7.4.1   Meta-Governance and Governance Networks: Adapting the Analytical Framework to Ethnic Policy

The case studies build on the general assumption that state and non-state actors create governance networks because both sides depend on each other's resources (see Berg-Nordlie et al., Chap. 2). A second basic conjecture guiding this chapter is that horizontal and vertical modes of governance form a fluid and variable mix. As has been frequently confirmed for Western democracies, governance networks rarely appear as self-regulating bodies but instead need to be governed by the state authorities to achieve the desired outcome. Correspondingly, it is supposed that regional authorities in Russia employ a versatile toolkit of instruments in order to govern the platforms in ethnic policy, ranging from the classical hierarchical tools to coercion but also to collaborative ways of interaction.

In order to grasp these interactions between state and non-state actors, some basic tools of 'meta-governance' are distinguished in the following (Vabo and Røiseland 2012). Like the other chapters in this book, this one refers to the analytical framework (NATO) after the four ideal-typical policy tools (Hood 1983; see Berg-Nordlie et al., Chap. 2): nodality, authority, treasure, and organisation. In our study, this framework is first and foremost applied to the regional level since that is where the legal responsibility for initiating and managing platforms in ethnic and youth policy is located. Yet, Russian federal authorities often encroach upon subnational issues. Multilevel aspects are therefore taken into account whenever it is appropriate and necessary for understanding the context in which the ethnic platforms operate (see Fig. 7.1). Furthermore, it is illustrated whether regional and federal authorities apply the instruments to govern networks in a 'soft' or 'hard' manner.

Due to the strong asymmetries shaping the relations between state and civil society to the disadvantage of the non-state actors, state authorities are usually suggested as holding a nodal position within the networks. *Nodality* denotes the ability of actors to spread information among the other network participants (Hood 1983: 6). If authorities are earnestly interested in resolving ethnic conflicts, they should communicate and exchange information with the representatives of ethnic organisations. Interestingly, regional target programs dedicated to ethnic issues frankly admit that information is a scarce resource and often exclusively provided by non-state actors (see above). By changing the background assumption in this way, it can be supposed that the position of state actors in the platforms is not necessarily as central as assumed by government-biased theories.

Authority, again, implies the ability of a government to force non-state actors into a certain behaviour. The authoritative rule is strongly associated with regulations and legislation and often accompanied by negative sanctions (Vabo and Røiseland 2012: 4). In a hybrid regime like Russia, however, it is often more than just law or the 'shadow' of hierarchy which is cast on governance networks. Considering that the rule of law is realised deficiently in Russia, coercive or repressive instruments, all tending to impair or even disconnect networks, are of high relevance even if they are not applied immediately. The mere opportunity that they *could* be used may prompt actors to adjust their behaviour in advance. Such constellations, however, tend to diminish the benefits of collaborating with non-state actors, first and foremost because unbiased information and expert knowledge can hardly be achieved. Empirically, these indirect effects are difficult to assess. But it can be expected that state authorities avoid applying or even referring to 'hard' tools of authority, as long as they are truly interested in collaboration. Correspondingly, modern theories discussing the nature of hybrid and authoritarian regimes emphasise that rulers usually prefer meeting the majority public preferences, using incentives, or manipulating public opinion instead of resorting to blanket repression (Petrov et al. 2014: 2).

The same is true for another tool labelled '*treasure*' in the NATO-framework. In order to realise public goals, state authorities often promote governance networks by funding private actors. In keeping with the efforts to create a 'constructive' and loyal civil society, regional and federal budgets provide financial means for domestic NGOs. Conversely, the concurrent Russian government's efforts to control NGOs receiving subsidies from abroad ('Foreign Agents Law') illustrate that governments may also link 'treasure' to legal instruments ('authority') in order to dry up NGOs financially. Governments rarely rely on '*treasure*' alone but combine it with other tools such as authority and nodality (Hood 1983: 49), as the following case studies will demonstrate.

Principally, governments have the choice of resorting to their own organisational resources and acting directly through their administration instead of using governance networks. '*Organisation*' therefore confers strong resources to governments because it is left to their discretion as to whether or not they share resources with private actors. It was convincingly argued that 'organisation' is a prerequisite for applying the three other resources so that a clear and selective distinction between organisation and the other tools to govern networks cannot be drawn (Vabo and Røiseland 2012, see Berg-Nordlie et al., Chap. 2). Nonetheless, it is more than 'just a simple derivative' of them (Hood 1983: 6). An aspect strongly confining the use of organisational tools is state capacity. In this view, the platforms in ethnic policy can be interpreted as a means of supplementing the limited organisational capacities of the state.

Figure 7.1 depicts these meta-governance strategies and illustrates how the governing of networks is embedded into the context of the Russian federal system. The federal aspect is especially relevant for understanding ethnic policy since it is at the heart of multilevel relations. Federal authorities may show a certain interest in having ethnic platforms established at regional level, as far as they are truly interested in participating in the resources of ethnic NGOs and other non-state actors. Accordingly, the two arrows in

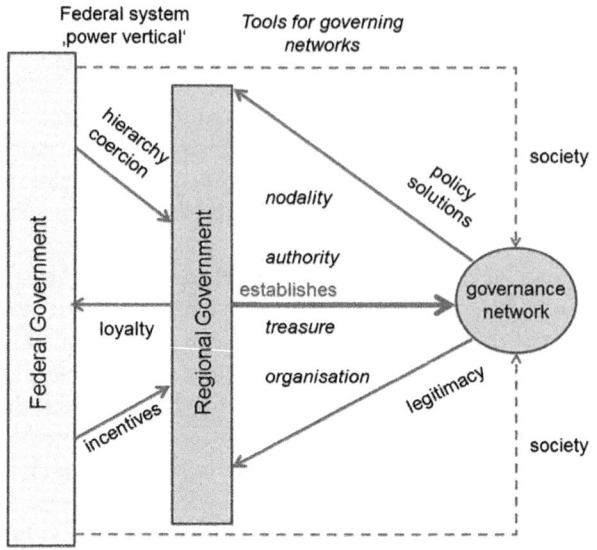

Fig. 7.1   Meta-governance in the Russian multilevel context. *Source* Own production referring to (Hood 1983; Vabo and Røiseland 2012: 4)

Fig. 7.1 running from the federal to the regional government suggest that the federal government can direct regional authorities either by resorting to hierarchical or even coercive instruments related to the 'power vertical', or by using subtler incentives. More specifically, federal authorities strive for achieving their goals by giving instructions to subnational governments, for instance by passing laws, by taking hand in regional elite selection, by transferring financial means, etc. The dashed arrows connecting the federal government and the governance network symbolise that the federal government's influence, if at all, on the network is more indirect than immediate. The arrows running from the governance network to regional governments again illustrate that networks are basically designed to deliver policy solutions which are tailored to regional needs and to enhance legitimacy. The federal government expects regional authorities to transfer the results of network strategies successfully to the federal government and to demonstrate loyalty. In order to produce the desired policy solutions, the regional government applies the above-mentioned NATO-tools. This can be done in a 'hard' or 'soft' way.

7.4.2   The Regional Context

As regards ethnic policy, since the 1990s Krasnodar and Stavropol' have had to cope with disadvantageous initial conditions. Regional authorities were faced with severe ethnic conflicts and reacted restrictively to illegal migration (Foxall 2014). In *Krasnodar*, the former governor Nikolai Kondratenko drew upon ethnic conflicts in order to mobilise the Cossacks as his power base, and massively discriminated against other ethnic groups. Aleksandr Tkachev, who was elected governor in 2001 and served as 'hand-picked successor' of Kondratenko, continued this policy and made the Cossacks his quasi-state agents. Both governors, who were initially attached to the Russian Communist Party, frequently quarrelled with the federal government. They presented themselves as guarantors of regional interests 'against a predatory national government' and politicised ethnic issues in order to strengthen their position vis-à-vis the federal government (Light 2016: 124, 134). Tkachev even proposed creating '..."filtration camps"...throughout the territory to detain and deport illegal migrants with non-Slavic surnames' (Swerdlow 2006: 1839). Regional authorities passed several laws restricting illegal migration and declared some ethnic groups as unwanted. Law enforcement agencies undertook regular passport controls and arrested people without registration. Lacking permanent registration, migrants were not employed by local businesses and did not receive education or social support. In law No. 9-KZ of June 23, 1996, for instance, discrimination against 'migrants' was given legal form since it stipulated the need of a 10-year settlement to become registered. According to law No. 460-KZ adopted in April 11, 2002, ethnic minorities were considered to be collectively responsible for violations of arrival and residence regulations (Popov and Kuznetsov 2008: 233, 234). Ethnic discrimination even attracted international attention after the USA had invited and nationalised about 12,000 Meskhetian Turks settling in Krasnodar *krai*. This ethnic group had been exiled to Central Asia under Stalin and moved to Krasnodar after massive pogroms had taken place in the Ferghana Valley in 1989 and 1990 (Popov and Kuznetsov 2008: 234–235). Even though the Meskhetian Turks possessed the legal status of Russian citizens, their treatment in Krasnodar rendered them de facto stateless persons (Swerdlow 2006: 1842).

The official policy of the governor handed lower officials carte blanche for discriminating migrants in Krasnodar (Light 2016: 125). Some discriminating laws were later abolished through pressure from the federal government; the federal Ministry of Justice removed discriminating parts of the regional legislation (Mikirova 2016: 133). In the early 2000s however, Krasnodar was still regarded as a region hallmarked by tense ethnic conflicts and rightly considered to be one of the most problematic regions in Russia. After assessing the situation in Krasnodar *krai*, observers came to the conclusion that Tkachev was not driven by blind xenophobia, but followed deliberate political calculations. By mobilising the citizens with anti-migrant resentments, the governor tried to compel the federal government to accept him as leader (Light 2016: 131), to legitimise his rule and strengthen his regional regime. In fact, Tkachev, who finally joined 'United Russia' in 2003 and headed the party list for the elections to the national parliament, became one of the strong political figures in North Caucasus and succeeded in staying in office until 2015. Since then, he has been Federal Minister of Agriculture.

Before the Kremlin tried to interfere into this tense situation, the regional administration had not pursued close collaboration with ethnic NGOs. Neither was it inclined to involve ethnic civil society organisations in order to extinguish the conflicts. The situation did not change until the federal government decided to smooth ethnic tensions in order to promote Krasnodar's economic and social development and to curb some of the governor's excesses (Light 2016: 140). It is to be mentioned, however, that ethnic NGOs were already in the 1990s more active than their counterparts in Stavropol' and had tried to convince the regional administration that civil society participation was indispensable for mediating and preventing ethnic conflicts (Mikirova 2016; Light 2016: 128). The regional civil society landscape was, in fact, more diverse; in 2007 more than 120 ethnic NGOs resided in the Krasnodar region (compared to about 90 in Stavropol'). In the report of the Public Chamber on the state of civil society published in 2008, Krasnodar ranged higher than Stavropol' regarding the regional level of public activity.[18] After Krasnodar had become a preferred object of the Kremlin's economic development strategy, the NGOs' intentions to calm down the precarious situation began to correspond at least to the federal government's preferences. The Kremlin enforced collaboration between regional authorities and NGOs in order to pacify the region: 'There were protest applications to the president, and they (the federal authorities) began to pressurise the regional authorities'.[19] The regional administration headed by governor Tkachev obtained instructions to alter its course. It commenced incorporating civil society organisations; for instance, the tense relations with the Armenian community could be improved. In 2005, for the first time the governor met with representatives of 40 ethnic NGOs (Mikirova 2016: 136). Different from Stavropol', where the platforms continued playing a negligible role in settling ethnic conflicts, NGOs finally became a more relevant partner for state actors within the investigated platforms. In 2007, the Federation Council of the Federal Assembly mentioned the experiences of Krasnodar with ethnic policy as a benchmark for other regions (Mikirova 2016: 137). This, however, is not to say that the regional government gave up its anti-migrant approach or that the governor changed his aggressive rhetoric. In 2012, for instance, Tkachev began to form a militia of about 1000 Cossacks in order to eliminate illegal migration and uphold public order, thereby explicitly referring to the situation in Stavropol': in his view, the neighbouring region was regarded as being unable to fulfil its function for filtering and stopping migrants on their way to Krasnodar. Moreover, he fuelled the debate by emphasising that the Russian population in Stavropol' would no longer accept the massive influx of non-Russian migrants.[20]

In *Stavropol' krai*, the federal government did not pursue a development strategy similar to that in Krasnodar (Mikirova 2016), although the region occupies a notable role for the Kremlin due to its geopolitical position in the North Caucasus. Researchers observed a remarkable negligence of regional authorities in interethnic relations. Observers highlight a regional 'tradition of silence' originating from the Soviet past and an understanding of ethnic tensions as being normal for everyday life (Mikirova 2016: 138). In the 1990s, racist organisations received more official support than in other regions in southern Russia, thereby gradually becoming an arm of the regional government (Foxall 2012). Cossack units patrolling the Chechen border were joined by Russian nationalists. Nevertheless, the regional government did not adopt an overtly xenophobic policy comparable to that in Krasnodar, but sought to use the migration issue mainly as a leverage to extract resources from the federal budget (Light 2016: 137). In May 2007, however, ethnic tensions escalated. The region witnessed mass unrests involving some hundred persons and pogroms after two Russians and a Chechen had been killed in a dispute between Slavic and Caucasian adolescents. For weeks, Stavropol' experienced intermittent rioting, while its regional government was unable to get the situation under control and restore order again (Foxall 2013: 159). In 2009, President Dmitry Medvedev stressed that the security situation in North Caucasus was one of the most serious internal problems in Russia. Media analysis conducted around the event illustrate that the official multicultural approach visible in the federal government's ethnic policy did not correspond to its real attitude which in fact promoted dissociative 'ethnic nationalism in both subtle and overt ways' (Schenk 2012: 797). In 2010, after having experienced terrorist attacks and youth riots again, about 10,000 citizens signed an appeal calling on President Medvedev to remove Stavropol' *krai* from the North Caucasus Federal District with its majority of ethnic republics (Foxall 2011: 13).

The political context for establishing ethnic platforms in Stavropol' *krai* was particularly complicated since the region had been politically unstable for years due to the struggle between political elites. Dmitri Kuz'min, elected mayor of the city of Stavropol' and leader of the Kremlin-attached party, 'A Just Russia', competed with Alexandr Chernogorov who had an affiliation with the 'People's Patriotic Union of Russia' which, again, was associated with the Communist Party before the 2007 regional parliamentary elections. Compared to the incumbents in Krasnodar, he was a less powerful political figure and had limited negotiation power. As a re-nominated governor, Chernogorov was supported by the governing hegemonic party 'United Russia' in 2007 due to its pragmatic approach (DeBardeleben and Zherebtsov 2010: 96–99). However, his relations with the hegemonic party deteriorated because he excluded its candidates when forming the government; he reinforced its own personal network instead. 'A Just Russia' finally won the regional parliamentary elections because voters had made the election a vote against the unpopular Chernogorov. Both sides accused each other of not having at hand solutions for coping with the ethnic tensions. The election results not only questioned the concept of 'managed pluralism', according to which party competition can be successfully manufactured by the Kremlin's administration, but also demonstrated Chernogorv's inability to head the regional party branch. The conflict between the parliamentary and the executive branches could be reconciled after Kuz'min had been threatened with a prison sentence and left the country. Chernogorov finally had to give up his office. After Chernogorov had been ousted, Valery Gaevskii, who mainly relied on local cadres but had also worked as deputy minister in the federal government before, was appointed governor.

After the conflict between the legislative and the executive branch had been settled, regional authorities began to draw more attention to ethnic conflicts and established negotiation platforms in ethnic policy. However, different from the Krasnodar regional administration, which defined itself as 'the developers, implementers and performers of regional ethnic policy',[21] the Stravropol' administration still was more reluctant in playing such an active role. Significantly, the head of committee for interethnic relations did not even accept the invitation of one of the relevant NGOs representing a considerable number of ethnic groups residing in the region.

7.4.3   Ethnic Platforms in Use—Interregional Differences

Formally, the two platforms in Stavropol' originated in order to take over basic functions in ethnic policy. The main tasks of the platform S1 *'Advisory Body for Interethnic Affairs'* (S1, see Table 7.1) were fixed in the resolution of the governor of Stavropol' *krai*, 'On the Advisory Body for Interethnic Affairs to the Governor' (2005). The document mentioned the preventing of ethnic conflicts, the preserving of ethnic cultures, and the developing of more harmonious ethnic relations among the different groups. The *'Youth Advisory Body for Interethnic Affairs'* (S2), which was created after the riots in 2007, was also expected to formulate proposals concerning how ethnic, cultural and educational programs for developing youth ethnic policy could be implemented in the region. For both platforms, it was stipulated that the bodies should take part in academic research and that consultations should be held with NGOs and religious organisations to achieve the aforementioned goals. More specifically, the platforms were designed to discuss bills relevant to ethnic questions, to inform the population about the state activities in them; they were also expected to explain the aims of ethnic policy to the media (Mikirova 2016: 166–168).

However, from the beginning the proper functioning of the platforms was ill-fated. The confrontation between both rivalling political camps fuelled the competition between ethnic NGOs in *Stavropol'*. Both party camps established their own, loyal NGO within each ethnic group. This split enforced the fragmentation of civil society groups along party lines, weakened the NGOs on the whole since they were not able to form coalitions, and diminished their weight vis-à-vis the state authorities. In addition, GONGOs were founded by the state administration in order to create private actors attached to the state. Moreover, in the platform *'Advisory Body for Interethnic Affairs'* (S1), Slavic NGOs were not willing to interact with other ethnic organisations.

The Kremlin did not pursue an economic development strategy in Stavropol' comparable to the one in Krasnodar. Moreover, regional and organisational factors exacerbated the emergence of collaborative interactions between state and non-state actors. Between 2006 and 2009, no regional law precisely regulating the cooperation with NGOs within the platforms had been issued in Stavropol'. Although a respective law was drafted in 2007 (see above), it did not pass the regional parliament because of budgetary restrictions. The framework regulating the composition of platforms thus remained rudimentary until 2010. Regional state agents were able to exploit these gaps in current regional legislation in order to avoid bona fide negotiations within the platforms.

Within the NATO-framework, it can be concluded that '*authority*' was not used in order to frame collaboration in a constructive manner but rather to avoid or feign negotiations (see Tables 7.1, 7.2). Throughout the empirical fieldwork, ethnic NGOs in Stavropol' constantly remained in a weaker position than in Krasnodar. Due to their limited financial capabilities, they were forced to spend more time and effort on their own financial survival than on their political and societal goals. As they did not receive financial support from the regional budget ('*treasure*') until 2010, they usually did not even possess an office but were forced to meet in private apartments. Moreover, representatives of NGOs complained that the distribution of financial aid was not transparent. Ethnic NGOs also lacked IT equipment and professional staff. Often, there was nothing else for them to do but to rely on volunteers. Compared to their counterparts in Krasnodar, they had little access to institutions and thus hardly ever participated in policy-making. As the heads of ethnic NGOs changed frequently, personal continuity remained limited. The regional government did not accept ethnic NGOs as partners qualified for developing problem-solving strategies in order to avoid the reasons of ethnic conflicts. Significantly, it was— at best—interested in using NGOs to relieve already existing tensions. Because of this indifference, meetings were not held regularly. The platform S1 ('*Advisory Body for Interethnic Affairs*') in Stavropol' (see Table 7.1) met only about once a year without holding any intermediate meetings of working groups; the platform S2 ('*Youth Advisory Body for Interethnic Affairs*') dealing with inter-ethnic issues of adolescents (see Table 7.1) came together about every three months. Both platforms featured weak organisational structures and were considered to be used only in emergencies.

The composition and the regulations of the negotiation platforms indicate that the formal functions and tasks could be fulfilled insufficiently. In both bodies, decisions were made by majority vote. Normative prescriptions provided no criteria for membership, no information on who was to set the agenda and no regulations on how the bodies were to be run. In general, of course, there is no obligation to implement recommendations given by the platforms. Due to the insufficient regulations, however, state actors were given the opportunity to determine the rules by themselves. Correspondingly, authorities decided ad hoc and on their own which NGOs and experts were invited. The representatives of ethnic NGOs were exclusively nominated and handpicked by the administration. In S1, for instance, more than half of the participants nominated by the state were in fact state actors (Mikirova 2016: 176, see Table 7.1). Changes in composition were decided by the governor alone; NGOs were not even informed that they were no longer members of the platforms. Significantly, participant selection was used as a distinct technique of *authority* to steer and control the networks. Whereas the majority of members came from civil society organisations in S2, state actors clearly dominated the scenery in platform S1: as the meta-governor, the *krai*'s governor headed the platform. Accordingly, critical voices stressed that meetings were only convened 'to illuminate the figure of the governor', as one interviewee put it.[22] Chairing the platform is, in fact, a strong technique to direct and censor the activities of the other network participants (see Berg-Nordlie et al., Chap. 2). Similarly, other representatives of NGOs stressed that the only role of NGOs in the platforms was to increase the legitimacy of state actions (Mikirova 2016: 179).

In a similar vein, the head of the 'Committee for Interethnic and Cossack Affairs' in the regional administration chaired platform S2, thus keeping the organisation under the control of the state. GONGOs were incorporated in both bodies so that any open and problem-oriented debate on ethnic conflicts was limited. In general, it is questionable whether compromises found within the network will be acknowledged by the membership, if participants are not selected by their own constituencies. Therefore, it is no wonder that representatives of NGOs did not or just half-heartedly support the recommendations adopted by the platforms in Stavropol'.

Generally, actors drafting the first proposal are able to predetermine the range of later decisions. Agenda-setting is a strong tool in the hands of a network-governor. Unsurprisingly, the agenda was set and decisions were prepared and made exclusively by the regional authorities in Stavropol'. Since NGOs were confronted with the agenda at the earliest during the meeting, they could not exert effective influence upon which issues were to be discussed. As a consequence, the relationships between the state actors and NGOs were shaped by mutual mistrust. During the ethnic tensions

Stavropol' *krai* was faced with between 2007 and 2009, the authorities initiated checks of those ethnic NGOs openly advancing their own positions. Participating in the platforms was theoretically possible; in practice, however, it was limited (Mikirova 2016: 180, 182). A representative of an ethnic NGO characterised the relations between state and non-state actors as follows: 'Is this normal politics? ...We cannot participate in anything...It is not possible to work with the authorities. They manipulate and deceive. In fact, we don't participate'.[23]

To put it in a nutshell, authorities in Stavropol' region created Potemkin villages feigning harmonious ethnic relations. Whereas in platform S2 the state actors aimed at getting at least some consultancy and information from loyal NGOs and therefore established a dialogue which, however, remained under state control, the paternalistic features were stronger in platform S1. Nevertheless, regional rulers at least realised 'the need to present the territory as "stable" in order to secure a place for itself in the changing landscape of power in post-Soviet Russia' (Foxall 2015: 125). Finally, NGOs took part in the meetings in order to obtain at least some information on what was on the government's agenda and to gain marginal government support. Information as a resource (*nodality*) was mostly on the part of the administration which decided autonomously which pieces were given to NGOs. Ethnic NGOs were barely appreciated as a source for getting unbiased information. As imitation and control remained the dominant features shaping the platforms in Stavropol', the resources of ethnic NGOs were not exploited in order to establish efficiently working governance networks. Therefore, it is not surprising that in the end neither S1 nor S2 were able to manage ethnic conflicts effectively.

Organisation, membership and regulations of the platforms in *Krasnodar* differed remarkably from their counterparts in Stavropol' *krai*.[24] Significantly, both platforms examined in this study were not set up by the regional governor and his administration, which had been on a hostile course against ethnic minorities and migrants for years. That the regional governor did not chair the platform was probably conducive to the functioning of the advisory bodies. The '*platform for ethnic issues*' in Krasnodar (K1, see Table 7.1) was founded by the NGO 'Centre of Ethnic Cultures'. This NGO, which was established as an umbrella organisation, was initiated by NGOs and the Krasnodar city administration in 1992. By 2007, it had already comprised more than 30 ethnic NGOs. The leaders of the NGOs were acknowledged authorities within their corresponding groups. After 2000, the Centre gradually changed its initial functions and finally became a platform for interactions with state actors; but different from the other platforms analysed in this chapter it preserved its more informal structure (Mikirova 2016: 170). As its main tasks, the preservation of ethnic groups living in Krasnodar *krai*, the strengthening of interethnic dialogue and peace as well as the protection of rights of ethnic minorities can be mentioned. The '*Advisory Body for Socially Important Issues*' in Krasnodar (K2, see Table 7.1), again, which is an advisory body to the regional department of the Federal Interior Ministry, was initiated by this department in 2005. Its tasks are similar to that of K1, although special emphasis was laid on the fight against extremism among ethnic youth groups through cooperation between state actors and NGOs. In K2, state actors were not allowed to be formal members, but instead participated in the meetings as experts, among them representatives of departments for Cossack affairs, for interaction with public and religious organisations, etc. (Mikirova 2016: 187). In both cases, the cooperation between state and private actors was based on a rather sound legal basis making interactions more predictable than in Stavropol'. Meetings were held frequently: K1 met at least twice a month. Although plenary sessions of K2 took place only twice a year (this is even less frequently than in Stavropol'), the working groups of this platform continually came together. In the working groups, the majority of members were non-state actors. However, state actors could principally take a leading position in the working groups, since the heads are elected by the groups in an open vote. In the main body, state actors had the status of experts and thus were not allowed to vote. Decisions in the platforms were taken by majority vote and had recommendation status.

The composition of the platforms differed significantly from those established in Stavropol'. Critical, albeit not 'antagonistic' NGOs were invited to the meetings,[25] since the state authorities appreciated their expert knowledge and regarded the reputation of the leaders within their ethnic groups as a source of legitimacy. Agendas were jointly elaborated in platform K2. Every member had the right to amend the agenda, which was distributed at least seven days before the meetings (Mikirova 2016: 173). If there was disagreement among the members, a mediation committee could be convened in order to settle open questions. For platform K1, the procedures for agenda-setting and decision-making were not explicitly defined. But in fact, NGOs made the agenda, appointed implementers, and invited state actors. Both platforms were chaired by a representative of an ethnic NGO (K1) or an independent expert (K2); the state and administrative actors refrained from guiding the network directly and, regarding meta-governance techniques, applied a remarkably softer version of *authority* than in Stavropol'. Accordingly, the participants on the side of non-state actors were appointed by the ethnic NGOs and not handpicked by state authorities. The interviewed members of NGOs confirmed that state representatives were willing to rest decisions on the NGOs' suggestions and accept their recommendations as guidelines for authoritative decisions. Representatives of the regional administration would not try to dominate the discussion so that problems could be deliberated candidly. Some state actors even explicitly confined their role to that of an observer. By participating in the networks, NGOs not just delivered legitimacy, consultative and coordinate resources to the state, but got—albeit limited —access to policymaking in return. The implementation of decisions was shared between state and non-state actors.

Altogether, *authority* was applied in smaller doses. In contrast to the practice in Stavropol', the regional administration refrained from adopting the role of a network governor in both platforms but delegated this role to non-state actors. The presence of state actors, however, increased the likelihood that decisions of the platforms were implemented after the meetings. Regional authorities did not essentially operate through their own administration in Krasnodar, whereas state authorities in Stavropol' acted through their own *organisation* while networks were more or less mimicked. Different from the platforms in Stavropol', their counterparts in Krasnodar featured characteristics of *horizontal* governance: 'We (the NGOs) and they (the regional administration and the security services) are on the right track. Problems are discussed and solved jointly'.[26] Mikirova (2016: 189) concludes that in contrast to Stavropol', where the platforms just simulated teamwork in order to increase the legitimacy of the regional government, the corresponding bodies in Krasnodar exhibited remarkable non-hierarchical features. The participating NGOs can best be characterised as 'cooperative' forces: 'Solely playing opposition (...) is not effective (...). If you want to move something, you should be somewhat willing to act within the system'.[27]

Unsurprisingly, the financial situation of NGOs was better than in Stavropol'. NGOs usually possessed offices, staff and professional equipment (*treasure*). Unlike in the neighbouring region, their activities were supported by regional funding programs even before 2007 and partly financed by the regional budget. It may be debated whether state funding subverts the independence of non-state actors. In fact, it seems unrealistic to expect NGOs to survive without such funding.

By specifying which tools were chosen and how they were applied in Krasnodar and Stavropol', Table 7.2 reveals marked interregional differences. After the federal government had issued orders to the Krasnodar regional government and had taken a hand in establishing cooperation with non-state actors, a comparatively 'softer' version of meta-governance (see Berg-Nordlie et al., Chap. 2) was adopted by the regional administration in Krasnodar. Yet, the platforms should not be understood as an embodiment of self-regulating networks formulating generally binding rules subsequently adopted by the state. Even in the 'softly' governed platforms in

Table 7.2 Meta-governance: tools for governing platforms in Krasnodar and Stavropol

Tools	Krasnodar	Stavropol'
Nodality	Information and expertise on the part of strong non-state actors; no central position of state actors in the platforms; non-state actors as network governors	Information and expertise on the part of state actors, weak NGOs; state actors as network governors
Authority	Instructions of federal authorities to the regional ones, application of 'power vertical' in order to establish horizontal governance modes at regional level	No corresponding federal instructions
	Authority used as a soft tool at regional level; state does not overtly dominate non-state actors	Authority used as a hard tool at regional level; state actors dominate non-state actors
	Regional legislation to establish platforms, some gaps	Regional legislation with regulatory gaps (until 2010), allows state actors to define the working of platforms
Treasure	Funding given to loyal and critical NGOs; state widely abstains from creating asymmetries between NGOs	Less funding given to NGOs (until 2010); if so, non-critical NGOs are preferred
Organisation	Regional and federal authorities do not mainly operate through state administration	Regional authorities operate through their own administration while networks are more or less imitated

Source Own compilation, based on Mikirova (2016)

Krasnodar, the state actors kept a basic role in the background. Although they more or less took their 'hands off' from the everyday working of the networks, authorities could have applied harder tools in order to shape the platforms to their advantage. In contrast to the practice in Krasnodar, the instruments explored in Stavropol' were used in a more hierarchical manner. There, the platforms more or less imitated governance networks and were shaped by mutual mistrust and asymmetrical relationships, leading to a network type which is labelled as 'mimicked' in the final chapter of this book (see Kropp and Aasland, Chap. 9).

Multilevel relations and governance networks were neatly interwoven in both regions, but overall created different constellations. In neither case did the state appear as a unitary actor. A major factor favouring horizontal governance in Krasnodar was the federal government's interest in attracting national and international investments and improving the region's infrastructure. Mediating ethnic tensions was a constitutive part of this strategy. The Kremlin enforced its development strategy by resorting to some vertical tools of authority in Krasnodar, although it remained reluctant to intervene into the discriminating policies of the regional governor (Light 2016: 115–147). Paradoxically, however, by applying the instruments of the 'power *vertical*' the Kremlin tried to facilitate a *horizontal* governance mode. While in Krasnodar a close coalition between the federal state and investors tended to spawn hierarchical relations with civil society actors in environmental policy (see Schuhmann and Kropp, Chap. 4; Kropp and Schuhmann 2016), the same constellation supported governance networks in ethnic policy. This finding again illustrates that policy does matter, because it considerably shapes actor constellations (see Kropp and Aasland, Chap. 9). Another relevant factor promoting horizontal networks in Krasnodar was the rather high level of NGOs' activity, something which had existed from the outset.

Vice versa, a regional economic strategy related to such an important event as the Winter Olympics in 2014 was not on the top of the federal government's priority list for Stavropol' *krai*, and the governor remained a weaker and rather unimportant political figure at the federal stage. Hence, if regional authorities in Stavropol' had really been interested in collaboration, they would have had the opportunity to revive the platforms and establish true collaborations with ethnic NGOs. However, the lack of overt discrimination against migrants shaping the early 2000s (Light 2016) does not imply that the regional administration actively invigorated the platforms. Although the Kremlin intervened into the heated situation around the 2007 riots in Stavropol' and also withdrew subnational rulers, it did not take a hand in the platforms. Random factors further complicated their effectivity. The outlined conflicts between the two branches of government and party camps exacerbated the fragmentation of ethnic NGOs and impaired their ability to form coalitions with other organisations. In any case, NGOs were weaker and less active than their counterparts in Krasnodar.

Obviously, regional authorities in Stavropol' were interested in curtailing the existing ethnic conflicts, but lacked the administrative capacity, political authority, trust, and ideas of how to effectively use the platforms in order to manage and prevent ethnic conflicts. Consequently, the case studies conducted in Stavropol' pose the question why authorities undertook efforts to imitate networks while in the end remaining rather inactive. Considering this puzzle, isomorphism suggests a denotation of these bodies which has not yet been highlighted by governance network theory (see Kropp and Aasland, Chap. 9). Institutional and organisational models such as governance networks, may serve as blueprints 'travelling' through different political contexts. Political actors spend considerable resources on emulating such models because they hope to increase legitimacy by adopting widely acknowledged solutions (Meyer and Rowan 1977). The theory also explains the low effectivity of the ethnic platforms in Stavropol'. Regional rulers did not substantially change their governance style and continued governing through the state organisation while feigning collaboration with private actors.

7.5 Concluding Discussion

The empirical findings provide the opportunity to reason about some theoretical and empirical implications. *Firstly*, it was shown that the platforms in Krasnodar resemble the type of softly state-managed networks, whereas their counterparts in Stavropol' are close to the type of mimicked networks, which remained ineffective in the end. Nonetheless, the empirical findings reveal that although these 'mimicked' networks were not able to settle or prevent ethnic tensions, they did nonetheless fulfil some systemic functions. By establishing ethnic platforms, regional incumbents demonstrated their readiness to conform to the model of managed civil society involvement imposed by the federal government. Moreover, they signalled to the public that some collaboration with non-state actors had been set off and that the voice of ethnic NGOs had been heard—although the heads of ethnic NGOs in Stavropol' complained about the 'dummy' character of the platforms. As was shown, however, even in such bodies actors were able to exchange at least some resources.

Thus, in establishing governance networks, regional incumbents respond to their 'sandwich position' typical for the recentralised Russian federal setting: they are expected to prevent political tensions, protests and riots, but also to strengthen legitimacy and deliver the desired policy results to the federal authorities (see Fig. 7.1). Not surprisingly, the governors in both regions did not actively promote the involvement of ethnic NGOs. They rather suspected collaboration with non-state actors, the more so as ethnic issues are closely related to security questions and regarded as a threat to the Russian state's integrity. Significantly, in Krasnodar, where the governor did not cease from playing the ethnic card, it was not the regional authorities initiating the platforms, but rather the NGOs and the regional department of the Federal Interior Ministry. Regional authorities had not been interested in utilising the platforms until the federal government signalled its will to activate the bodies for developing the region. Yet, despite the indisputable relevance of the federal government, the case studies revealed that subnational policy approaches dedicated to cope with ethnic issues vary significantly, even under the conditions of strongly 'verticalised' relations between the federal centre and the federal subjects. Specific 'regional' factors seem to explain much of the variation; this is a *second* lesson to be drawn when comparing the use of platforms in ethnic policy across regions.

Thirdly, our findings induce us to remain sceptical when considering the sustainability of governance networks. Network participants, including state actors, may continue with ethnic platforms, once they have experienced them as effective working bodies. However, it still has to be clarified what will happen when the federal government—as meta-governor—no longer appears as the main driver of the platforms. Given that regional authorities have low interest in getting on with governance networks, it seems plausible that network activities may expire or just carry symbolic value. In order to review such developments and further evaluate causal links, long-term observations which go beyond the scope of this article are necessary. As a research strategy, it would be useful replicating some case studies, particularly those conducted in Krasnodar. There, it could be reassessed whether or not the interest of federal authorities in running ethnic platforms decreased after the Winter Olympics in 2014, and whether or not the regional authorities have sustained these working bodies.

NOTES

1. *Perepis naselenija* 2010, http://www.gks.ru/free_doc/new_site/perepis2010/croc/perepis_itogi1612.htm. (accessed October 10, 2016).
2. See for instance report on the state of civil society in the Russian Federation 2007, the public chamber of the Russian Federation, Moscow 2007: 47.
3. *Perepis naselenija* 2010, http://www.gks.ru/free_doc/new_site/perepis2010/croc/perepis_itogi1612.htm (accessed October 10, 2016).
4. In 2002, the proportion of ethnic Russians in Krasnodar accounted for 86.6% of the population. Other large ethnic groups are Armenians and Ukrainians. The ethnic composition was similar in Stavropol', where ethnic Russians made up 81.6% of the regional population (80.9% in 2010). See All-Russian population census of 2002, http://www.perepis2002.ru/index.html?id=17 , see also *perepis naselenija* 2010; Mikirova (2016): 70–74.
5. 'Target programs for the economic development of the economy of the Krasnodar region', see for example http://fcp.economy.gov.ru/cgi-bin/cis/fcp.cgi/Fcp/Title/ and http://economy.krasnodar.ru/gos-prog-kk/perech-gp/, accessed April 2, 2017.
6. For the Circassian question see Richmond (2013), Markedonov (2014: 11–15).
7. The other six federal subjects being part of the North Caucasus Federal District are ethnic republics (Chechnya, Dagestan, Ingushetia, Kabardino-Balkaria, Karachaevo-Cherkessia, North Ossetia-Alania).
8. In addition, the last Chechen war (1999–2009) restored the Russian control over the renegade territory and warned the leadership of ethnic republics not to try dissociating from Moscow.
9. Interview 39, NGO, Stavropol. All interviews cited in the following were conducted by Karina Mikirova. For information about the interviews, see Mikirova 2016.
10. http://eng.state.kremlin.ru/council/28/news, accessed October 19, 2016.
11. See also http://www.tandfonline.com/doi/abs/10.2753/RUP1061-1940520102?journalCode=mrup20, retrieved March 11, 2017.
12. http://www.komitet2-4.km.duma.gov.ru/file.xp?idb=3633724&fn=%EF%EB%E0%ED.pdf&size=651339, accessed August 16, 2016.
13. Interview 38, NGO, Stavropol'.
14. The ECAs allow ethnic groups to claim a degree of freedom in handling their own (cultural) affairs. ECAs (NCAs) form the basis of non-territorial organisation of ethnic groups. Regarding their organisational form, however, they possess fewer rights than ordinary NGOs. For more information, see Osipov (2013).

15. For detailed description of regional laws on ethnic issues and NGOs see Mikirova (2016).
16. Law of Krasnodar region No. 1284-KZ (25 June 2007) 'On approval of the regional target program 'harmonisation of interethnic relationships and the development of ethnic cultures in the Krasnodar region in 2008'; 2006 target program of the Stavropol' region 'On the development of ethnic and inter-religious relations in the Stavropol' region from 2007 to 2009'.
17. *Obshchestvennaja palata Rossijskoj Federatsii*, see http://www.oprf.ru/, accessed August 8, 2016.
18. https://www.oprf.ru/files/Doklad-OPRF-2008-ENGL_300409_2.pdf, accessed February 9, 2017.
19. Interview 18, NGO, Krasnodar.
20. https://www.wsws.org/de/articles/2012/08/kosa-a22.html, accessed February 9, 2017.
21. Interview 26, administrative actor, Krasnodar.
22. Interview 48, regional administration, Stavropol'.
23. Interview 39, NGO, Stavropol'.
24. Interview 13, NGO, Krasnodar; 41, ex-member of the ethnic advisory body to the governor, Stavropol'.
25. Interviews 23, 24 with NGOs, Krasnodar; 26 with regional administration, Krasnodar.
26. Interview 21 with NGO, Krasnodar.
27. Interview 12, NGO Krasnodar.

REFERENCES

Braginskaia, Ekaterina. 2012. Domestication or Representation? Russia and the Institutionalisation of Islam in Comparative Perspective. *Europe-Asia Studies* 64 (3): 597–620.

Brancati, D. 2009. *Peace by Design: Managing Intrastate Conflict through Decentralization*. Oxford: Oxford University Press.

Cheskin, Ammon, and Luke March. 2015. State-Society Relations in Contemporary Russia: New Forms of Political and Social Contention. *East European Politics* 31 (3): 261–273.

Davies, Jonathan S. 2011. *Challenging Governance Theory. From Networks to Hegemony*. Bristol: The Policy Press.

DeBardeleben, Joan, and Michail Zherebtsov. 2010. The Transition to Managerial Patronage in Russia's Regions. In *The Politics of Sub-National Authoritarianism in Russia*, ed. Vladimir Gel'man, Cameron Ross, 85–105. Aldershot: Ashgate.

Deryugin, Alexander, and Galina Kurlandskaya. 2007. The Russian Federation. In *The Practice of Fiscal Federalism: Comparative Perspectives*, ed. Anwar Shah, John Kincaid, 235–261. Montreal.

Evans, Alfred B. 2008. The First Steps of Russia's Public Chamber: Representation or Coordination? *Demokratizatsiya* 16: 345–362.

Foxall, Andrew. 2010. Discourses of Demonisation: Chechens, Russians, and the Stavropol' Riots of 2007. *Geopolitics* 15: 684–704.

Foxall, Andrew. 2011. Recent Developments in Inter-Ethnic Relations in Stavropol'skii krai. *Russian Analytical Digest* 93: 12–14.

Foxall, Andrew. 2012. Post-Soviet Ethnic Relations in Stavropol'skii Krai, Russia: 'A Melting Pot or Boiling Shaft'? *Europe-Asia Studies* 64 (9): 1758–1779.

Foxall, Andrew. 2014. Performing Ethnic Relations in Russia's North Caucasus: Regional Spectacles in Stavropol' krai. *Central Asian Survey* 33 (1): 47–61.

Foxall, Andrew. 2015. *Ethnic Relations in Post-Soviet Russia. Russians and Non-Russians in the North Caucasus*. London, New York: Routledge.

Gel'man, Vladimir. 2010. The Dynamics of Sub-National Authoritarianism: Russia in Comparative Perspective. In *The Politics of Sub-National Authoritarianism in Russia*, ed. Vladimir Gel'man, Cameron Ross, 1–18. Farnham: Ashgate.

Gel'man, Vladimir, and Sergei Ryzhenkov. 2011. Local Regimes, Sub-national Governance and the 'Power Vertical' in Contemporary Russia. *Europe-Asia Studies* 63: 449–465.

Gerring, John. 2008. Case Selection for Case-Study Analysis: Qualitative and Quantitative Techniques. In *The Oxford Handbook of Political Methodology*, ed. J.M. Box-Steffensmeier, H.E. Brady, and D. Collier, 645–684. Oxford: Oxford University Press.

Hood, Brian C. 1983. *The Tools of Government*. London: Macmillan.

Kropp, Sabine, and Johannes Schumann. 2016. Governance networks and vertical power in Russia – Environmental impact assessments and collaboration between state and non-state actors. *East European Politics* 32 (2): 192–214.

Light, Matthew. 2016. *Fragile Migration Rights. Freedom of Movement in Post-Soviet Russia*. Abingdon: Routledge.

Markedonov, Sergey. 2014. *The 2014 Sochi Olympics. A Patchwork of Challenges*. Centre for Strategic and International Studies Report. Lanham etc.: Rowman & Littlefield.

Meyer, John W., and Brian Rowan. 1977. Institutionalized Organizations: Formal Structures as Myth and Ceremony. *American Journal of Sociology* 83: 340–363.

Mikirova, Karina. 2016. *Governance Structures for Regional Ethnic Policy in the Russian Federation. Interactions Between State and Non-State Actors Within Negotiation Platforms*. Berlin: Wissenschaftlicher Verlag.

Ospiov, Alexander. 2013. National-Cultural Autonomy in Russia. A Matter of Legal Regulation or the Symbolic Construction of an Ethnic Mosaic? In *Managing Ethnic Diversity in Russia,* ed. Oleh Protsyk, Benedikt Harzl, 62–84. Abingdon: Routledge.

Petrov, Nikolay, Maria Lipman, and Henry E. Hale. 2014. Three Dilemmas of Hybrid Regime Governance: Russia from Putin to Putin. *Post-Soviet Affairs* 30: 1–16.

Popov, Anton, and Igor Kuznetsov. 2008. Ethnic Discrimination and the Discourse of 'Indigenization': The Regional Regime, 'Indigenous Majority' and Ethnic Minorities in Krasnodar Krai in Russia. *Nationalities Papers: The Journal of Nationalism and Ethnicity* 36 (2): 223–252.

Reisinger, William M. 2013. *Russia's Regions and Comparative Subnational Politics.* Houndmills: Routledge.

Reuter, Ora John. 2010. The Politics of Dominant Party Formation: United Russia and Russia's Governors. *Europe-Asia Studies* 62: 293–327.

Richmond, Walter. 2013. Preparations for the Sochi Olympics. In *The Fire Below. How the Caucasus Shaped Russia*, ed. Robert Bruce Ware, 203–223. New York: Bloomsbury.

Richter, James. 2009a. The Ministry of Civil Society? The Public Chambers in the Regions. *Problems of Post-Communism* 56: 7–20.

Richter, James. 2009b. Putin and the Public Chamber. *Post-Soviet Affairs* 25: 40–66.

Ross, Cameron. 2010. Federalism and Inter-Governmental Relations in Russia. *Journal of Communist Studies and Transition Politics* 26 (2): 165–187.

Savva, M.V. 2008. *Dialog obščestva i vlasti kak mechanism profilaktiki ėkstremizma. Sbornik statej: Métodiki profilaktiki ėkstremisma v molodežnoj srede, ėkspertnyj podchod*, Krasnodar.

Savva, Mikhail, Valerii Tishkov. 2012. Civil Society Institutions and Peacemaking. *Russian Social Science Review* 53 (3): 60–87.

Schenk, Caress. 2012. Nationalism in the Russian Media: Content Analysis of Newspaper Coverage Surrounding Conflict in Stavropol, 24 May–7 June 2007. *Nationalities Papers: The Journal of Nationalism and Ethnicity* 40 (5): 783–805.

Sharafutdinova, Gulnaz. 2009. Subnational Governance in Russia: How Putin Changed the Contract with His Agents and the Problems It Created for Medvedev. *Publius: The Journal of Federalism* 40: 672–696.

Smyth, Regina, Anna Lowry, and Brandon Wilkening. 2007. Engineering Victory: Institutional Reform, Informal Institutions, and the Formation of a Hegemonic Party Regime in the Russian Federation. *Post-Soviet Affairs* 23: 118–137.

Swerdlow, Steve. 2006. Understanding Post-Soviet Ethnic Discrimination and the Effective Use of U.S. Refugee Resettlement: The Case of the Meskhetian Turks of Krasnodar Krai. *California Law Journal* 94 (6): 1827–1878.

Vabo, Signy Irene, and Asbjørn Røiseland. 2012. Conceptualizing the Tools of Government in Urban Network Governance. *International Journal of Public Administration* 35: 1–13.

Wolff, Stefan. 2011. Managing Ethnic Conflict: The Merits and Perils of Territorial Accommodation. *Political Studies Review* 9: 26–41.

Yin, Robert K. 2014. *Case Study Research and Methods*, 5th ed. London: Sage.

CHAPTER 8

Substitution in Sápmi. Meta-Governance and Conflicts Over Representation in Regional Indigenous Governance

Mikkel Berg-Nordlie

8.1   INTRODUCTION

The chapter sheds light on regional governance in the field of indigenous politics through a detailed study of reforms of indigenous participation structures in the Murmansk Region 2006–2014. The chapter begins by accounting in brief for data gathering and methodology, and continues by describing key aspects of Russia's indigenous policy field, as well as giving key information about the indigenous people of Murmansk Region, the Sámi. Following this, it discusses three governance networks created by regional authorities with the stated intention of facilitating the indigenous group's possibilities to advise them on indigenous policy, and the conflicts that arose about these governance networks. Focus lies on the authorities' attempts to metagovern networks, the attempts of a non-state network of reformist activists to escape meta-governance through the establishment of a more independent representative organ, the securitisation of the conflict, and the eventual substitution of the reformists' self-organised political

M. Berg-Nordlie (✉)
Department for International Studies and Migration, NIBR Institute of Oslo and Akershus University College, Holbergs Gate 1, 0166 Oslo, Norway
e-mail: Mikkel.berg-nordlie@nibr.hioa.no

© The Author(s) 2018
S. Kropp et al. (eds.), *Governance in Russian Regions*,
DOI 10.1007/978-3-319-61702-2_8

entity. The chapter refers to meta-governance techniques discussed in Chap. 2—*framing (formal, economic, rhetorical)* and *participant regulation (direct participation, participant selection)*. The closing discussion describes the functions of the formal governance networks observed, and comments on the events accounted for in light of four basic steering resources: *nodality, authority, treasure,* and *organisation.* These resources, as well as a typology of governance network functions, are also introduced and discussed in Chap. 2.[1]

8.2   DATA AND METHODOLOGY

The author has been gathering and analysing data on Russian indigenous politics, and Sámi politics in particular since 2009. This work has been financed by various actors: mainly the Norwegian Research Council (the Sámi Research Program and the Russia/High North Research Program), but also the NIBR Institute of Oslo and Akershus University College, and the Arctic University of Norway. Data gathering has taken the form of both short and extended field works (ranging between one week and two months), interviews, scrutiny of relevant media, document studies, and studies of existing literature. Ethical standards in research on indigenous peoples is a subject of much academic debate, with a particular focus on securing research participants' free, prior, and informed consent (Alver and Øyen 2007: 24–39; Drugge 2016a, b; Ingierd and Fossum 2014; NESH 2016: B7–8; Niemi and Semb 2009; Olsen 2016: 29–30; Túnon et al. 2016: 67). To ensure this, the research projects' basis and planned output were presented to the interviewees, who were given the possibility of asking further questions about the research. They often did—questions reflecting rising insecurities about Western actors, or about being seen as involved with these. It was sometimes necessary to clarify in detail the relationship of my home institutions to the Norwegian state structures and the origin and purpose of the projects. This was mainly an issue during the initial phase of data gathering. Later interviews were more characterised by the nature of my research having become known. Interviewees' consent were further secured by their being given opportunity to check quotes prior to their first publication and to correct or retract these.

8.3   Russian Indigenous Policy and the Sámi

8.3.1   The Construction of Russia's Category of Indigenousness

There is no universal definition of 'indigenous peoples', but one wide-spread usage considers it as referring to ethnic groups with a historical experience of seeing their homelands forcibly incorporated by a state not under their control and subsequently becoming a subjugated group within that state (deCosta 2015). Under such a definition, Russia has a vast number of peoples that could be considered indigenous. Nevertheless, the Russian term generally translated as 'indigenous' refers to a smaller subset of Russia's ethnic groups. In 1925, a list was enacted at the Union level that placed certain peoples of the realm into a common category. The basis for this categorisation was small-numberedness, inhabiting areas seen as peripheral, association with certain rural traditional economic activities, or a semi-settled/nomadic lifestyle (Kalte 2003: 23; Kryazhkov 2010: 45; Sokolovski 2000: 105–108; Sokolovskiy 2011: 242; Øverland and Blakkisrud 2006: 182–183). This categorisation was informed by the intention of giving targeted support to the realm's 'weakest' peoples, those seen as having the longest way to go towards 'Communism'. Policy towards this delimited set of peoples was split off from general ethnic minority policy, forming a separate policy field which, after an initial period of high activity during the 1920s, was subsequently given little attention and very weak institutionalisation. In 2000, a federal-level list was again enacted, encompassing peoples considered 'native, small-numbered peoples (of the North)' (*korennye malochislennye narody (severa)*, often abbreviated as KMN or KMNS). The spirit of 1925 was retained by the definition of KMNs: ethnic groups inhabiting territories also inhabited by their ancestors, numbering less than 50,000, and maintaining traditional ways of life and economic activities (Berg-Nordlie 2015b; Øverland and Blakkisrud 2006: 172–174; Sokolovski 2000: 105–108; Sokolovskiy 2011: 242).

8.3.2   Participation in Governance by RAIPON and Other Indigenous Representatives

During the Russian Federation's first decade, indigenous policy was given little priority at the federal level. Around the turn of the millennium, three federal laws were enacted, forming the legal basis for Russian indigenous policy: *On Guarantees of Rights for Indigenous Peoples* (1999) among other things confirmed regions' rights to create councils of indigenous representatives under the executive (Sect. 5.8), and the right of indigenous peoples to delegate 'authorised representatives' to such councils (Sect. 8.7). *On General Principles for the Organisation of Obshchinas* (2000) regulated the establishment of kin- and community-based entities for the practice of traditional economic activities. Of lesser importance to this chapter, *On Territories for Traditional Nature Use* (2001) regulated the creation of special areas where indigenous peoples could practice their traditional livelihoods. Indigenous representative bodies, *obshchinas*, and TTPs did already exist in certain regions, but there was now Federation-wide, streamlining legislation. Much of Russian indigenous political debate in the current millennium has concerned these laws (Berezhkov 2012; Bowring 2013: 30–31; Kryazhkov 2015; Guarantees 2009; Obshchinas 2000; TTP 2001; Øverland and Blakkisrud 2006).

At the federal level, the de facto representative of indigenous interests has been a non-state actor: RAIPON, the umbrella organisation for NGOs of KMN-status peoples. RAIPON has combined protest activity, border-transcending networking, and informational work, with lobbying towards and cooperating with the authorities. Through its status as a Federation-wide organisation, RAIPON has had the right to propose changes to federal law and to take part in federal-level formal governance networks, including the Public Chamber[2] (Berezhkov 2012: 6–24; IWGIA 1991: 17–18; Sleptsov 2005: 66–67; Yetylen 1996: 83–94). As for state-based actors, the first decade of the Russian Federation saw a prolonged period of institutional instability in federal-level indigenous policy: responsibility for the policy field repeatedly changed hands until it was anchored in the Ministry of Regional Development in 2004 (Øverland and Blakkisrud 2006), where it stayed until the ministry's abolishment in 2014. Responsibility was then given to the Ministry of Culture.

While federal-level representation is of great importance, it has been considered as crucial by Russian indigenous peoples to achieve representation at the regional level. Models for indigenous participation in regional politics vary from place to place, having emerged from local processes involving regions and peoples with different characteristics. Different participation mechanisms include NGOs directly representing the indigenous population, the authorities accepting councils created from below as authorised representatives of local indigenous peoples, the authorities creating representation councils of their own, and arrangements for indigenous interest representation within regional parliaments. The large degree of variation makes it difficult to talk about any 'normal model' as regards formal arrangements for indigenous participation in Russian regional politics (Berezhkov 2012; Kalte 2003: 70–72; Kryazhkov 2005: 68–73, 343–352; 2012: 29; 2015; Turaev 2005: 82–83; Todishev 2005: 58–63; Zakharov 2005: 91–92).

8.3.3   Securitisation, Industry, and RAIPON's Struggle for Survival

In Chap. 7, Kropp and Schuhmann described securitisation in the general 'national policy' field, stemming from authorities' association of ethnic minorities with centrifugal forces, suspicions of disloyalty to the centre, and violent conflict. The groups today classified as KMNs have not avoided this securitisation altogether, even though their small numbers and the 'peripherality' inherent in their definition has generally tended to make them —and the indigenous policy field as such—seen as a lesser concern by the central authorities (Berg-Nordlie 2015b). A definite challenge to the 'small peoples of the North' has been state-orchestrated drives for economic development. This has brought land-alienating industrialisation, demographic swamping through colonisation, and forced resettlement (Fondahl 1993: 487; Overland and Berg-Nordlie 2012: 36; Vinogradova 2010: 134; Øverland and Blakkisrud 2006: 167–168). As the North is seen as more economically important, the geographic area and consequently its ethnic politics also becomes more securitised. During the current millennium, the North is again being discussed in the language of economic and military-strategic importance, and indigenous activists have experienced accusations that rights-based politics 'blackmail' industries of national importance (Berg-Nordlie 2015b). As discussed in Chap. 2, rising geo-political instability has made Russia less hospitable for critical NGOs that engage in international networking. These developments are challenging for the Russian indigenous NGO sector which during the post-Soviet era integrated itself into international indigenous networks, and which include many organisations that have engaged in disputes related to industrial resource extraction. It is from this background that we must consider the experiences of RAIPON, 2009–2013.

RAIPON began to receive negative attention from the Ministry of Justice already in 2009, formally not over its foreign contacts or its open criticism of industrial ventures on indigenous land, but over technicalities regarding the legality of the organisation's statutes (Berezhkov 2012: 23–30). This should be considered in the context of Russian law often being applied selectively to remove 'troublesome' actors from the political game board, while refraining from using these laws against actors considered 'loyal' (Bækken 2013: 1–6, 59–67, 204–210; 2015). Indeed, during the process that followed, a former RAIPON vice president accused the Ministry of Justice of clandestinely working on behalf of forces within the Ministry of Regional Development that wanted to curb RAIPON's influence (Berezhkov 2012, 2013).[3] The Ministry first threatened to withdraw RAIPON's important formal status as a federation-wide organisation and then in 2012 suspended the organisation. In 2013, it was allowed to resume its activities, but had to change its statutes: its president now had to be elected by a two-thirds majority. During that year's federation-wide RAIPON congress, the winner of the majority vote had to run again against the second-most popular candidate—a *Duma* deputy from the regime's party *Yedinnaya Rossiya*, representing the gas-rich Yamalo-Nenets region. Foreign observers and press were asked to leave the premises and in a closed session between elections, the most popular candidate withdrew his candidacy. After the election, most of RAIPON's employees were laid off, and the organisation became less visible in public debate. Following 2013, IWGIA refers to RAIPON as 'operating under tight state control' (2014: 31–33; 2015: 33–35; 2016: 42).

8.3.4   *The Sámi People and the East/West Divide*

The Sámi is an indigenous nation whose homeland, Sápmi, has been divided by four states—Finland, Norway, Russia, and Sweden. The border-transcending aspect of this indigenous group has facilitated a spread of ideas about indigenous governance that have clashed with Russian ideas and practices, a fact of some importance to this case. Russian Sámi history has been impacted by their home, the Kola Peninsula, proving to be of key strategic significance to Russia during the 1900s,[4] and by the fact that the majority of the ethnic group lives in Western states. Sámi political activism has on several occasions been treated as a security concern, sometimes with deadly outcomes for activists (Berg-Nordlie 2015b). Since the *Perestroika*, strong Sámi activist networks have been built across the former Iron Curtain. Two aspects of this networking are of high relevance to the chapter: Firstly, during the post-Soviet economic collapse a dominant discourse was established among the Western Sámi—that they have a moral imperative to show support, including economic assistance but also political solidarity, to the Russian Sámi (Berg-Nordlie 2011a, b, 2015c; Overland and Berg-Nordlie 2012). Secondly, that pan-Sámi networking in some cases transcends the state/non-state divide. The Russian Sámi are represented in Barents WGIP (Working Group of Indigenous Peoples), a body with an advisory function towards the Barents Euro-Arctic Council and the Barents Regional Council —these are respectively government-level and region-level cooperation regimes for Russia and the Western states Finland, Norway, and Sweden.[5] The Russian Sámi have also joined the Sámi Council, which is an international union of Sámi NGOs, but which also receives financial support from the home states of the Western Sámi. Furthermore, the Russian Sámi send participatory observers to the Sámi Parliamentary Council, a common structure for the three Western *Sámediggi*s (Berg-Nordlie 2013). The latter are the representative organs of the Western Sámi: state-created and state-regulated organs governed by elected representatives of ethnically Sámi citizens of Finland, Norway, and Sweden (Bergh and Saglie 2015; Berg-Nordlie 2015c; Falch et al. 2015; Josefsen et al 2015; Mörkenstam et al. 2016; Nyyssönen 2015; Pettersen 2015). While interrelations between the Nordic states and Russia improved after the fall of the USSR, the security structures operating in the Murmansk Region continued to show a certain interest in the Russian Sámi and their border-transcending ethno-politics, and suspicions and accusations of Sámi separatism continued to resurface (Berg-Nordlie 2015a; Larsson-Kalvemo 1995; Overland and Berg-Nordlie 2012). Securitisation and geopolitical tensions should generally be kept in mind when analysing Russian indigenous politics, but in the specific subfield of Russian Sámi politics, these aspects have particular explanatory power.

8.3.5   *Russian Sámi Civil Society and Murmansk Region's Indigenous Governance*

Before moving over to the three governance networks established 2006–2014, and the conflicts that surround them, the reader needs to acquire a small overview of Murmansk Region's indigenous politics. The two main ethno-political organisations are *AKS* (est. 1989) and *OOSMO* (1998), both region-covering NGOs with a 'catch-all' vision, i.e. they are open to all Sámi of Murmansk Region. The two NGOs enjoy the same level of representation in pan-Sámi affairs, but only AKS is a RAIPON member. Since 2002, Sámi *obshchina*s have been established in the region, being considered as a possible vessel for the re-introduction of traditional Sámi small-scale, family-based reindeer herding after its Soviet-Era disruption. The actual activity level and orientation of these organisations varies widely. Some exist mainly on paper, some are primarily involved in ethno-tourism, others more oriented towards reindeer herding, etc. (Berg-Nordlie 2015a; Overland and Berg-Nordlie 2012; Vladimirova 2005, 2011). Many other Russian Sámi organisations and organisation types exist, but the above will be in focus here. As detailed elsewhere (Berg-Nordlie 2015a, b), indigenous governance in Murmansk Region was (much like at the federal level) characterised by unstable institutionalisation prior to an administrative reform in 2004. Before this, responsibility for indigenous policy was continually moved about in the system, and interaction with indigenous civil society happened in a rather non-systematised fashion, often limited to ad hoc discussions with leaders of indigenous NGOs (Gutsol and Riabova 2002; Kalte 2003; Vinogradova 2005). The regional charter of 1998 did, however, establish that the regional state organs had to 'cooperate' with the indigenous people in the realisation of their rights (Charter 2015, Sect. 21.2). In 2004, responsibility for indigenous political coordination and the implementation of indigenous policy was given to the Northern Peoples' Centre, a 'state regional institution' (*gosudarstvennoe oblastnoe byudzhetnoe uchrezhdenie*) operating under a committee of the regional government[6,7] (this type of institution is described in Chap. 2). The 2004 reform would prove to 'stick': the Centre remained the regional authorities' indigenous governance agency, working in an implementing capacity and networking with both Sámi civil society and other state organs.

8.4   META-GOVERNANCE AND CONFLICTS OVER GOVERNANCE STRUCTURES IN MURMANSK REGION, 2006–2014

8.4.1   Model 1: The Coordination Council—and the First Congress

3In 2006, the Northern Peoples' Centre established the first formal governance network aimed at ensuring indigenous civil society input: the Coordination Council (*Koordinatsionniy sovet*).[8] The meta-governance technique of participant selection was notably absent in this model: the state bound itself to invite only leaders or deputy leaders of the indigenous NGOs, in practice allowing these to choose their own representatives without outside interference (Centre 2006). Apart from this, the region's formal framing of the network allowed them wide room for meta-governance: the Council's influence was formally regulated as advisory, and to a rather low-level institution that in itself only had an implementing and participatory function.

The governance network was not given any organisational or economic resources of its own but depended on the Centre's staff, localities, and finances. The Centre's leader furthermore participated directly in proceedings (Centre 2006). Somewhat unexpectedly for the regional authorities, a significant number of indigenous activists rejected this model for indigenous participation. Instead, the creation of the Council became the catalyst for a sudden and quite forceful campaign for the import of a Western model of indigenous governance.

Murmansk Region's indigenous civil society had undergone a schism in 1998, when OOSMO was established, and had since then become increasingly fractured (Overland and Berg-Nordlie 2012). In the absence of a unifying non-state 'node', regional authorities enjoyed a heightened degree of nodality in indigenous governance, particularly after the establishment of the Centre. In the short run, the creation of the Council further institutionalised this nodality, since the Centre now gathered the many (at the time eighteen) indigenous civil society formations around itself as a 'hub'. However, the Council was eventually also used as an arena for the formation of a new nodal network of activists, which had other ideas about how indigenous governance should be organised. The creation of the Coordination Council had emboldened certain activists, who now perceived that further reform was realistic. From 2007, AKS and OOSMO, and key activists from other organisations, worked together for what they called a *saamskiy parlament* or 'Sámi Parliament'—an oft-used translation of *Sámediggi* (Berg-Nordlie 2011b; Sovkina 2008). After two decades of border-transcending networking, many Russian Sámi activists considered the Sámediggis as being the 'go-to' model for Sámi representation. When comparing this to the model for indigenous participation offered by the region, many concluded that the domestic variant fell short: it was accused of being inadequately democratic and for giving too little influence to indigenous representatives.[9]

> Many decisions that the council made were not listened to by the regional authorities, important questions were not solved. As we know, the interests of the Sámi and the authorities do not always coincide (Sharshina and Yakovleva 2008).

> The Coordination Council should have decided matters, and the Centre executed its decisions. That would have been a Sámi Parliament. Except that in the Council there were only the leaders of the organisations, not elected people (Reform network activist, 2009).

Regional authorities exhibited skepticism about these developments, as did certain indigenous activists. Some of the latter were skeptical of the two big NGOs and, in the prolongation of this, any project spearheaded by those organisations. Others saw the Sámediggi model as unfit for Russia, for a variety of reasons. Some saw the demand as unrealistic and only serving to provoke the authorities unnecessarily. Others again disagreed that ethnically-elected representatives should have the kind of power that they believed the Western Sámediggis possessed—beliefs that were often quite erroneous (for example the idea that the Sámediggis have legislative authority), but which were also subscribed to by some activists *for* a Russian 'Sámi Parliament'. Skeptics were found among many *obshchina*-based actors, but not exclusively in that sector (Berg-Nordlie 2015a). The authorities eventually decided that the issue should be discussed at 'the First Congress of the Sámi of Murmansk Region' (2008). Before that Congress was held, the Centre disbanded the Coordination Council. The Council had by then essentially rebelled against the authorities' framing of its mandate as an advisory structure, when a majority of participants present at one session voted for a declaration that it constituted the 'highest authority of the Russian Sámi until the holding of the First Congress' (Sovkina 2008). Such a denial of the regional authorities' framing is somewhat typical of the movement for a Russian 'Sámi Parliament'. The discourse promoting such a reform rejected the authorities' relatively paternalistic framing of indigenous representation as constituted by state-organised channels to provide user-group input about the authorities' indigenous policy decisions—and instead articulated ideas about indige-nous representation that emphasised indigenous empowerment and direct election of indigenous representatives.

Participants at the First Congress were to be elected by local groups of indigenous persons. However, disagreements arose as to whether or not the regional authorities were giving inadequate information to indigenous communities before elections, resulting in a skewed turnout. In some places, activists organised alternative elections. When the Congress did take place, disputes arose as to the legitimacy of some participants (Berg-Nordlie 2011b). The First Congress was organised on the region's authority and utilised its treasure and organisation—but, nevertheless, the authorities did not manage to effectively influence the outcome: their suggestion of a council of elected indigenous representatives that had to be approved by the provincial Government was voted down. A majority sided with the position promoted by the cross-organisational network of indigenous activists. The Congress requested a Russian 'Sámi Parliament' and to work for such an organ appointed a 'Council of Authorised Representatives'—henceforth referred to as 'SUPS' after the Russian acronym for *Sovet upolnomochyonnykh pred-staviteley Saamov* (a name referring to the concept of 'authorised representation' in the *Law on Guarantees of Rights*) (LP 2008; Sharshina and Yakovleva 2008; SUPS 2008).[10] RAIPON was quick to voice support for SUPS.[11] The reformist network had essentially managed to utilise the region's resources, in addition to the resources already inherent in their own organisations and networking, to promote the creation of an organ of which the regional authorities were not ready to approve.

8.4.2 Model 2: The Council of Representatives—and the Second Congress

The first reaction of regional officials was to rhetorically 'reframe' the authority of the First Congress, stating to the media that

> ...violations of procedure – participation in the voting by citizens of Sámi ethnicity who were not original delegates, have forced the organs of the executive power to consider this Congress rather [just] a gathering of citizens (...) [W]e will work with them [SUPS] as we would with yet another civil society formation (Regional government official, 2008; LP 2008).

Following the First Congress, several Centre staff including the leader left their posts, and the Centre was eventually transferred to another regional government committee. In 2009, the regional authorities established the Council of Indigenous Representatives under the Murmansk Region Government (*Sovet predstaviteley korennykh malochislennykh narodov severa pri pravitel'stve Murmanskoy oblasti*, henceforth: the Council of Representatives) (Postanovlenie 2009). The Council of Representatives is subject to substantial state meta-governance. Firstly, it was framed to be advisory and participatory only—although notably the new council's advisory activity formally occurs towards a higher level of the regional hierarchy than the old council, as it is placed directly under the Government and not under the Centre. Participant selection is practiced, although somewhat 'softly': Council members are selected by the Governor, but after nominations by organisations in the *obshchina* sector. The Council also includes a member of the region's Public Chamber who is to be part of the indigenous population. The representative of the Public Chamber headed the Council of Representatives between 2011 and 2015. The Council was not regulated to possess economic means under its own control or indeed any organisational resources apart from those brought in by its members. The Northern Peoples' Centre was set to manage the organisational affairs of the Council while still ultimately answering to its 'founder' (*uchreditel'*), the regional government. Through its retained nodality the Centre, and by extension the government, obviously has a significant potential to influence Council activities. Finally, direct participation is part of the Council's structure through the participation of a vice governor. Staff of other state agencies have also taken part in Council meetings (Berg-Nordlie 2015a).

As discussed in Chap. 2, it is quite common for state-based actors in Russia to allow civil society groups the right to nominate participants in governance networks, but reserve for themselves the power to ultimately choose who participates. This can be considered a 'security hatch' of sorts, allowing the authorities to remove or block the participation of any actor that steps out of line (Aasland et al. 2016; Berg-Nordlie and Tkach 2016; Davies et al. 2016). What makes the Council of Representatives stand out is that only *obshchina*s are allowed to participate. One of the Council's functions is to advise the Government on how to allocate support to their type of organisation and it is perhaps not so strange that *obshchina*s are given prioritised access to a governance network with that function. However, keeping in mind the context of the Council's creation, it is noteworthy that the formal delimitation of eligible participants did in practice sideline AKS and OOSMO—organisations whose activists were central in the reformist network and which had deeper involvement in East-West transcending political networks.

SUPS continued operating as Russian Sámi representatives, referring to their mandate from the First Congress. They were widely accepted as such among Western Sámi activists—as should be expected, since activists accustomed to democratic procedures would be hard-pressed not to respect the First Congress' majority decision. In addition, one should note that some of SUPS' members had strong networks among Western Sámi. For example, one member was a former leader of the border-transcending Sámi Council, and the SUPS leader had represented the Russian Sámi in the Barents WGIP since 2007 (WGIP 2007). The reformist network dominated the information flow about the conflict out of Russia, not just because of pre-existing networks with Western activists, but also because the regional authorities and activists aligned with these did not prioritise informational work targeting the Western Sámi. Some even saw Western

Sámi support for the reformists as confirming suspicions that the campaign for a Russian Sámediggi 'originated abroad... [T]he roots of the idea lie in the West' (Russian Sámi activist 2010).

These suspicions were not weakened when, the year after her election, the SUPS leader began to work at the Barents Indigenous Peoples' Office (BIPO)—an indigenous information and service centre that also functions as WGIP's secretariat. Russia participates in the Barents Cooperation, and hence one may question how a Barents-based structure could be considered as suspect by Russians. While serving indigenous peoples in both Russia and the West, BIPO is financed by the Norwegian Sámediggi and administered by the Norwegian Barents Secretariat, the latter again being owned by Norway's three northernmost counties.[12] That state-based entities such as the Sámediggis and the counties may operate autonomously from the central state on the international arena is an alien idea to many in Russia, who assume that actors under state financing or administration toe the line set down by the state. The strengthening of BIPO by one employee was stated explicitly by the initiative-taker (WGIP) as rooted in a need to be 'following up the political work among the Sámi on the Russian side' (*Prosjektkatalog* 2009). When a position described as such was given to the SUPS leader, it does becomes understandable that some would conclude that actors in the West were working actively to support the decision of the First Congress' majority. It is another matter that such activist-driven international support was enlarged discursively in Russia to a grand conspiracy in which, as one widely circulated newspaper text put it, 'the Sámi are the new card of the West in the battle over the Arctic'.[13] In 2010, SUPS organised a 'Second Congress of the Sámi of Murmansk Region'. Beforehand, SUPS and the Norwegian Sámediggi had sent a joint application for funding of this congress to the Norwegian Barents Secretariat. The Secretariat's funding programme is targeted towards supporting Norwegian-Russian joint projects, particularly those protecting indigenous interests, and they agreed to partly finance the conference that was to 'discuss matters of regional significance, inform the population about the activity of Murmansk Region's public authorities' executive organs, and implement societal self-governance' (*Prosjektkatalog* 2010). The Norwegian Sámediggi also contributed funds to the Second Congress (Sámediggi 2010). In the event, the Second Congress elected what it referred to as a Russian 'Sámi Parliament'—*Saamskiy parlament* (Russian) or *Kuèllnègk nyoark sám' sobbar* (Kildin Sámi). The Sámi name purposely invoked the "*Kuèllnègknjarrk Sobbar*" (Kola Peninsula Assembly), an Imperial-Era organ of local self-government that was at this time being discursively constructed as 'the first   Parliament' (more on this in Berg-Nordlie 2015b). The Sobbar was tasked with working for official recognition during a four-year period (SUPS 2010). It did not formally register as any type of civil society formation—partly because activists considered that registering it as an NGO may have precluded it from being recognised as an authorised body of representatives, and partly to avoid being subjected to selective law enforcement over formalities.[14]

The reformist network had enjoyed high nodality in Russian Sámi civil society by virtue of uniting activists from all major organisations. This status was seriously weakened when, in 2010, a new AKS leader was elected who had earlier pioneered the establishment of *obshchina*s in Murmansk Region, and voiced support for the *obshchina*-based Council of Representatives.

> I don't know how representative this new organ is. (...) I support the idea of unifying all the Sámi organisations on the Kola Peninsula, but in Murmansk there already is a council that promotes Sámi issues... (AKS leader 2010)

That the Sobbar could not anymore claim to unite all the main Russian Sámi civil society organisations was also picked up by Western Sámi media, and the dominant narrative about the Russian Sámi struggling to get a Sámediggi was gradually challenged by discourse on 'great disagreement' over the issue.[15] Despite the withdrawal of support from RAIPON's local member organisation, AKS, the reformist network retained good relations with the umbrella organisation itself. In 2012, a competence-raising study trip to the Norwegian Sámediggi for Sobbar and RAIPON activists was organised jointly by RAIPON and a Norwegian indigenous institution[16] with involvement from Barents WGIP. The organisers applied for, and received, financing from the Norwegian Barents Secretariat's programme for Russian-Norwegian indigenous projects (Berezhkov 2012; Prosjektkatalog 2012).

As established in Chap. 2, Russian authorities are interested in feedback on their policy, but want to crack down on 'dissentful contention'—i.e. criticism seen as targeting the regime or its core interests—particularly if it is practiced by groups connected to international networks. The reformist network began to fit the bill. It refused to fall in line with the regional authorities' ideas about how indigenous government should be organised, criticised regional indigenous policy, its leadership was deeply involved with networks of co-ethnics in the West during a time of rising geopolitical instability, received support from these networks, and lobbied for what was seen as the import of Western political models. In 2012, named Sobbar activists were accused by a regional media spokesman of trying to 'form a separatist mood among the Sámi people', and for using indigenous politics in a bid to secure themselves 'rents' from industries and transportation in the region. It was claimed that the 'initiator of [the reformist network's] activities are foreign organisations' and that the Sobbar's activities were 'coordinated from abroad'. To back up these accusations, Norwegian Sámediggi support was referred to, and WGIP was mentioned as an arena used for unwanted activities.[17] This statement echoed the rising tendency to discuss Western-Russian civil society cooperation in the language of foreign agency, the notion of 'indigenous blackmail' against industry, and (more case-specifically) previous discourse about Russian Sámi activists as a fifth column for the West. The statement obviously signified a hardening of fronts, but the breach between the authorities and the reformist network's activists was not total: reformist activists participated in cooperation with the Centre, in open Council meetings, and in working groups under the Council. In addition to being a pragmatic way of attempting to participate in policy-deliberation, the activists took care to describe this as Sobbar activities, utilising their participation symbolically to underscore the readiness of the Sobbar to assume indigenous governance responsibilities. The authorities, meanwhile, did not recognise the Sobbar, on the basis that it was not formally registered anywhere, and would refer to this as only the participation of individual activists.

8.4.3   Model 3: The New Sobbar—and the Third Congress

In 2014, the post-Soviet geopolitical climate reached an all-time low as the Ukrainian crisis exploded, with Russia annexing Crimea and Western sanctions against Russia. That same year, the UN World Conference on Indigenous Peoples was to be held in New York. Several delegates from Russia experienced obstructions when attempting to reach this meeting, including the Sobbar leader whose car's tyres were slashed in the night, and when her replacement car was pulled over by the police on the way to the airport, her passport was stolen by an unidentified assailant (IWGIA 2015: 33–35). When the Sobbar leader tried to attend the Norwegian Sámediggi's 25th anniversary, she was denied exit, formally for unrelated reasons.[18] In November, the reformist network attempted to take back AKS. This at first appeared successful, since the Sobbar leader was elected the new AKS leader, but regional authorities refused to recognise the election as valid since she had not received two-thirds of the votes. They determined that the incumbent would retain the post until an extraordinary general assembly was to be held.[19] That assembly was held in 2015, and re-elected the incumbent unchallenged.[20] By that time, the reformist network had suffered a much more serious defeat.

In accordance with the Sobbar's framing document (established by the Second Congress), it had to seek renewed legitimacy after four years. The network began to prepare for a 'Third Congress' and invited the regional authorities to participate. The authorities, however, set down their own committee to plan for a Sámi Congress with AKS and the Council of Representatives. In the event, the congress held in November 2014 (after the AKS leadership elections), was organised not by the incumbent Sobbar, but by the committee set down by the authorities.[21] There was no direct selection of participants, but the organisers assigned quotas for voting delegates to various organisations. Some organisations—such as AKS and OOSMO—were given specific mention and specific quotas, but the list also gave one representative to each *obshchina* and to 'all other legal entities established on Murmansk Region's territory by ethnic Sámi'. That the number of AKS and OOSMO delegates was fixed, in practice limited the influence of these two largest organisation, whereas the small but many organisations were positioned to pack a significant collective punching power (Artieva 2014; Third Congress 2014a, b). The resultant congress was sympathetic to the state-based actors' positions on how regional indigenous governance should be organised. This turnout was not just due to the authorities having been at liberty to influence who participated; it must also be considered in the context of the events leading up to the Third Congress. During seven years of activism for a 'Sámi Parliament', the authorities had demonstrated that they were both positioned and dispositioned to ignore that request. Furthermore, the current geopolitical situation made the import of an indigenous representation model from the West difficult to imagine. Through direct participation in the proceedings, representatives of the authorities—both regional and federal—made this abundantly clear. One regional parliament representative claimed from the podium that Russia was being led into ethnic division by people receiving money from abroad.[22] Another blow to the reformist network—although it had been obvious that after 2013, the reformist network could no longer count on RAIPON's support—was the presence of the new RAIPON leader in his capacity as an envoy from the federal *Duma*.[23]

At this congress and afterwards, interesting discursive shifts could be observed. Opponents of the reformist network now discussed the *Kuèllnègk nyoark sám' sobbar* as having existed, but as having failed to perform the tasks with which the Second Congress charged them, among other things through the choice of not registering the Sobbar formally.[24] When the authority of the Third Congress was discussed, some positions from the First Congress were reversed, as some reformist activists argued that this Congress was a 'conference' that did not have the right to choose Sámi representatives, while the state-based actors strongly voiced the opposite opinion.

'...if you doubt that this Congress is a Congress then you automatically dele-gitimise—educated people, people having received education in Norway [indicates Sobbar leader], understand this—then you delegitimise the decisions of the Second Congress, and the First Congress...' (A. V. Zhuravskij, Ministry of Culture)[25]

The Third Congress eventually elected nine individuals to be the representatives of the Russian Sámi. This body was given the name *Saamskoe sobranie "Sám' sobbar"* ('the Sámi Assembly *Sám' sobbar*') and was described as replacing the *Kuèllnègk nyoark sám' sobbar*. Several members of the old Sobbar ran for election to the new Sobbar, but only one of them garnered enough votes. Leadership of the Sobbar was given to the person who had received the largest number of votes—the same person who had led the Northern Peoples' Centre 2004–2008. After 2008, he had been active in the NGO 'Sámi Nature Fund', where the Council of Representatives' leader was also involved.[26] In the aftermath of the Third Congress, two members of the new Sobbar were chosen as deputy leaders: the AKS leader and the Council of Representatives' leader.[27] In this last of the three formalised governance networks[28] accounted for here, we observe that, technically, there has been no participant selection. However, the formal framing of the selection process can be said to have de facto disadvantaged certain actors and been in the favor of others. We also observe that the resultant governance network involves people with whom regional authorities are comfortable, and that have close connections with them—while activists associated with the reformist network have largely been sidelined. The authorities do not participate directly in the Sobbar as they do in the Council of Representatives, but representatives of regional organs have been known to take part in discussions at Sobbar meetings.[29] As for organisational or economic resources, the Sobbar has not received any such to dispose of unilaterally.

In the aftermath of the Third Congress, central activists in the reformist network denied that the Third Council legitimately dissolved the old Sobbar, and began to try garnering support for this position in Russian and Western Sápmi. So far, successes have been limited. Supporters of the new Sobbar argue that the old Sobbar's members legitimised the Third Congress by running for elections and voting (Yakovlev 2014). At the grass roots level, the momentum around the campaign for a Russian Sámediggi has been noticeably reduced after the Third Congress. In the West, the Barents structures have accepted as legitimate the decisions of Third Congress, just as they accepted the decisions of the First and Second Congress. These decisions included the removing of the old Sobbar leader from Barents WGIP (BIPC 2015). Of the core structures for border-transcending indigenous networking in the north, WGIP had given the Sobbar its most substantial recognition: in a document from 2013, the Russian Sámi representative in the working group was even referred to as having been appointed by the Sobbar (WGIP 2013). For comparison, the Sámi Parliamentary Council never formally recognised the Sobbar as a Sámediggi analogue, despite requests from the former. Ultimately, the Sámediggis were unwilling to accept as an equal partner an organ that, unlike them, had no state recognition.[30] Immediately after the Third Congress, leaders of the Finnish and Swedish Sámediggis made statements in support of the old Sobbar,[31] but since then there has been relative silence over the matter. At the March 2015 meeting of the Sámi Parliamentary Council, statements were made to the effect that there is no Sámediggi in Russia.[32] It is noteworthy that immediately after the Third Congress, the Council of Representatives' leader sent out a letter explaining their position on the old and new Sobbars. The letter also came in an English-language version that was circulated abroad by sympathisers. New Sobbar members have also participated in border-transcending indigenous events in the West. Representatives of the old Sobbar are still active on the arena of border-transcending Sámi politics, but they are no longer alone on it.

What occurred in 2014 was that the authorities dealt a blow to the informal reformist network and the *Kuèllnegk nyoark sám' sobbar* through a form of substitution. The new organ adopted the symbolically significant name utilised by the reformist network, and partly mimicked the old organ's structure: a 'Sámi Congress' elects a council of nine representatives to a 'Sobbar'—although instead of a congress by constituency-elected representatives, this model was a congress of organisations represented in accordance with a quota system. The organ of the network that came to be seen as too dissentful and too connected to foreign actors, was substituted by one dominated by persons well-connected to the authorities.

8.5 CLOSING DISCUSSION

This chapter has accounted for three different formal governance networks established by Murmansk Region in the indigenous policy field, and the emergence of an informal network of reformists working for the introduction of an altogether different model for indigenous participation in indigenous governance. The Coordination Council (2006–2008), the Council of Representatives (2009–), and *Sám' sobbar* (2014–) are similar in that they fulfil the same functions when compared to the model presented in Chap. 2 (cf. Aasland et al. 2016). None of them are *decision-making*, or for that matter involved in *monitoring*. To a certain extent it is possible to say that they take part in *implementation*, since they give advice to state organs on policy-implementation. However, the main tasks of these formal governance networks are to be *advisory* organs to the regional authorities, while the latter retain all rights to make indigenous policy decisions. All of the above could be said to be in line with general tendencies in state-organised Russian indigenous representation practices, although it is difficult to isolate an essential 'norm' out from the different arrangements for indigenous participation found in different regions. The first of the mentioned governance networks had an aspect of *coordination* as it constituted an attempt to unify the multitude of indigenous organisations operating in Murmansk Region at the time. This worked a little too well for the authorities' tastes, but simultaneously not well enough: the main NGOs and some key actors from other smaller groups unified around the need for wholesale reform of the indigenous representation system—while a significant number of Sámi activists still disagreed with the nature of the proposed reform. This unification around a reformist political program also brought indigenous activists into a clash with the regional authorities. The two next formal governance networks to be established had *conflict management* as one of its core functions. We are not talking here about conflict management in the sense that these networks were forums for negotiation or mediation between actors in conflict, rather they appeared tailored to manage the conflict by sidelining one party. This particularly concerns the Council of Representatives, but also the Third Congress was organised and held in a manner that made it likely the resultant indigenous representation council would not be dominated by activists that the authorities found unacceptable.

We may also relate what we have observed to the NATO model introduced in Chap. 2, drawn from Hood (1983) and Vabo and Røiseland (2012). *Nodality* was utilised relatively strongly by the authorities. They did not monopolise the information flow, but state-based actors and their allies did utilise their strong position to promote their own discourses about which indigenous representatives were legitimate, or for that matter, trustworthy. The First Congress was at one point discussed as lacking decision-making authority, SUPS and the Sobbar were treated as functionally non-existent due to lacking registration, the legitimacy of the Second Congress was questioned, and some activists were accused of operating on behalf of foreign actors. The reformist network used its own very strong position abroad to promote its own discourses, but gradually the opposing party also began to get their message across to Western audiences—particularly after 2010 with the change of leadership in AKS. The authorities' reaction against the reformist network could be read as trying to counterwork the emergence of a node in Russian *Sámi* civil society that was outside of state control. However, their reaction is adequately explained by the politics dominating within that rival node. What was seen as undesirable was not the fact of a non-state 'hub' uniting various civil society actors, so much as reform activists' insistence on elected indigenous representation with the autonomy to criticise the authorities publicly, and the connections between critical non-state actors and Western actors. *Authority* was practiced in a 'soft' manner over the Coordination Council, where civil society was allowed to choose its own representatives, but in a more 'hard' manner over the Council of Representatives established in the wake of the Coordination Council's abolishment. As for the *Sám' sobbar*, direct selection of participants was not practiced, but the formal regulations' quotas for representation played a part in causing the eventual result—in addition to, among other things, the direct participation of state-based actors in the proceedings. Under 'hard authority', the model utilised in this book also places 'informal use of power' (Chaps. 2 and 8). It can be methodologically and ethically difficult to state outright that law has been applied selectively. Nevertheless, attention should be paid to the problems over formalities encountered by reformist activists in 2014 —particularly what occurred after the AKS leadership election in 2014, since this bears some interesting similarities to the experience of RAIPON in 2013. As for *treasure*, the outset of the period saw this resource utilised softly. The formal governance networks were not given economic resources under their own control. However, as had been usual throughout the 1990s, funding from Western Sápmi was generally available to the Russian Sámi, in particular for border-transcending projects. The reformist network utilised this opportunity, as had been common for activists in the Russian Sámi revival movement. Regional authorities' public reactions to this support, as well as the looming threat of the Foreign Agent law from 2012, served as a disincentive for domestic actors to apply for further foreign support, making the situation approach the hard form of treasury-usage. Finally, regarding *organisation*, this chapter has looked at the management of political structures rather than 'task accomplishment'—but the advisory nature of all the state-regulated governance networks does result in a situation where the regional authorities are essentially free to ignore input and solve issues through their own organisational resources. At another level, hard utilisation of organisation is also demonstrated by the authorities' treatment of the councils elected at the First and Second Congress: when offered representatives that they found unacceptable, the regional authorities were able to, and did, chose to not involve them indigenous governance.

Finally, it should be noted that the conflict described in this chapter was not just about how to organise indigenous participation in regional indigenous governance, but also about distrust rooted in geopolitical conflict. From the very beginning, scepticism towards Western actors and ideas coloured the authorities', and some indigenous activists', responses to the reformist network. As geopolitical tension kept building and the Russian state apparatus increasingly reacted negatively against non-state actors with ties to foreign actors, reactions against the reformist network became harder. The indigenous nation dealt with in this chapter is at particular risk of being securitised, due to its East/West-transcending aspect, but the experiences described nevertheless reflect challenges faced by Russian indigenous civil society in general during a period of increasing global tension. It also provides a case study of strategies utilised in a situation where the authorities' need for formal input-channels clashes with the perceived need to keep certain actors out, and when different actors' ideas about representation and participation collide.

NOTES

1. The chapter draws partly on data from previous publications by the author, but also contains previously unpublished data. The material is subjected to new analysis in line with theory presented in Chap. 2. The chapter incorporates some text from the PhD thesis "Russian Sámi representation in Russian and pan-Sámi politics, 1992–2014" delivered for consideration at the Arctic University of Norway in February 2017 (method/ethics, empirical data, analysis).
2. See Chap. 2 for more on the Public Chamber.
3. According to the vice president's own account, Russian security structures attempted to recruit him as an agent inside RAIPON in 2010. Fearing reprisals after turning them down, he escaped to Norway with his family in 2011, enrolling as a student at the Arctic University of Norway. In 2013, Russian authorities demanded to have him extradited for alleged economic crimes. In 2015, he was given political asylum in Norway. (Berezhkov 2013; Nrk.no: Begjært utlevert av Putin—Fikk asyl i Norge, https://www.nrk.no/sapmi/russisk-urfolksaktivist-fikk-politisk-asyl-1.12155531).
4. The Kola Peninsula was invaded from the west in both world wars, and was heavily fortified during the Cold War due to the direct border between NATO and the USSR (more on this in Berg-Nordlie 2015b).
5. Beac.st: *Working group of indigenous peoples* (http://www.beac.st/en/Working-Groups/Working-Group-of-Indigenous-Peoples#members).
6. Originally *Tsentr korennykh malochislennykh narodov Severa* ("Centre of the Native, Small-Numbered Peoples of the North"), now the more ambiguous *Murmanskiy tsentr narodov Severa* ('Murmansk Centre of the Northern peoples'). On the face of it, this seems to indicate that the centre now has a broader field of activity than just Sámi issues. For this reason, the new name is occasionally criticised. In practice, the Centre's activity is still oriented toward Sámi issues (Gov-murman.ru: *Gosudarstvennoe oblastnoe byudzhetnoe uchrezhdenie "Murmanskiy tsentr narodov Severa"*, http://www.gov-murman.ru/region/saami/mcns/); *Ustav gosudarstvennoe oblastnoe...*, http://www.gov-murman.ru/region/saami/mcns/ustav.pdf). Originally, the Centre was nested under the Department for Local Governments and Legislative Issues, but after the First Congress (see below) it changed hands to the Committee for Contacts with Civil Society Organisations and Youth Affairs (Berg-Nordlie 2015a).
7. Originally institutionalised as a 'gosudarstvennoe oblastnoe uchrezhdenie', but later made a 'gosudarstvennoe oblastnoe *byudzhetnoe* uchrezhdenie', a terminology in line with that of Federal Law FZ-83 (2010) which regulates this type of institution.

8. Ansipira.npolar.no: *V Murmanskoy oblasti sozdan koordinatsionniy sovet korennykh malochislennykh narodov Severa* (http://ansipra.npolar.no/russian/Bulletin/Bulletin15R.pdf)

9. Further reasons for the desire to establish a Russian Sámediggi are explored in Berg-Nordlie (2011a, 2013, 2015a, b).

10. Finnmarken.no: *Vil ha russisk sameting*, www.finnmarken.no/Utenriks/article4020187.ece; Nrk.no: *Kola-samer vil ha eget sameting*, http://img.nrk.no/kanal/nrk_sami_radio/1.6206117.

11. Raipon.info: *Saami*, www.raipon.info/index.php/narody/narody-severa-sibiri-i-dalengo-vostoka-rf/252-2009-08-20-13-54-58.

12. Barents.no: *Eies av Nord-Norge*, https://barents.no/nb/om-oss/eies-av-nord-norge; Sametinget.no: *Barentssamarbeidet*, https://www.sametinget.no/Tjenester/Internasjonalt-arbeid/Barentssamarbeidet.

13. Finugor.ru.: *Saamy – novaya karta Zapada...*, http://www.finugor.ru/node/16207.

14. Csipn.ru: *Fond saamskogo naslediya i razvitiya..*, http://www.csipn.ru/glavnaya/region-news/286-fond-saamskogo-naslediya-i-razvitiya-eto-ne-reklama-my-rabotaem#.WKBwn6IRrBw.

15. Nrk.no: *Kola-samer vil ha eget sameting* (http://img.nrk.no/kanal/nrk_sami_radio/1.6206117); *Sterke kvinner uenige om sameting*, www.nrk.no/kanal/nrk_sapmi/1.7563483.

16. The Centre for Northern Peoples (*Davvi álbmogiid guovddáš*). Despite similarities in name, not connected to Murmansk Region's Northern Peoples' Centre (Senterfornordligefolk.no: *Murmansk Sámi Parliament på studiebesøk i Norge,* http://www.senterfornordligefolk.no/murmansk-sami-parliament-paa-studiebesoek-i-norge.5096433-146031.html).

17. 7 × 7.ru: *9 avgusta vo vsem mire...* (http://7x7-journal.ru/item/20144).

18. Nrk.no: *Sovkina hindret i å delta i Sametignets 25-årsjubileum* (http://www.nrk.no/sapmi/sovkina-nektet-utreise-fra-russland-igjen-1.11988898).

19. Nrk.no: *All makt til Valentina Sovkina* (http://www.nrk.no/sapmi/all-makt-til-valentina-sovkina-1.12050798), *Valget av Sovkina er kjent ugyldig* (http://www.nrk.no/sapmi/sovkina-er-ikke-godkjent-som-ny-leder-1.12070201).

20. Gov-murman.ru: *Izbran prezident Associacii kol'skikh saamov* (http://www.gov-murman.ru/region/saami/saami_news/74956/); 7 × 7-journal.ru: *Kol'skie saami vybrali novogo prezidenta* (http://7x7-journal.ru/item/55594).

21. Saamisups.ucoz.ru: *3 S"yezd Kol'skikh saamov 2014. Sozdanie iniciativnoy gruppy* (http://saamisups.ucoz.ru/publ/tretij_sezd_saamov_murmanskoj_oblasti/3_sezd_kolskikh_saamov_2014_sozdanie_iniciativnoj_gruppy/5-1-0-103); Nazaccent.ru: *Rossijskie saamy obsudyat na s"yezde noviy zakon i upravlyayuščiy organ* (http://nazaccent.ru/content/11187-rossijskie-saamy-

obsudyat-na-sezde-kto.html); Nazzaccent.ru: *Izmenyon format S"yezda saamov* (http://nazaccent.ru/content/13935-murmanskie-chinovniki-izmenili-format-sezda-saamov.html).

22. Youtube.com: *Vediščeva, N. N. Na s"yezde saamov. Obvinenie. Polnost'yu* (https://www.youtube.com/watch?v=c5xuJjrpG_I); Duma-murman.ru: *Vedishcheva Nataliya Nikolayeva* (http://www.duma-murman.ru/structure/deputies/vedisheva/); Finugor.ru: *III S"yezd rossiyskikh saami: ne po polozheniyu, pod davleniem chinovnikov, s obvineniyami v "rabote na Zapad"* (http://finugor.ru/iii-sezd-rossiiskikh-saami-ne-po-polozheniyu-pod-davleniem-chinovnikov-s-obvineniyami-v-rabote-na-za).

23. Gov-murman.ru: *Protokol III s"yezda korennogo naroda Kol'skogo Severa – saamov* (http://www.gov-murman.ru/bitrix/redirect.php?event1=file&event2=download&event3=Position.tiff&goto=/upload/iblock/1b8/Position.tiff).

24. Nazaccent.ru: *Saamy na s"yezde reshili sozdat' obshcherossiyskiy sojuz naroda* (http://nazaccent.ru/content/13964-saamy-na-sezde-reshili-sozdat-obsher ossijskij.html); Nazaccent.ru: *V Murmanske i Lovozere v Den' saamov podnyal nacional'niy flag* (http://nazaccent.ru/content/14741-v-murmanske-i-lovozere-v-den.html); Nazaccent.ru: *Rossiyskie saamy obsudyat na s"yezde noviy zakon i upravlyayushchiy organ* (http://nazaccent.ru/content/11187-rossijskie-saamy-obsudyat-na-sezde-kto.html).

25. Youtube.com: *Zhuravskij A. V. na s"yezde Saamov* (https://www.youtube.com/watch?v=QVORdPRkExo)

26. Moroshka.ucoz.ru: *Ustav fonda*, http://moroshka.ucoz.org/index/0-41.

27. This person has since retired as leader of the Council of Representatives. According to the protocol of the proceedings, a representative of the regional government declared at the close of the congress that all those elected to the Sobbar would form part of the Council of Representatives. However, the Council of Representatives has continued to exist as a formally separate governance network. According to interviewees it is now considered as a representative organ of the obshchinas and mainly dealing with issues related to these, but the formal delimitation of responsibilities between the Sobbar and the Council of Representatives is difficult to understand, since regulative documents about the new Sobbar have yet to be posted on the regional authorities' website. Gov-murman.ru: *V Murmanske sostojalas' pervaya vstrecha chlenov Saamskogo Sobraniya "Sám' Sobbar"* (http://www.gov-murman.ru/region/saami/decisions_kmns_congress/news_saami_assembly/66949); B-port.com: *Gubernator Murmanskoy oblasti Marina Kovtun provela rabochuyu vstrechu predstavitelyam Saamskogo sobrania Sám' Sobbar* (http://www.b-port.com/officially/item/146513.html).

28. Documents regulating the new *Sobbar*'s functions and structure are absent from the regional authorities' website. It is nevertheless treated here as

'formalised' in the sense that the regional authorities organised the congress that elected it, and have publicly recognized it as the representative organ of the Russian Sámi.

29. See f.ex. Gov-murman.ru: *V Lovozere sostoyalos' zasedanie Saamskogo sobrania « Sam' Sobbar »* (http://www.gov-murman.ru/region/saami/decisions_kmns_congress/news_saami_assembly/191427/).

30. Nrk.no: - *På tide at vi får bli med.* (https://www.nrk.no/sapmi/samer-i-russland-vil-inn-i-spr-1.7870404).

31. 7 × 7-journal: *V Saamskom parlamente Kol'skogo poluostrova vozmushcheny sozdaniem podkontrol'noy mestnym vlastyami organizatsii-dvoynika* (http://7x7-journal.ru/item/50717); *Valget av Sovkina er kjent ugyldig* (http://www.nrk.no/sapmi/sovkina-er-ikke-godkjent-som-ny-leder-1.12 070201); Finugor.ru: *Lidery saamskikh parlamentov Finlyandii i Shvecii nazvali Sojuz rossijskikh saami marionetochnym organom* (http://finugor.ru/lidery-saamskikh-parlamentov-finlyandii-i-shvetsii-nazvali-soyuz-rossiis kikh-saami-marionetochnym-or); Yle.fi: *Valentina Sovkina: Sápmelaččat Ruoššas besset dušše duhkoraddat smávva áššiiguin* (http://yle.fi/uutiset/valentina_sovkina_sapmelaccat_ruossas_besset_dusse_duhkoraddat_smavva_assiiguin/7661356).

32. Yle.fi: *Mii civkit SPR dievasčoahkkimis Oulus* (http://yle.fi/uutiset/mii_civkit_spr_dievascoahkkimis_oulus/7877617).

References

Aasland, Aadne, Mikkel Berg-Nordlie, and Elena Bogdanova. 2016. Encouraged but controlled: governance networks in Russian regions. *East European Politics* 32 (2): 148–169.

Alver, B.G., and Ø. Øyen. 2007. Challenges of Research Ethics: An Introduction. *FF Communications* 140 (292): 11–55.

Artieva, A. 2014. Saamskiy parlament Kol'skogo poluostrova: bor'ba za pravo nasamoopre-delenie. *Barentsobserver* November 20, 2014. http://barentsobserver.com/ru/opinion/2014/11/saamskiy-parlament-kolskogo-poluostrova-borba-za-pravo-na-samoopredelenie-20-11.

Berezhkov, D. 2012. *The Study of the Indigenous Peoples' Participation in Decision Making in Russia Federation.* Report, Davvi álbmogiid guovddáš/Senter for nordlige folk/Center of Northern People RAIPON.

Berezhkov, D. 2013. New Political Realities for the Indigenous Movement in Russia. *FDCIP 2013. Forum for Development Cooperation with Indigenous Peoples Conference Report.*

Berg-Nordlie, M. 2011a. Need and Misery in the Eastern Periphery. Nordic Sámi Discourseson the Russian Sámi. *Acta Borealia* 28 (1): 19–36.

Berg-Nordlie, M. 2011b. Striving to Unite. The Russian Sámi and the Nordic Sámi Parliament model. *Arctic Review on Law and Politics* 2 (1): 52–76.

Berg-Nordlie, M. 2013. The Iron Curtain through Sápmi. Pan-Sámi Politics, Nordic Cooperation and the Russian Sámi. In *L'image du Sápmi II, Études comparées. Textes réunis par Kajsa Andersson. Humanistica Oerebroensia. Artes et linguae*, ed. K. Andersson. Örebro: Örebro University.

Berg-Nordlie, M. 2015a. Who Shall Represent the Sámi? Indigenous Governance in Murmansk Region and the Nordic Sámi Parliament Model. In *Indigenous Policy. Institutions, Representation, Mobilisation*, ed. Mikkel Berg-Nordlie, Jo Saglie, and Ann Sullivan. Colchester: ECPR Press.

Berg-Nordlie, M. 2015b. Two centuries of Russian Sámi policy: arrangements for autonomy and participation seen in light of Imperial, Soviet and indigenous minority policy 1822–2014. *Acta Borealia* 32 (1): 40–67.

Berg-Nordlie, M. 2015c. Representasjon i Sápmi. Fire stater, fire tilnærminger til inklusjon av urfolk i samstyring. In *Den samepolitiske utviklingen på 2000-tallet*, ed. B. Bjerkli, and P. Selle. Oslo: Gyldendal.

Berg-Nordlie, Mikkel, and Olga Tkach. 2016. You are Responsible for Your People: The Role of Diaspora Leaders in the Governance of Immigrant Integration in Russia. *Demokratizatsiya* 24 (2): 173–198.

Bergh, J., and J. Saglie. 2015. Partisystem og skillelinjer i samepolitikken. In *Samer, makt og demokrati. Sametinget og den nye samiske offentligheten*, ed. B. Bjerkli, and P. Selle. Oslo: Gyldendal.

Bowring, Bill. 2013. Russian Legislation in the Area of Minority Rights. In *Managing Ethnic Diversity in Russia*, ed. Oleg Protsykh, and Benedikt Harzl, 15–36. New York: Routledge.

Bækken, H. 2013. Selective Law Enforcement in Russian Politics 2007-2011, *Legal Action for Extra-legal Purposes*. Ph.D. thesis, Faculty of Humanities, University of Oslo.

Centre. 2006. *Koordinatsyonniy sovet pri gosudarstvennom oblastnom uchrezhdenii 'Murmanskiy oblastnoy tsentr korennykh malochislennykh narodov Severa'.* (Regulative document, Coordination Council).

Charter. 2015. *Ustav Murmanskoy oblasti (s izmeneniyami na: 25.12.2015).* (Murmansk Region's charter).

Davies, Jonathan S., Jørn Holm-Hansen, Vadim Kononenko, and Asbjørn Røiseland. 2016. Network Governance in Russia: An Analytical Framework. *East European Politics* 32 (2): 131–147.

deCosta, R. 2015. States' Definitions of Indigenous Peoples: A Survey of Practices. In *Indigenous Policy. Institutions, Representation, Mobilisation*, ed. Mikkel Berg-Nordlie, Jo Saglie, and Ann Sullivan. Colchester: ECPR Press.

Drugge, A.-L. 2016a. How Can We do it Right? Ethical Uncertainty in Swedish Sámi Research. *Journal of Aacemic Ethics* August 2016: 1–17.

Drugge, A.-L. (ed.) 2016b. *Ethics in Indigenous Research. Past Experiences – Future Challenges*. Umeå: Vaartoe.

Falch, T., P. Selle, and K. Strømsnes. 2015. The Sámi: 25 years of Indigenous Authority in Norway. *Ethnopolitics* 15 (1): 125–143.

Fondahl, Gail. 1993. Siberia: Native Peoples and Newcomers. In *Nations and Politics in the Soviet Successor States*, ed. Ian Bremmer, and Raymond Taras, 477–510. Cambridge: Cambridge University Press.

Guarantees. 2009. Federal'niy zakon ot 30.04.99 N 82-FZ (Red. ot 05.04.2009) .... http://docs.procspb.ru/content/base/77555 (Law on Guarantees of Rights).

Gutsol, Natalia, and Larissa Riabova. 2002. Kola Saami and Regional Development. In *Conflict and Cooperation in the North*, ed. Kristiina Karppi, and Johan Eriksson, 313–342. Umeå: Norrlands Universitetsforlag.

Hood, Christopher. 1983. *The Tools of Government*. London: Macmillan.

Ingierd, H., and H.J. Fossum. 2014. *Etniske grupper*, NESH. (https://www.etikkom.no/FBIB/Temaer/Forskning-pa-bestemte-grupper/Etniske-grupper/).

IWGIA (International Working Group for Indigenous Affairs). 1991. The Association of Small Peoples of the Northern Soviet Union. Convention of the 26. International Work Group for Indigenous Affairs Newsletter No. 2, November/December 1991.

IWGIA. 2014. *The Indigenous World 2014*. Copenhagen: IWGIA.

IWGIA. 2015. *The Indigenous World 2015*. Copenhagen: IWGIA.

IWGIA. 2016. *The Indigenous World 2016*. Copenhagen: IWGIA.

Jakovlev, A. 2014. *III Congress of the Saami – the indigenous people of the Kola Peninsula*. [Letter circulated online, English version].

Josefsen, E., U. Mörkenstam, and J. Saglie. 2015. Different Institutions Within Similar States: The Norwegian and Swedish *Sámediggis*. *Ethnopolitics* 14 (1): 32–51.

Kalte, Zinaida. 2003. *Politiko-pravovye aspekty razvitiya korennogo malochislennogo naroda rossiyskoy federatsii – Saami*. Russia: Political Science diss., Russian Academy of State Agencies.

Kryazhkov, Vladimir. 2005. The Example of Khanty-Mansi Okrug. In *An Indigenous Parliament? Realities and Perspectives in Russia an the Circumpolar North*, ed. Kathrin Wessendorf, 28–38. Copenhagen: IWGIA.

Kryazhkov, Vladimir. 2010. *Korennye malochislennye narody Severa v rossiyskom prave*. Moskva: Izdatelstvo NORMA.

Kryazhkov, Vladimir. 2012. Rossiyskoe zakonodatel'stvo o severnykh narodakh I pravoprimeitel'naya praktika: sostoyanie I perspektivi. *Gosudarstvo I pravo* 5: 27–35.

Kryazhkov, V. 2015. Legal Regulation of the Relations Between Indigenous Small-Numbered Peoples of the North and Subsoil Users in the Russian Federation. *Northern Review* 39.

Larsson-Kalvemo, Astrid. 1995. 'Fighting for Survival.' Överlevelsesstrategier i nya omständigheter bland samerna på Kolahalvön. Master thesis, University of Tromsø, Tromsø.

LP. 2008. Sijt sobbar – sto let spustja. *Lovozerskaja Pravda* 26.12.08.

Mörkenstam, U., S. Dahlberg, J. Bergh, and J. Saglie. 2016. Valdeltagande, skiljelinker och legitimitet: en jämförelse med Norge. In *Sametingsval. Väljare, partier och media*, (eds.), R. Nilsson, S. Dahlberg, and U. Mörkenstam. Stockholm: Santérus.

NESH, De nasjonale forskningsetiske komiteene. 2016. *Guidelines for Research Ethics in the Social Sciences, Humanities, Law and Theology.*

Niemi, E., and A.J. Semb. 2009. *Forskningsetisk kontekst: Historisk urett og forskning som overgrep.*, NESH 2009 (https://www.etikkom.no/fbib/temaer/forskning-pa-bestemte-grupper/etniske-grupper/forskningsetisk-kontekst-historisk-urett-og-forskning-som-overgrep/).

Nyyssönen, J. 2015. Det samiske politiske etablissementet og motmobliseringen – konflikter om etniske kategorier i Finland. In *Samepolitikkens* utvikling, ed. B. Bjerkli, and P. Selle. Oslo: Gyldendal.

Obshchinas. 2000. Federalniy zakon ot 20 iyulya 2000 g. N 104-FZ Ob obshchikh printsipakh.... http://base.garant.ru/182356/. (Obshchna Law).

Olsen, T.A. 2016. Responsibility, Reciprocity and Respect. On the Ethics of (self-) Representation and Advocacy in Indigenous studies. In *Ethics in Indigenous Research. Past Experiences – Future Challenges*, A.-L. Drugge (2016b, ed). Umeå: Vaartoe.

Overland, I., and M. Berg-Nordlie. 2012. *Bridging Divides. Ethno-Political Leadership Among the Russian Sámi.* New York: Berghahn Books.

Øverland, Indra., and Helge Blakkisrud. 2006. The Evolution of Indigenous Policy in the Post-Soviet North. In *Tackling Space. Politics and the Russian North*, ed. Helge Blakkisrud and Geir Hønneland, 163–192. Lanham: University Press of America.

Pettersen, T. 2015. The Sámediggi Electoral Roll in Norway: Framework, Growth and Geographical Shifts. In *Indigenous politics. Institutions, representation, mobilisation*, ed. M. Berg-Nordlie, J. Saglie and A. Sullivan. Colchester: ECPR.

Postanovlenie. 2009. *Postanovlenie o sovete predstaviteleh korennykh malochislennykh narodov Severa pri pravitel'stve Murmanskoy oblasti:* http://www.gov-murman.ru/region/saami/convocation/.

Prosjektkatalog. 2009. *Prosjektkatalog Administrative bevilgninger Barentssekretariatet* (Grants from the Norwegian Barents Secretariat, 2009).

Prosjektkatalog. 2010. *PROSJEKTKATALOG SMÅPROSJEKT (adm. bev.) FOKUS 2010 juni-desember* (Grants from the Norwegian Barents Secretariat, 2010).

Prosjektkatalog. 2012. *PROSJEKTKATALOG 2012, URFOLK. Norwegian Barents Secretariat.* (Grants from the Norwegian Barents Secretriat, 2012).

Sámediggi. 2010. *SUPS MO Rådet for de fullmektige samiske representanter i Murmansk oblast – Avvikling av 2. samiske kongress i Murmansk – tilskudd* (Grant from the Norwegian Sámediggi, 2010).

Sharshina, N., and Ye. Yakovleva. 2008. *Perviy s''yezd saamov Rossii: Doroga k realizatsii vozmozhnostey.*

Sleptsov, Anatoly. N. 2005. RAIPON as Authorized Agency Representing the Rights of Indigenous Peoples. In *An Indigenous Parliament? Realities and Perspectives in Russia and the Circumpolar North*, ed. Kathrin Wessendorf, 66–67. Copenhagen: IWGIA.

Sokolovski, S.V. 2000. The Construction of 'Indigenousness' in Russian Science, Politics, and Law. *The Journal of Legal Pluralism and Unofficial Law* 32 (45): 91–113.

Sokolovskiy, S.V. 2011. Russian Legal Concepts and the Demography of Indigenous Peoples. In *Indigenous Peoples and Demography. The Complex Relation Between Identitiy and Statistics*, ed. P. Axelsson and P. Sköld. New York: Berghahn.

Sovkina, V. 2008. *Saamskij Parlament.* [Presentation of the Sami Parliament project by reform activists].

Third Congress. 2014a. Polozhenie o s''yezde korennogo naroda Kol'skogo Severa – saamov. http://gov-murman.ru/region/saami/decisions_kmns_congress/docs_saami_assembly/.

Third Congress. 2014b. Programma s''yezda korennogo naroda Severa – saamov. http://gov-murman.ru/region/saami/decisions_kmns_congress/docs_saami_assembly/.

Todishev, Mikhail. 2005. Indigenous Peoples and the Electoral System of the Russian Federation. In *An Indigenous Parliament? Realities and Perspectives in Russia and the Circumpolar North*, ed. Kathrin Wessendorf, 52–65. Copenhagen: IWGIA.

TTP. 2001. Federalniy zakon ot 7 maya 2001 g. N 49-FZ... (TTP law) http://base.garant.ru/12122856. (TTP Law).

Túnon, H., Kvarnström, M. & H. Lerner. 2016. "Ethical Codes of Conduct for Research Related to Indigenous Peoples and Local Communities—Core Principles, Challenges and Opportunities. In *Ethics in Indigenous Research. Past Experiences—Future Challenges*, ed. A.-L. Drugge. Umeå: Vaartoe.

Turaev, Vadim. 2005. The Examples of Amur and Khabarovsk. In *An Indigenous Parliament? Realities and Perspectives in Russia and the Circumpolar North*, ed. Kathrin Wessendorf, 74–87. Copenhagen: IWGIA.

Vabo, S.I., and A. Røiseland. 2012. Conceptualizing the Tools of Government in Urban Network Governance. *International Journal of Public Administration* 35 (14): 934–946.

Vinogradova, Svetlana. 2005. *Saami kol'skogo poluostrova: osnovnye tendentsii sovremennoy zhisni*. Apatity: KNC RAN.

Vinogradova, Svetlana. 2010. Formirovanie gosudarstvennoy politiki v otnoshenii korennykh malochislennykh narodov Severa, Sibiri i Dal'nego vostoka: retrospektivniy analiz. *Trudy kol'skogo nauchnogo tsentra RAN 2*.

Vladimirova, V. 2005. Just Labor. Labor Ethic in a Post-Soviet Reindeer Herding Community. *Acta Universitatis Upsaliensis. Uppsala Studies in Cultural Anthropology No. 40*.

Vladimirova, V. 2011. We are Reindeer People, We Come from Reindeer'. Reindeer Herding in Representations of the Sami in Russia. *Acta Borealia* 28 (1): 89–113.

WGIP. 2007. *Annual Report 2007*.

WGIP. 2013. *Annual Report 2013*.

Yetylen, Vladimir. 1996. Self-government among the Small Peoples of the North. In *Anxious North. Indigenous Peoples in Soviet and Post-Soviet Russia. Selected Documents, Letters and Articles*, ed. Aleksandr Pika, Jens Dahl, and Inge Larsen, 83–94. Copenhagen: IWGIA.

Zakharov, Dmitry. 2005. The Example of Sakha (Yakutia). In *An Indigenous Parliament? Realities and Perspectives in Russia and the Circumpolar North*, ed. Kathrin Wessendorf, 88–98. Copenhagen: IWGIA.

CHAPTER 9

Patterns of Governance in Russia: Feedback of Empirical Findings into Governance Theory

Sabine Kropp and Aadne Aasland

9.1   Investigating Variance and Commonalities of Russian Governance Networks

As many hybrid and authoritarian regimes have consolidated over the past years, it is a worthwhile endeavour to investigate how authorities in such regimes cope with complex policy problems and how they try to achieve output legitimacy. In answering this question, this volume utilised network governance theory to analyse different arenas of contemporary Russian politics. In the encompassing literature on governance, networks are often considered to be characteristic of modern democracies which create and nurture such bodies in order to enhance the quality of decisions by involving

S. Kropp (✉)
Otto Suhr Institute of Political Science, Chair of German Politics,
Freie Universität Berlin, Ihnestraße 22, 14195 Berlin, Germany
e-mail: sabine.kropp@fu-berlin.de

A. Aasland
The Norwegian Institute for Urban and Regional Research (NIBR),
Oslo and Akershus University College of Applied Sciences, St. Olavs Plass,
Po box 4, 0130 Oslo, Norway
e-mail: aadne.aasland@nibr.hioa.no

© The Author(s) 2018   219
S. Kropp et al. (eds.), *Governance in Russian Regions*,
DOI 10.1007/978-3-319-61702-2_9

non-state actors into policy-making, and to increase legitimacy among affected parts of the populace. In the recent past, however, authoritarian and hybrid regimes, such as those in China and Russia, have also experimented with governance networks, thus further substantiating the assumption that network governance is a pervasive phenomenon not solely associated with liberal democratic regimes (see Chap. 2). Correspondingly, it is the overarching argument of this book that governance networks can be found almost everywhere in today's politics. For the purpose of our analysis, formalised governance networks which bring together various types of non-state actors and state authorities in order to cope with everyday policy problems were examined. Within such networks, horizontal relations among the actors, some rather rudimentary and others more distinct, emerge. As a matter of course, the Russian state exerts a strong role as network manager and is able to dominate interactions

(see below; for further definition of the concept and its difference and relatedness to other types of Russian informal networks see Chap. 2).

The basic objective of this chapter is to systematise the empirical observations provided by the case studies in this volume and to contribute to a form of network governance theory that fits into various regime contexts and sheds the normative baggage of—the often unrealistic— assumptions taken from a liberal-democratic context. In doing so, some conclusions about network governance in hybrid and authoritarian regimes can be drawn: why do these governance networks emerge; what is their practical functioning; and how do they relate to hierarchical modes of governing?

Strikingly, the need for a 'managed', 'constructive' or 'consenting' civil society has become part of official Russian discourse on state-society relations and is manifest in everyday political practice (Aasland et al. 2016; Myhre and Berg-Nordlie 2016). In Russia, civil society participation within governance networks is designed to substitute the weak problem-solving capacity of the representative-democratic institutions. Even in a markedly recentralised system, it holds true that complex problems cannot be solved adequately by resorting to hierarchy, command and coercion alone or by simply applying decrees coming 'from above'. Governance networks can be investigated in regimes that are very different from each other, because similar and complex social, political and economic issues occur (Van Bueren et al. 2003) irrespective of the regime type. Not coincidentally, all policy issues selected for this book are somewhat 'wicked' (Head 2008): they either feature a high level of social or political conflict, cut across policy sectors and demand coordination, or they are salient in that policy solutions considerably affect the authorities' legitimacy. Significantly, in all case studies collected in this volume, state authorities were faced with a situation where they could not solve certain problems without involving non-state actors, or where such actors were incorporated or given an arena to participate in order to secure stability. This general evidence, however, does not imply that all governance networks were used in order to enhance effective policy solutions. Increasing effectivity and problem-solving capacity is not always the primary goal of actors establishing and maintaining networks. Accordingly, some of the case studies confirm the conventional wisdom that organisations may sometimes just be symbolic (Boxenbaum and Jonsson 2013: 81; see below).

Besides having some striking commonalities, the networks examined in this book cover a considerable range of regional as well as policy- and case-related variations. To find policy-related differences is not really surprising because policy studies have frequently emphasised that actor constellations are essentially formed by the characteristics of the respective policy (Lowi 1972: 299). Correspondingly, the chapters give evidence that the composition and use of governance networks vary from one policy to another. At the same time, however, the empirical data uncovered significant variance within one and the same policy field. For this reason, in order to encompass both differences and similarities, it was not only necessary to compare networks across policies, but also to investigate various networks in one and the same policy issue—comparing different regions, or during different points in time.

Examining second-tier, regional administrative entities facilitates an operationalisation of different strategic contexts in which networking actors operate. The Russian federation offers a kind of living laboratory for exploring such regional variation, as it features a large number of federal subjects shaped by enormous economic and political asymmetries, and a system that still allows for policy solutions tailored to regional and local needs. To illustrate this subnational variance, all chapters but Chap. 8 examined one policy issue in two regions. But also in the Chap. 8, three different cases could be compared because the study took place over a prolonged period and hence investigated different systems for indigenous representation at various points in time. Altogether, the research design underlying the inquiries in this book allowed for the carving out of varying subnational governance styles.

Within the outline of this research design, which combines regional and cross-sectoral comparisons, some case-related differences also became conspicuous (see e.g. Chap. 4). Under the basic ideas of neo-institutionalism, this finding is not really surprising: all strands of neo-institutionalism unanimously highlight the role of actors constructing rules which, again, constitute actors (Scott 2014: 81; Hall and Taylor 1993; Scharpf 1997). Actors have various interests and preferences and understand their roles within networks differently; rules constituting networks are thus interpreted in various ways. In other words, one should be aware that a residual and contingent 'actor-related factor' continues to shape individual cases, even though it is possible to carve out *typical* patterns of Russian governance.

These common characteristics of network governance in Russia are discussed in the following section of this chapter. First and foremost, they relate to the *dominant role of the state*. Although the Russian state is often reliant on the resources of private actors, it stands out that strong asymmetries sculpt most interactions of state and non-state actors within the networks. To secure its prominent position, the state applies an extensive variety of hard and soft meta-governance tools for controlling networks. In the same section, the *functions* of Russian governance networks are reconsidered. Subsequently, it is discussed how the Russian institutional context, which is shaped by a high degree of fragmentation, impacts subnational governance networks in that it provides 'access points' for non-state actors (Bouwen 2004). Networks are not only anchored into the multi-layered, albeit strongly recentralised federal setting, but also interact with various, sometimes even competing, authorities representing different portfolios and pursuing diverging policy objectives at the different territorial levels. In recapitulating typical patterns of Russian network governance, theoretical generalisations about the nature of governance under the conditions of a hybrid regime can finally be drawn. In this way, through detailed empirical comparisons, the book allows for feeding back into general governance theory in the final section of this chapter.

9.2   Types of Russian Governance Networks

By sorting the rich empirical material generated by the case studies, both differences and commonalities of governance networks become distinct and visible, thereby allowing for developing typologies on a more abstract level. The networks are categorised by focusing on the dominant position of the state within the networks as well as showing the functions networks fulfil in the policy process.

9.2.1 State Dominance Within the Networks

At the most general level, it can be summarised that nearly all networks investigated in this book were more or less dominated by state authorities. Russian civil society interacts with powerful—albeit resource-dependent—state actors. Referring to the NATO-model (introduced in Chap. 2) we observe that—in terms of treasury, authority, and organisation—the state practices a mix of 'hard' and 'soft' meta-governance tools (Vabo and Røiseland 2012). The state retains a monopoly on decision-making authority, since Russian governance networks are never given real, formalised decision-making power. Organisational resources are not just used to exert influence inside networks, but also allow state employees to make decisions disregarding networks' input if they see fit. As to treasury: the state is a central source of financial support for Russian civil society, the more so as it has been reducing the supplements from foreign donors during recent years. The result of this is that the authorities also hold a strong nodal position within networks, a position from where they can spread informational resources and dominate communication channels. Their monopoly on authority, combined with the reduction of rival treasuries, make Russian state institutions focal points for providing orientation for civil society actors who try to exert influence and obtain funding. State actors use organisational resources in order to have staff employed which works with the policy issues in question, thereby further strengthening nodality. Ministries, state services, and state-owned institutions (see, for example, Chaps. 7, 8) become the hubs around which much of civil society activity revolve. Finally, nodality in public discursive processes is enhanced by Russian media paying acute attention to messages sent out by the state, while it is much more difficult—although not totally impossible—for non-state actors to break through with their discourse (cf. Myhre and Berg-Nordlie 2016).

Governance networks can in general be placed on a continuum ranging from self-regulated via state-managed, to purely 'mimicked' bodies. In self-regulating networks, either non-state actors negotiate policy solutions autonomously or representatives of the state participate on an equal footing with the non-state actors in the network. The state authorities refrain from applying hard meta-governance tools to dominate the horizontal interactions. However, even in democracies this ideal-type of network is rather uncommon, and so one should not expect to find many of such bodies in hybrid regimes like Russia either (Davies et al. 2016). Unsurprisingly, there are just a few cases in our Russian sample: for instance, one of the platforms designed to moderate and prevent ethnic conflicts in Krasnodar (Chap. 7) and a few of the networks regulating child care in Samara and St. Petersburg (Chap. 6), resemble this network model. In these cases, the very purpose of the network is to come up with suggestions that the regional and local councils are obliged to consider—but of course not necessarily to approve.

In the indigenous policy case (Chap. 8), one of the governance networks even formally fulfils the self-regulating model. However, due to the informal mechanisms, it is accused of having been constituted in a manner that made it improbable from the outset that this body would display 'dissentful' contention (Cheskin and March 2015) or other unwanted behaviour, thus in practice not threatening state control. In a few cases (see above), the state facilitated or established networks, but subsequently confined its own role to more or less that of an observer. This happened, for example, during some public hearings held to conduct environmental impact assessments (EIAs, see Chap. 4). In other cases, again, the networks were initiated and led by non-state actors, and the state actors were invited as participants without taking on a dominating role. Although few of these networks could be considered authentically self-regulating bodies, they at least ensured 'effective consultancy' (see Chap. 2), i.e., the advice and expertise provided by non-state actors were used as the basis for subsequent decision-making or problem-solving. On the described continuum, these networks still fall within the range of soft state dominance, but can be placed closer to the pole of self-regulation. In all investigated cases, however, state authorities would have had the opportunity and power to intervene if they deemed it useful or appropriate. Despite the generally strong role of state authorities, the mentioned cases, however, point up that soft forms of meta-governance do still appear in the context of the Russian hybrid regime.

In contrast, mimicked networks, which are located at the other pole of the continuum, can be understood as a phenomenon in which authorities establish a requested organisational model but either undercut its influence or staff it with actors who kow-tow to state interests. By establishing and using governance networks, these bodies technically fulfil demands from above (in the state hierarchy), from below (grassroots), or from outside (international obligations or rules set by foreign partners), but no real policy is being developed and the substantial input and representational function is missing. Networks are often called 'faked' by activists and politicians who oppose them, but we here use objective criteria to categorise networks as 'mimicked': if the non-state actors are fully dependent on the state, and if the network has no other relevant function than to conform to the demanded organisational model.

In fact, rich evidence for such forged networks could be found. They were, for example, at work in Stavropol, where the regional government was not willing to incorporate autonomous non-state actors effectively into the network, but rather preferred to imitate network governance in order to demonstrate at least some activity to the citizens and to the federal government (see Chap. 7). They also occurred during the implementation of the environmental impact assessments (Chap. 4). Within these mandatory networks, collaboration with non-state actors was dodged whenever state actors had their own stakes in projects of high economic value. At other times, though, it is more difficult to conclude as to whether or not a network should be classified as 'mimicked'. Two of the networks for indigenous policy given in Chap. 8, for example, were created to meet demands from below, but at least one of them based itself on members that can be said to have been dependent on the state authorities. The third network, again, is created in a manner that makes participants formally independent of the state, but is nevertheless accused of being 'mimicked' because of the informal selection processes disadvantaging non-state actors.

These findings pose the question why actors spend considerable transaction costs for establishing and maintaining these mimicked networks that, in terms of problem-solving capacity, seem to be strikingly ineffective. A simple, but obvious answer is: state actors create and nurture such bodies for they are considered as the proper way things should be done. Civil society involvement is somewhat taken for granted and enforced by legislation in today's Russia; actors tend to stick to such generalised expectations, even if they are not willing to trigger networks. Also, international programs have actively spread policy instruments, among others civil society involvement, to the Soviet successor states, including Russia. Large Russian industries (which, sometimes, also operate in Western countries) employ professional staff for health, safety and environmental risk management and are usually well informed about prevalent policy instruments and approaches; international NGOs also exchange knowledge about experiences in their field (the EIA issues illustrate the diffusion of such instruments). Such processes are accompanied by constant academic exchanges among experts, who sometimes even draft the laws for Russian ministries such as the ministry of the environment (*Minprirody*). Thus, network governance may be distributed simultaneously through various channels. Moreover, through creating governance networks, the state fulfils the expectations of civil society organisations and their constituencies —and deflects potential criticism for side-lining these interests.

To further theorise this argument, isomorphism provides a suitable approach for grasping such processes of imitation (Meyer and Rowan 1977). The theory points to the widespread observation that institutional designers and political leaders copy acknowledged organisational models and institutions—not necessarily because they are perceived as an adequate tool, but simply because actors respond strategically to institutional or other external pressures. By incorporating elements from the institutional environment, an organisation may become 'imbued' with legitimacy (Wooten and Hoffman 2013: 132). In a similar vein, it was emphasised that processes of imitation make organisations 'more similar without necessarily making them more efficient' (DiMaggio and Powell 1983: 147).

The copying of prevalent models leads to a remarkable uniformity in organisational structure. At the same time, actors often tend to keep the already existing rules and routines of organisations alive because they have to cope with conflicts between contradicting institutional and political pressures. Activities of participants therefore often keep 'decoupled' from formal structures (Scott 2014: 185). As a result, a 'new', officially sanctioned organisational model—in this study the governance networks—may become more or less detached from the authorities' real operations and everyday strategies which exist independently from the established structures. Thus the theory gives reasons why governance networks seem to triumph and successfully travel throughout political systems, although not always fulfilling substantial functions. On the other hand, however, it seems not to be completely impossible that even such 'sleeping' networks can be activated at some indefinite future date.

Generally, networks in Russia feature strong asymmetries between state and non-state actors. They are shaped by distinct hierarchies between the knots forming the particular network. Within this general category of state dominance, however, there is leeway for some diversity of conceptualisation, so that different degrees of state dominance can be categorised somewhere between the two poles of the continuum. These degrees refer to the way networks are governed by the state. In the basic concept of meta-governance underlying the case studies (Chap. 2), the concept of state-dominated networks can be reflected as whether (and why) the state applies predominantly hard or soft tools on to the networks.

On this note, we distinguish two subtypes of state-dominated governance networks: one labelled as being 'strongly dominated', and the other designated as being 'softly dominated' (see Fig. 9.1). In the first scenario, state authorities predominantly resort to means of coercion and command, either explicitly or implicitly as well as selectively. In the second, the main emphasis is on the use of incentives and on developing strategies that

self-regulated ══════════════ state-dominated ══════════════ mimicked

softly dominated	strongly dominated
N: State has a relatively central position in terms of information and communication transfer	**N:** State monopolises flow of information and communication and utilises this to push agenda, block unwanted signalling from non-state actors, overwhelm actors and public with own rhetoric.
A: Enabling and non-binding regulations	**A:** Restrictive regulations, violation of rules (informal use of power)
Representatives selected or nominated by non-state actors	Representatives selected by state authorities; state-dominated NGOs
T: Funding or financial aid by the state; funding not widely used to censor, external funding available	**T:** No or very limited funding, or state monopolises funding. Uses this to marginalise unwanted actors, cultivate wanted actors.
O: Tasks are accomplished by the network, inside the network.	**O:** Tasks are accomplished through state organisation external to the network or through state organisation within the network.

Fig. 9.1 Subtypes of Russian state-dominated governance networks

enable a deeper collaboration with NGOs. Accordingly, Fig. 9.1 takes up the considerations of Chap. 2, depicting that nodality, authority, treasure and organisation—the four components of the NATO model (Hood 1983)—can be applied differently to each network. Note that even though some important tools are compiled in the figure, it cannot provide a comprehensive list, for the empirical diversity is inexhaustible.

Where to draw the line between softly and strongly (hard) state-dominated networks is not always clear. As a rule of thumb, a governance network is characterised as 'strongly state-dominated' if hard tools are predominantly applied onto a network, and as 'softly state-dominated' if the soft tools dwarf the hard ones. Of course, meta-governance strategies of authorities tend to feature a mix of hard and soft tools, and the mix can change over time. For instance, state actors may refrain from selecting the representatives of NGOs, but state grants and subsidies can nevertheless be limited and regulations may be restrictive. Given such a case, a network is nevertheless categorised as 'strongly' dominated by the state. There were examples of some state-loyal or state-dominated NGOs being given control over the nomination of candidates, thereby excluding more critical organisations or individuals from network participations. Regulations of quotas from different types of organisations are, for example, another way of manipulating network membership. Thus, hard and soft tools can be difficult to discern for an outside observer as the mere possibility, sometimes hidden or implicit, of using them may induce the NGOs to act in a certain way.

Despite the overarching state dominance characterising most Russian governance networks, the findings reinforce one of the basic theoretical assumptions of governance theory: it highlights that authorities substantially depend on the resources of non-state actors. Sometimes the involvement of non-state actors is needed to accomplish specific policy goals; at other times their incorporation into networks is mainly aimed at preventing public criticism; while at other times again the state is seeking legitimacy by being appreciated by actors from below, above or outside as incorporating certain interest groups. In all these cases, the non-state actors possess resources— even if their very agreement to be present in a network is 'for show'—that are needed by the state. The state's dependence on non-state actors is neither contradictory to the finding of state dominance, nor really surprising. State actors—whether in democracies or in hybrid and authoritarian regimes— need to gather information and expertise, coordinate resources, and try to enhance legitimacy by collaborating with civil society.

9.2.2   *Network Functions*

Governance networks can also be classified as to their functions. Table 9.1 gives an overview about types of functions performed by governance networks in the six policies examined. Authoritative decisions are hardly ever made by these bodies; the *decision-making* function of Russian governance networks has, in fact, remained rudimentary. The environmental impact assessments (EIAs) are an exception because the involvement of NGOs, which have to sign the minutes of the meetings, is stipulated by law. However, as the empirical findings reveal, participation of non-state actors was nevertheless undermined in a number of EIAs (Chap. 4). Some limited, or indirect, decision-making authority was also observed within indigenous policy and child welfare.

The basic finding, which highlights the weak decision-making capacity of networks, is not really surprising. It is not the norm in Western contexts either that decision-making power is downright devolved to governance networks. It would seriously affect the quality of democracy if private actors, whose legitimacy is much weaker than that of the elected representatives, would have the last say. Accordingly, critical assessments of network governance highlight that the democratic performance of networks needs to be anchored in representative institutions; by no means do governance networks lead to an end to sovereign rule in democracies (Héritier and Lehmkuhl 2008; Bekkers et al. 2007). These statements, however, get a different twist in hybrid regimes because in such contexts governance networks may become one of the few arenas where unbiased inputs are formulated by non-state actors (depending, of course, on the composition of networks).

It is glaringly conspicuous that the *implementation* function of Russian networks is more common than the decision-making function. For example, socially oriented organisations, with their special status among Russian NGOs, are given the task to implement welfare services for the state, as the chapters on HIV policies (Chap. 3) and child welfare (Chap. 6) illustrate. This is the result of low state capacity, an ideology of state retrenchment in the social sphere, and civil society's easier access to hard-to-reach target groups and, at times, by the limited scope of developing innovative and cost-efficient methods. But this result is specific for social policy and, given noticeable policy differences, needs further contextualisation. By looking at the other policy issues examined in this book, it becomes evident that networks rarely contribute to the implementation of policies. Decisions are regularly executed by the state's own administration (Table 9.1).

Table 9.1 Governance networks typology

	HIV/Drug prevention	Environmental impact assessment	Climate change adaptation	Child welfare	Ethnic policy	Indigenous governance
Type of network						
Self-regulation	No	No	No	Partially	Partially	No
Soft state-dominance	Common	Common	Common	Most common	Yes	Networks have features of both soft and hard tools
Hard state-dominance	Most common	Common	Most common	Common	Yes	
Mimicked	No	Common	No	No	Yes	Partially
Network function						
Decision-making	No	Yes, but limited	No	No	No	No
Consultancy/advice	Yes	Yes	Yes	Yes	Yes	Yes
Implementation	Yes	No	No	Yes	Little	Some
Co-ordination	Yes	Yes	Yes	Yes	Yes	Yes
Monitoring/control	Little	Little	No	Partially	No	No
Conflict management	No	No	No	No	Yes	Yes

The network function which is arguably the hardest to assess is *legitimacy*: the purpose of it is undisputed, but its effects are diffuse. According to the problem-centred strand of network governance theory, the state garners broader (input as well as output) legitimacy when incorporating private actors (Chap. 2). In harmony with this, the case studies collected in this book suggest that in those networks, in which representatives were accepted as cooperation partners by the authorities (albeit not always on an equal footing), NGOs more often uttered supportive views of policy-making around their policy issue than they did in mimicked networks. Russian media, for their part, present governance networks as useful and as a widespread and natural approach to policy-making (Myhre and Berg-Nordlie 2016). Chapter 6 shows how child welfare is a sentimentalised policy area in Russia that brings 'all good forces' together for the sake of the children, thereby legitimising state policy. In Chap. 8 we observe that despite all the conflicts surrounding state-indigenous governance networks, the authorities are committed for purposes of legitimacy and rule-fulfilment to having organs that formally constitute indigenous representation.

Yet, how networks effectively impact on the citizens' support for the regime has to remain an open question, the more so as the membership of most Russian NGOs is small and has limited capacity to sustainably influence citizens. It also remains an unresolved question whether the mimicked networks can generate any legitimacy at all, or whether the citizens are able to read the hidden agenda behind these networks. In the interviews, representatives of NGOs in virtually all policy areas evaluated single governance networks as 'fake', and as attempts to conform to authoritative demands without being enlivened as true working bodies. However, other interviewees were more positively oriented, seeing in governance networks at least some chance to influence the authorities. Finally, it cannot be solidly evaluated whether mimicked networks contribute to enhance legitimacy or not, and if so, to what degree, because data revealing how citizens and elites assess the functioning and effectiveness of governance networks do not exist.

Apart from the outlined differences, some commonalities stand out. Just a few governance networks were designed to monitor the administrations; and even if the *monitoring* and *controlling* function was assigned to networks, state actors were still able to avoid or even undermine such activities, as for example the case studies on environmental impact assessments reveal (Chap. 4). Rarely were the informants able to give an account of whether and how the platforms' monitoring takes place in a systematic way, thereby underlining the ambiguity of these practices (see e.g. Chap. 3 on HIV and drug policy).

In contrast, all networks fulfil *coordinative* functions. This finding is not really surprising since coordination is a constitutive function of networks which are by definition designed to bring various types of actors together. Furthermore, the vertical, compartmentalised policy-making process in Russia, and underdeveloped practices of cross-sectoral collaboration between policy sectors necessitate mechanisms that can cope with this complexity (see below). This task is often fulfilled by policy network platforms which are set up to coordinate initiatives and designed to avoid the duplication of activities and which consequently distribute tasks and responsibilities among network members (all chapters give evidence of this). Another important coordination function of the platforms is simply to facilitate the exchange of information that both state and non-state actors need in order to perform their roles in the policy-making system. Coordination of measures directed towards specific population groups, which are sometimes hard to reach or approach by state authorities, was also a function frequently found within many network governance platforms—especially within social policies.

Furthermore, it should be noticed that nearly all networks exert some *consultative* and *advisory* functions, even though not all are used to gather 'effective consultancy', meaning that policies proposed by the network are in the end taken as basis for authoritative decisions. In general, research on governance networks has emphasised that expertise has become an important resource of non-state actors in the 'information society' and, from the view of state actors, for effective problem-solving (Mayntz 1993a). Only recently, though, has attention turned to the relevance of this resource for authoritarian regimes (Davies et al. 2016). Undoubtedly, information and expertise are invaluable resources for both democratic and non-democratic rulers. But it seems plausible that incumbents in hybrid and authoritarian regimes are particularly afflicted with the problem of having scarce information. Due to the strong hierarchies shaping non-democratic regimes, rulers cannot effectively gather (local) information, the more so because citizens and elites often hide their true opinions in front of the authorities (Wintrobe 1998). Lacking unbiased information and authentic feedback, incumbents face the difficulty of trying to calculate realistically the political effects of their decisions, and therefore tend to make decisions which miss the mark. In strongly centralised states such as

Russia, decision-making bodies at the top of the state hierarchy are typically overstrained—a problem which had already seriously impaired effective policy solutions in the former Soviet Union. The attempts of the Russian government to create and manage a 'constructive' civil society can be better understood against this backdrop: NGOs are expected to deliver expertise and critical assessments, but, at the same time, to remain loyal and keep within the limits defined by the state.

Considering these shortcomings, it is easy to grasp why consultancy and advice are the most prominent functions of Russian governance networks. NGOs are able to provide expertise and information which cannot sufficiently be produced by the representative institutions, not least of all because the latter are incorporated into the strict hierarchies of the 'power vertical'. Moreover, from the perspective of state actors, NGOs may not only deliver the desired policy expertise, but also bring in some politically relevant information (Webber 1992). As a kind of early-warning mechanism, non-state actors involved in networks signal to the authorities which policy solution may be accepted by the citizens and which may not. This, however, requires that NGOs are able to credibly represent any noteworthy group interest—a precondition which is not always a given. Moreover, the task is difficult to achieve, because if NGOs would signal discontent, this could easily be interpreted as a lack of loyalty and thus arouse suspicion. For this reason, critical NGOs have to cope with the risk that a clear line cannot be drawn between constructive criticism and 'consentful contention' (Cheskin and March 2015) on the one side and oppositional or antagonistic attitudes on the other.

From the perspective of the state actors, it is easier to keep discussions under control within networks than to provide space for critical public discourses, which may run out of control. Correspondingly, all case studies collected in this book corroborate that, even if incumbents appreciate the expertise and information provided by NGOs, they more or less exhibit an ambivalent attitude towards non-state actors providing *political* information. Consequently, rulers face a basic dilemma. They are reliant on the expertise of NGOs, but nonetheless aim to limit non-state actors' autonomy, which, again, is a prerequisite for developing the demanded resources. As support, our empirical data provide a wealth of evidence that the elites' attitudes towards governance networks remain ambiguous, hovering between the fear of putting authority at stake and the goal of producing effective policy outputs (Kropp and Schuhmann 2016).

Some networks have also *conflict management* as a core function (e.g. ethnic and indigenous policies, environmental impact assessments—see Table 9.1), in the sense that they should contribute to mitigating, negotiating and resolving conflicts in society. This does not mean, however, that the governance networks are set up to resolve conflicts among competing political interests. The platforms are not considered arenas for political interest representation, and non-state participants are usually seen as merited experts that work towards the common good rather than representatives that have a fixed mandate or represent certain non-state interests.

9.3   Fragmented Institutional Architecture as Context for Governance Networks

Governance networks must be understood in the institutional context in which they operate (Owen-Smith and Powell 2013); they usually bear a strong institutional footprint. In the following, the impact of two institutional elements able to provide and multiply 'access points' (Bouwen 2004) to NGOs is discussed: the multilevel setting and the sectoral organisation of government. Although the Russian system is shaped by tight hierarchies, it still provides a strongly fragmented institutional arrangement: responsibilities are not only distributed among various territorial levels, but also between sectorally-organised ministries and administrative tiers, which, again, link the different territorial entities to each other. All governance networks investigated in this book are somewhat anchored in this complex context which consists of different—not always coherent—and sometimes even conflicting institutional layers.

The Russian multilevel system operates as a context highly relevant for showing how governance networks are run. Local and regional network options are sustainably influenced by federal politics. These territorial interactions have been simplified by the metaphor of the 'power vertical', which comprises a toolkit of various instruments the federal government can apply to subnational governance networks. Besides the legal distribution of responsibilities fixed in the constitution and in federal laws, strategic behaviour and opportunity structures decisively shape federal-regional interactions. This even more so as actors often do not comply with the rules and as laws and regulations often contradict each other, leave space for interpretation, and are not resolutely enforced. Federal authorities in Russia are less constricted in encroaching on regional responsibilities than their counterparts in democratic federations, where the separation of powers principle shapes the relations between the federal units more strongly. Moreover, the regulatory idea of 'federal comity' (Burgess 2006), which provides the glue holding the territorial entities of a federation together and concomitantly prevents authorities from taking hand in the responsibilities of other federal units, exists as only a shadow in Russian politics.

As shown in some of the cases studied for this book, the federal government itself intervened in the cases, i.e. either directly into the formation and the everyday functioning of the networks (Chap. 7), or, in a few cases, it also undermined cooperative governance and squeezed out non-state actors (Chap. 4). Strikingly, such interventions do not follow comprehensible rules, but instead are undertaken if the authorities regard it as useful or necessary. Sometimes, federal authorities lack the capacity or simply see no need or have no motivation to intervene into the subnational networks (Chap. 7)— non-intervention is, indeed, also a common pattern. In addition, federal authorities may make less binding policy recommendations to which regional authorities may or may not choose to adhere. This was for example the case with needle exchange programmes for drug users, programmes which are strongly discouraged by federal authorities but nevertheless carried out by a few Russian regions (Chap. 3). In summary, it can be stated that federal interventions into subnational networks create most *diverse* linkages between the arenas of multilevel and network governance.

The effects of federal interventions on governance networks are by no means unambiguous. The enforcement of federal authority can lead either to the facilitation, the prevention or even to the virtual dissolution of existing governance networks. In reviewing the empirical data, a couple of basic strategic motives explaining why the federal government intervenes can be singled out. Firstly, some cases revealed that the federal government tends to encroach on the federal subject's jurisdictions, if the federal government aims at developing a region economically. Such processes were at work in Krasnodar, where the federal government intervened into regional policy-making in order to achieve improvements in ethnic conflict management by promoting networks (see Chap. 7). Secondly, the federal government may take influence upon subnational governance networks if federal actors have their own stakes in projects of high economic value, as Chap. 4 describing environmental impact assessments shows. Moreover, federal authorities do enforce public participation in EIA in order to reduce ecological conflicts and avert public discontent since it is feared that this could undermine the regime's legitimacy. Finally, in Chap. 8 we also observe that representatives of the federal authorities involve themselves in an alliance with regional authorities, in all likelihood due to the level of *securitisation* that indigenous policy had reached. The federal and regional authorities here worked in tandem with certain actors in civil society to sideline other civil society-based actors that were seen as having troubling connections to the West and very publicly engaging in dissenting contention.

The cases cited above give evidence that processes are, in fact, often vertically structured, in the sense that the federal government applies its power to the regional and local level where most networks are located. On the other hand, as the case of urban climate change adaptation in St. Petersburg in Chap. 5 illustrates, there is some leeway for initiatives taken by cities if the federal level exerts no strong pressure to opt for a certain solution. Even though bottom-up processes are much less significant, the data confirm that the federal government's capacity to intervene into regional policy-making processes is limited. Its constricted capacity also explains why the Russian government encroaches on regional networks in some cases, while it holds off in others.

Moreover, the case studies uncovered some patterns pointing to regional variations both within and across policy fields. Being a donor to the federal budget (such as St. Petersburg) rather than a recipient of federal subsidies (e.g. Samara) allows the former to operate more independently from the federal authorities. A more developed and diversified civil society landscape in some regions also correlates with stronger governance networks (see the networks in ethnic policy in Krasnodar, Chap. 7), though what comes first in the causal link is not always easy to establish. Furthermore, the geographic location and perceived security threats (ethnic strife, border issues, etc.) also affect the level of policy decentralisation and federal attempts to interfere in the regions, including infringement on governance networks. This picture is not unambiguous, however. As shown in Chap. 5 on climate change adaptation and Chap. 6 on child welfare, cross-border cooperation with Finland and Norway respectively has been conducive to regional networks formation and policy initiatives.

Hence, although this book is first and foremost concerned with governance networks, it still allows for some detailed insights in how features of multilevel governance interact with regional and local networks. The multilevel setup establishes an institutional context which increases the complexity of interactions (Chap. 2). It also gives non-state actors the—albeit limited—opportunity to ally with different state actors. The empirical evidence thus strongly corroborates the argument that the Russian state rarely appears as unitary actor or as a monolithic bloc. It should, indeed, be more adequately understood as multiple constellations of actors following particular territorial interests and policy preferences.

In addition, the data demonstrate that it is highly relevant how a certain problem is framed and which ministry is responsible. The sectoral organisation of Russian governments and executives at all territorial levels further reinforces institutional fragmentation. Politicians and bureaucrats belonging to different, often rivalling sectors and branches at the various territorial levels, do not always take the same positions, but often follow different ideas and concepts. They internalise various role definitions and develop specific identities revolving around their tasks. Whether HIV, for instance, is treated as a question of health policy or conceptualised as a matter of security decisively impacts the working of a respective network. As shown in Chap. 3, NGOs favouring harm reduction in the HIV sphere would be more inclined to establish alliances with health authorities rather than the drug ones. Likewise, in order to strengthen their position various state organisational units competing over policy may seek allies among respected non-state actors. Whether ecological expertise, for example, is seen as conducive for the sustainable development of a region or as hindrance to economic growth (or an obstacle for realising individual interests) also explains how a network is operated.

The examples demonstrate that single ministries featuring sectorally-organised administrations often frame the same problem in a different manner and consequently pursue diverging concepts and competing solutions. In this sense, studies on Western governments have pointed out that conflicts among ministries and administrations may sometimes be as fierce as among competing parties, but we see that these effects caused by sectoral organisation of government also occur in Russia. Even though most incumbents are members of the hegemonic 'United Russia', the case studies suggest that the role orientations of incumbents also relate to their responsibility for a particular policy issue—an attitude which they might share with non-state actors operating within the same policy. It is a question still unanswered whether or not administrators cultivate policy-specific orientations so strong that these roles even countervail territorial or party interests. Notwithstanding these questions, it can be nutshelled that the sectoral diversity within the Russian state organisation provides access to *different* state actors, and that institutional fragmentation tends to work in favour of governance networks.

9.4   FEEDBACK OF EMPIRICAL FINDINGS INTO GOVERNANCE THEORY

The conclusions drawn in the above sections corroborate that governance theory has proven very useful in aiding our understanding of Russian politics. It is the basic argument of this book that analysing Russian politics through the lenses of governance theory helps to gain a deeper understanding of what constitutes the nature of regime hybridity and 'new' authoritarianism (Hale 2011; Robertson 2012; Way 2010). Certainly the broader literature has suggested that it is a striking feature of the Russian regime that civil society has been co-opted and managed since the 2000s and that the activity of private actors 'is maintained within strictly defined state limits' (Cheskin and March 2015: 267). The Russian version of governance networks is specific insofar as it is applied both to mobilise participation and cooperation, *and* to keep civil society under control. The relevance of this dualistic concept is also confirmed by the entirety of the case studies. It thus seems worthwhile to dedicate some further theoretical reflections to this Janus-faced nature of governance networks at the end of this book. We argue that understanding the features and effects of governance networks in Russia requires simultaneous attention to both facets—cooperation and control.

In fact, the empirical findings transcend the reasons for explaining why and how governance networks are run in Russia in that they allow for taking the theory out of its original context and developing more general thoughts on governance theory. In reconstructing the composition and the interactions among actors within the Russian networks, it should be noticed that they do share some similarities with their western relatives. As in democracies, processes of resource exchange shape the Russian networks; this finding even holds true for the mimicked networks. Russian authorities noticeably depend on the resources of private actors, and non-state actors extract benefits from collaboration. Resource interdependence, again, reinforces the collaborative, officially sanctioned policy-making approach. In this understanding, networks are 'relevant pipes through which resources can circulate' (Owen-Smith and Powell 2013: 618).

It has been shown that most Russian networks are characterised by strong hierarchies leading to asymmetric relations which clearly work in favour of the state authorities. One may argue that these characteristics, which were subsumed under the label of 'state dominance', can also be regarded as typical for governance networks in established democracies. Even there, networks usually operate within the 'shadow of hierarchy' cast by the state (Scharpf 1994: 40), i.e. that the state configures the interactions between state and non-state actors, sets the ultimate rules, and makes the final decisions. For reasons of legitimacy, policy solutions proposed by networks are finally taken by the representative institutions. In this context, it was emphasised that resource dependence does not at all herald the weakness of the democratic state (Mayntz 1993b).

As Davies highlights in his sharp-cut criticism on democratic network governance (Davies 2011, 2012), both sides—state and non-state actors— do often not interact on an equal footing; there are strong asymmetries shaping the networks; and even though trust can be generated by the actors forming a network, it should not be understood as a necessary condition for explaining why such interactions emerge and are sustained. Actors within a network often do not pursue common goals either. Obviously, some prevalent ideas on governance networks turned out to be simply too idealistic (see Chap. 2). Thus it can be stated that irrespective of the regime type under consideration, conflicts, mistrust, and diverging preferences may shape the relations between actors forming a governance network—features which certainly have a negative impact on the functioning of networks.

Moreover, researchers meet with serious difficulty when trying to grasp the differences between governance networks in democratic regimes and hybrid or authoritarian ones by calculating the share of horizontal and vertical governance modes. It is simply impossible to quantify this mixture. It is also disputable as to whether horizontal modes outweigh the vertical ones or if they can be found more frequently in democracies, even though a higher frequency seems to be a plausible assumption. Obviously, the 'patterns of the mix' frequently described by governance network theory (Davies 2011: 57) can be found in both regime types. How, then, can we theorise the generative relationship between a regime type and governance networks?

A distinctive characteristic of Russian governance networks that deserves attention is related to the conspicuous proximity of civil society to the state. Loyal NGOs, which have become constituent for the 'managed' civil society, usually do not question the regime norms, but operate within the boundaries set by these norms and consequently direct their aspirations to the authorities' goals. There is widespread consensus that most NGOs have moved closer to the state in order to pursue their policies, thus blurring the borders between state and society (Fröhlich 2012). This observation was recently labelled as 'consentful contention' (Cheskin and March 2015), meaning that under the umbrella of the demanded constructive collaboration, private actors are expected to be loyal, but not necessarily subservient to the state, although they may also effect a critical stance. In general, it is nearly impossible to establish efficient, problem-oriented collaborations as long as hostile or even antagonistic orientations are prevalent. By contrast, if orientations are cooperative and if actors share the basic goal to enforce not only their self-interest but also to pursue common benefits (Scharpf 1997), it is possible to come to a 'productive symbiosis', wherein actors can understand each other as potential allies (Lewis 2013: 326). Then, civil society can participate in the rich resources of the state, and in return the state actors can make use of the expertise and other scarce resources provided by private actors. This, again, is exactly what the official Russian policy aims to achieve.

At this point of argumentation, one might demur that representatives in democracies prefer collaborating with non-antagonistic, constructive civil society actors as well. Moreover, it was highlighted that many NGOs in Western democracies depend on state funding, so that their proximity to the state cannot make the ultimate difference either. However, it is not only the range within which non-state actors' behaviour is still tolerated as constructive that is smaller in non-democratic regimes; the limits of this range are also not clear-cut. Even though it has become a kind of truism that the simple dichotomy between civil society's autonomy and extensive co-optation is too rough (Cheskin and March 2015: 270), it can be stated that the Russian authorities have considerable leeway to set (often contradictory) regulations or to bypass or even infringe on the rules if they consider such a move as being useful. Authorities in hybrid or authoritarian regimes are able to define both the opportunities enabling and the boundaries limiting non-state actors unilaterally and arbitrarily. In order to make non-state actors responsive (or, in some cases, amenable) to the authorities, it is not even necessary to apply coercive tools and repression explicitly onto networks. Often, the mere existence of such instruments is sufficient to achieve a symbiotic behaviour of non-state actors. Thus in hybrid and authoritarian regimes, governance networks operate under precarious conditions.

In other words, governance networks in democracies and autocracies or hybrid regimes may function in a similar manner on the operational level. But the default rule of law and arbitrariness, which goes along with a high level of uncertainty, carries some implications for the working of networks on a more general level. It is still an unanswered question whether and to what degree the Russian governance networks can contribute in the long run to developing innovative and effective policy solutions. New ideas are often concocted by minorities and groups which come from outside the mainstream and initially do not conform to the position of the current majority. In contrast, Russian authorities often have strong reservations against policy solutions deviating from what is considered to be appropriate. Much is decided by how 'hardline' the non-state actors are prepared to behave. The inclusion offered by the authorities involves the expectation of not making public 'nuisances' and refraining from certain moves which may be perceived as too radical. This expectation does not constitute a residual and contingent actor-related factor; rather it represents a pattern 'typical' for the Russian case. Authorities relate 'making nuisance' not only to a non-state actor's concrete behaviour, but also to a large extent whether the non-state actor's positions are in line with official policies or not. However, even in the view of Russian rulers there is no a priori divergence between the policy positions of non-state and state actors. The key question is what happens when such policy divergences actually occur. Chapter 4 suggests that state authorities switch to hard and coercive tools in cases in which essential conflicts, such as between economic vs. ecological interests, are on the agenda.

Another distinguishing feature of networks in Russia relates to the way horizontal, network-like collaborations are linked to the vertical tools of meta-governance. As described in the policy chapters, Russian authorities apply a wide range of soft as well as hard tools onto the networks. The use of soft tools seems to conform to the practice of democratic governance. Again, at first glance it is difficult to draw a clear line between network practices in different regime contexts. Authorities in non-democratic regimes aim at saving transaction costs by resorting to soft tools as well, and concomitantly try to delimitate the use of costly coercive or repressive instruments. If only 'constructive' and loyal NGOs are incorporated into governance networks, state actors have no manifest interest to resort to hard tools unless their attitude expresses a generalised mistrust vis-à-vis non-state actors. Put differently, a logical relation between the facilitation of a 'constructive' civil society on the one hand and the application of soft meta-governance tools on the other becomes empirically visible and theoretically conclusive. The case studies, however, also provide explanations for the usage of hard tools. Even though the main trend is the application of soft tools, we found several cases where the authorities selectively made use of hard tools or where they saw the need to set an example, such as in the application of the Foreign Agents law (Chap. 3). Moreover, hard tools were distinctly applied when state actors and (state-owned) enterprises had their own stakes in infrastructure projects or when security issues were affected. In these particular cases, NGOs were either squeezed out of collaboration or state actors resorted to repressive measures (Chaps. 4, 7, 8).

In conflating the different forms of governance networks to a typical pattern, it becomes evident that a state-dominated model whose function is to gather policy advice and coordinate actors prevails in Russia. Within this model, the existing networks oscillate between hard and soft state domination. This finding corresponds to the overall conception of a strong and independent Russian state whose sovereignty should not be permeated by antagonistic, fundamentally critical private actors. Different from networks in established democracies, where the positions and affiliations of participants are just partially under control of the network manager (Owen-Smith and Powell 2013: 601), it is constitutive for the Russian dualistic concept that state actors use these bodies not just to solve policy problems and enhance legitimacy, but also to keep civil society under control. Hence the Russian version of governance networks is probably more fragile and prone to violation: their existence and involvement of non-state actors can be questioned by the authorities.

Still, it is an open question whether governance networks are a model which is taken over due to its simple diffusion or whether it is an element already deeply rooted in the Russian institutional architecture. In any case, our empirical findings do corroborate that governance networks are a ubiquitous phenomenon and that they do fulfil concrete functions in the policy process in Russia. We contend that more than a simple cross-sectoral comparison is required in future research. Variations and similarities may become more apparent if network governance theory is not only taken out of its original context and applied to a hybrid, increasingly authoritarian regime as shown in the articles in this book, but is also guided by comparisons among different regime types.

References

Aasland, Aadne, Mikkel Berg-Nordlie, and Elena Bogdanova. 2016. Encouraged but Controlled: Governance Networks in Russian Regions. *East European Politics* 32 (2): 148–169.

Bekkers, Viktor, Geske Dijkstra, Arthur Edwards, and Menno Fenger. 2007. *Governance and the Democratic Deficit*. Hampshire: Ashgate.

Bouwen, Peter. 2004. Exchange access Good for Access. A Comparative Study of Business Lobbying in the EU Institutions. *European Journal of Political Research*, 43 (3): 337–69.

Boxenbaum, Eva, and Stefan Jonsson. 2013. Isomorphism, Diffusion and Decoupling. In *The Sage Handbook of Organizational Institutionalism*, eds. Royston Greenwood, Christine Oliver, Kerstin Sahlin, and Roy Suddaby, 78–98. Los Angeles, London: Sage.

Bueren, Van, M. Ellen, Erik-Hans Klijn, and Joop F.M. Koppenjan. 2003. Dealing with Wicked Problems in Networks: Analyzing an Environmental Debate from a Network Perspective. *Journal of Public Administration and Theory* 13 (2): 193–212.

Burgess, Michael. 2006. *Comparative Federalism Theory and Practice*. Abingdon: Routledge.

Cheskin, Ammon, and Luke March. 2015. State–Society Relations in Contemporary Russia: New Forms of Political and Social Contention. *East European Politics* 31 (3): 261–273.

Davies, Jonathan S. 2011. *Challenging Governance Theory. From Network to Hegemony*. Bristol: Policy Press.

Davies, Jonathan S. 2012. Network Governance Theory: A Gramscian Critique. *Environment and Planning* 44 (11): 2687–2704.

Davies, Jonathan S., Jørn Holm-Hansen, Vadim Kononenko, and Asbjørn Røiseland. 2016. Network Governance in Russia: An Analytical Framework. *East European Politics* 32 (2): 131–147.

DiMaggio, Paul J., and Walter W. Powell. 1983. The Iron Cage Revisited: Institutional Isomorphism and Collective Rationality in Organizational Fields. *American Sociological Review* 48 (2): 147–160.

Fröhlich, Christian. 2012. Civil Society and the State Intertwined: The Case of Disability NGOs in Russia. *East European Politics* 28 (4): 371–389.

Hale, Henry E. 2011. Hybrid regimes—When Autocracy and Democracy Mix. In *Dynamics of Democratization: Dictatorship, Development, and Diffusion*, ed. Nathan J. Brown, 23–45. Baltimore: John Hopkins University.

Hall, Peter, and Rosemary C.R. Taylor. 1996. Political Science and the Three New Institutionalisms. *Political Studies* 44 (5): 936–957.

Head, Brian W. 2008. Wicked Problems in Public Policy. *Public Policy* 3 (2): 101–118.

Heritiér, Adrienne, and Dirk Lehmkuhl. 2008. The Shadow of Hierarchy and New Modes of Governance. *Journal of Public Policy* 28: 1–17.

Hood, Christopher. 1983. *The Tools of Government*. London: Macmillan.

Kropp, Sabine, and Johannes Schumann. 2016. Governance Networks and Vertical Power in Russia—Environmental Impact Assessments and Collaboration Between State and Non-State Actors. *East European Politics* 32 (2): 192–214.

Lewis, David. 2013. Civil Society and the Authoritarian State: Cooperation, Contestation and Discourse. *Journal of Civil Society* 9 (3): 325–340.

Lowi, Theodore J. 1972. Four Systems of Policy, Politics, and Choice. *Public Administration Review* 33: 298–310.

Mayntz, Renate. 1993a. Modernization and the Logic of Interorganizational Networks. In *Societal Change Between Market and Organization*, eds. John Child, Michel Crozier, Renate Mayntz, et al., 3–18. Aldershot: Avebury.

Mayntz, Renate. 1993b. Policy-Netzwerke und die Logik von Verhandlungssystemen. *Politische Vierteljahresschrift*. Sonderheft 46, ed. Adrienne Héritier, 39–56. Policy-Analyse: Kritik und Neuorientierung.

Meyer, John W., and Brian Rowan. 1977. Institutional Organizations: Formal Structure as Myth and Ceremony. *American Journal of Sociology* 83: 340–363.

Myhre, Marthe, and Mikkel Berg-Nordlie. 2016. 'The state cannot help them all". Russian Media Discourse on the Inclusion of Non-state Actors In Governance. *East European Politics* 32 (2): 192–214.

Owen-Smith, Jason, and Walter W. Powell. 2013. Networks and Institutions. In *The Sage Handbook of Organizational Institutionalism*, ed. Royston Greenwood, Christine Oliver, Kerstin Sahlin, and Roy Suddaby, 596–643. Los Angeles, London: Sage.

Robertson, Graeme. 2010. *The Politics of Protest in Hybrid Regimes: Managing Dissent in Post-communist Russia*. Cambridge: Cambridge University Press.

Scharpf, Fritz W. 1994. Games Real Actors Could Play: Positive and Negative Coordination in Embedded Negotiations. *Journal of Theoretical Politics* 6 (1): 27–53.

Scharpf, Fritz W. 1997. *Games Real Actors Play. Actor-centered Institutionalism in Policy Research*. Boulder: Westview Press.

Scott, Richard W. 2014. *Institutions and Organizations. Ideas, Interests, and Identities*, 4th ed. Los Angeles et al.: Sage.

Vabo, Signy Irene, and Asbjørn Røiseland. 2012. Conceptualizing the Tools of Government In Urban Network Governance. *International Journal of Public Administration* 35 (14): 934–946.

Way, Lucian. 2010. The New Authoritarianism in the Former Soviet Union. *Communist and Post-Communist Studies* 43: 335–337.

Webber, Douglass. 1992. The Distribution and Use of Policy Knowledge in the Policy Process. In *Advances in Policy Studies since 1950*, eds. W. Dunn and R. M. Kelly, 383–418. New Brunswick.

Wintrobe, R. 1998. *The Political Economy of Dictatorship*. Cambridge: CUP.

Wooten, Melissa, and Andrew J. Hoffman. 2013. Organizational Fields: Past, Present and Future. In *The Sage Handbook of Organizational Institutionalism*, eds. Royston Greenwood, Christine Oliver, Kerstin Sahlin, and Roy Suddaby, 130–148. Los Angeles, London: Sage.

INDEX

A

Access points, 31, 222, 234
Adaption to climate change, 122
AIDS, 43, 46, 48–51, 58, 67
AIDS centres, 44, 48, 50, 56, 59, 65, 67
Authoritarianism, 3, 5, 8, 132, 153, 238

B

Barents Cooperation, 201
Business, civil society and state, 10, 73

C

Child rights, 131, 132, 134–136, 138, 140, 141, 145, 146, 149–151
Child welfare, 131–134, 136, 139, 141, 145, 146, 150–152, 229, 231, 236
Civil society, 2, 10, 12, 13, 19, 23, 24, 29, 30, 44, 45, 49, 51–55, 61, 63–67, 73, 74, 81, 82, 93, 97, 106, 107, 120, 123, 126, 132, 134, 136, 141, 142, 149, 164, 166, 169, 172, 175, 177, 182, 183, 196, 197, 200, 202, 203, 208, 209, 220, 223, 225, 228, 229, 233, 236, 238–240, 242
Climate change, 5, 32, 105–108, 111–119, 121–127, 236

Conflict management, 20, 32, 33, 156, 164, 166, 207, 234, 235
Constructive civil society, 240

D

Drug control authorities, 44, 58, 67
Drug users, 34, 44, 46–53, 55, 56, 58–60, 64, 66–68, 235

E

Emergencies, 176
Environmental Impact Assessments (EIA), 73–79, 81–94, 96, 97, 225, 229, 235
Environmental protection, 23, 76, 83, 88, 89, 94, 106, 113, 114, 116, 118, 120
Ethnic NGOs, 161, 162, 165–167, 169, 172, 173, 175–180, 182–184
Ethnic policy, 156, 157, 163–167, 169, 171, 173–175, 182, 184, 236

F

Federal encroachment, 31
Floods, 109, 110, 114–116, 119, 125
Foster families, 134, 136, 137, 149

G

GONGOs, 25, 51, 89, 167, 175, 177
Governance networks, 2–6, 8, 9,
    11–15, 17, 19–21, 24–29, 31–35,
    44, 53–55, 57, 58, 61–65, 67, 68,
    117, 125, 126, 131, 132, 150, 151,
    157, 163, 167–169, 178, 182–184,
    192, 195, 200, 205, 207, 209,
    220–224, 226–229, 231–236, 238,
    239, 241, 242

H

Hard governance tools, 74, 89, 94, 96,
    98, 223
Health authorities, 44, 56, 58, 63, 68,
    237
HIV, 5, 32, 34, 44–53, 55–61, 63–68,
    229, 232, 237
Housing, 23, 25, 106, 114, 140, 160
Hybrid regime, 5, 7, 16, 22, 35, 168,
    220, 222, 224, 229, 238, 241, 242

I

Imitated networks, 182
Indigenous, 32, 33, 107, 164,
    189–197, 199, 201–204, 206–209,
    224, 225, 229, 231, 236
Indigenous peoples, 191, 192, 195,
    201
Indigenous representation, 5, 198, 204,
    207, 221, 231
Informality, 9, 26, 27
Institutional fragmentation, 237, 238
Irkutsk, 33, 75, 83–85
Iron Curtain, 194
Isomorphism, 183, 226

K

KMN, 191, 193
Krasnodar, 33, 75, 83, 86, 89, 90, 92,
    93, 157, 160, 161, 164, 165,
    171–175, 178, 180–184, 224, 235,
    236

M

Managed democracy, 22, 24
Mandatory negotiations, 73
Meta-governance, 4, 9, 14–19, 25, 35,
    44, 56, 74, 78, 80–82, 84, 86, 89,
    94, 97, 114, 127, 157, 167–169,
    180, 181, 189, 196, 199, 222–224,
    227, 228, 241, 242
Method triangulation, 34, 162
Multilevel governance, 30, 31, 236
Multilevel system, 29, 34, 234
Municipal infrastructure, 114, 118, 125
Murmansk, 32, 189, 195–199, 201,
    202, 204, 207

N

Natural Disasters, 51
Negative impact on the environment,
    76
Network functions
    conflict management, 32
    consultation, 79, 175
    coordination, 12, 53, 207, 232
    decision-making, 1, 13, 18, 20, 53
    implementation, 15, 27, 44, 53
    monitoring, 55, 231
Network governance, 2, 8–11, 13–16,
    18, 19, 21, 26, 27, 33, 44, 106, 107,
    115, 124, 125, 131–133, 150, 219,

220, 222, 225, 226, 229, 231, 232,
    239, 242
NGOs, 10, 18, 22, 23, 25, 26, 30, 31,
    34, 46, 47, 49–52, 58, 67, 68,
    74–88, 90–94, 96–98, 131, 133,
    141–143, 149, 157, 165, 166, 169,
    172, 175–178, 180, 182, 184, 192,
    193, 195, 196, 198, 207, 225, 228,
    229, 231, 233, 234, 237, 239–242
North Caucasus, 157, 160, 161, 164,
    172–174

O

Obshchina, 192, 195, 198–200, 202,
    204

P

Placement of children, 136, 138
Platforms, 21, 23, 34, 66, 131, 145,
    150, 151, 157, 161, 165, 166, 168,
    169, 173–179, 181–183, 232, 234
Policy field, 21, 32, 33, 44, 53, 55, 68,
    107, 156, 189, 191, 192, 221, 236
Policy system, 44
Public chamber, 23, 52, 142–144, 150,
    151, 166, 172, 199
Public health, 50, 58, 67, 114
Putinism, 141

R

RAIPON, 192–195, 202, 204, 208
Rule of law, 27, 98, 168, 241

Russian (Federation), 43, 49, 75, 122,
    135, 140, 142, 144, 164, 166, 191,
    192, 221

S

Samara, 33, 44, 49–53, 57–59, 63–66,
    224, 236
Sámediggi, 195, 197, 198, 201–203,
    206
Sámi, 189, 190, 194, 195, 197, 198,
    200–209
Securitization, 189, 193, 195
Sistema, 26
Sobbar, 201–206, 208
Soft governance tools, 84, 94
St. Petersburg, 32, 44, 49–53, 57–60,
    63–66, 236
State dominated networks, 25, 227,
    228
Stavropol, 157, 160, 161, 165,
    171–180, 182, 183, 225
Substitution, 22, 46, 48, 58, 141, 189,
    206

U

Urban planning, 113–115, 119, 125

V

Volunteerism, 131, 147

Printed by Printforce, the Netherlands